STUDY GUIDE

for use with

HUMAN ADJUSTMENT

John Santrock

University of Texas at Dallas

Prepared by

Kathleen Field
Terry Pettijohn

The Ohio State University at Marion

Boston   Burr Ridge, IL   Dubuque, IA   Madison, WI   New York   San Francisco   St. Louis
Bangkok   Bogotá   Caracas   Kuala Lumpur   Lisbon   London   Madrid   Mexico City
Milan   Montreal   New Delhi   Santiago   Seoul   Singapore   Sydney   Taipei   Toronto

The McGraw·Hill Companies

Mc Graw Hill **Higher Education**

STUDENT STUDY GUIDE TO ACCOMPANY HUMAN ADJUSTMENT
Published by McGraw-Hill, a business unit of The McGraw-Hill Companies, Inc., 1221 Avenue of the
Americas, New York, NY, 10020. Copyright © 2006 by The McGraw-Hill Companies, Inc. All rights
reserved. No part of this publication may be reproduced or distributed in any form or by any means, or
stored in a database or retrieval system, without the prior written consent of The McGraw-Hill Companies,
Inc., including, but not limited to, in any network or other electronic storage or transmission, or broadcast
for distance learning. Some ancillaries, including electronic and print components, may not be available to
customers outside the United States.

This book is printed on acid-free paper.

1 2 3 4 5 6 7 8 9 0 QPD/QPD 0 9 8 7 6 5

ISBN 0-07-312415-X

Editor in Chief: *Emily Barrosse*
Publisher: *Stephen Rutter*
Senior Sponsoring Editor: *John T. Wannemacher*
Marketing Manager: *Melissa Caughlin*
Director of Development: *Judith Kromm*
Managing Editor: *Jean Dal Porto*
Project Manager: *Rick Hecker*
Art Director: *Jeanne Schreiber*
Design Manager: *Laurie J. Entringer*
Art Manager: *Robin Mouat*
Photo Research Coordinator: *Alexandra Ambrose*
Senior Print Supplements Producer: *Louis Swaim*
Media Project Manager: *Alexander Rohrs*
Senior Production Supervisor: *Carol A. Bielski*
Media Producer: *Stephanie George*
Permissions Editor: *Marty Granahan*
Composition: 10/11 *Times New Roman by Alan Noyes*
Printing: PMS *Black*

www.mhhe.com

Contents

PREFACE

This *Student Study Guide* was developed to help you understand and learn the principles and applications that are presented in *Human Adjustment* by John W. Santrock. It also should help you to integrate what you learn in the classroom with what you learn in the textbook, to prepare for tests, and to apply what you learn to your life.

Each chapter of this study guide includes the following features:

- **Chapter Outline.** This detailed outline provides an overview of the textbook chapter and can prepare you for studying the chapter.
- **Learning Goals.** For each chapter in the textbook, the author established Learning Goals, and those goals are included here. There is a goal for each major section of the textbook chapter. These goals provide a guide for your study and form the structure of the Guided Review.
- **Guided Review.** To help you master the content presented in the textbook, the Guided Review goes over the main ideas and facts discussed in the chapter in the same order as the textbook.
- **Key Terms.** Psychology, like every discipline, has its own terminology, which you need to master in order to understand the concepts and information developed by the discipline. The Key Terms section asks you to recall definitions and to write examples of the concepts. You can find the

definitions in the margins of the textbook in the same order as they are listed here.
- **Practice Tests.** There are two multiple-choice tests (Test A and Test B) for each chapter. Practice Test A should help you assess your preliminary knowledge of the material; Practice Test B is at the end of the chapter to provide a final check of your understanding.
- **Identifying Concepts.** This section is designed to help you strengthen your ability to recognize important theories, people, and concepts discussed in the chapter.
- **Understanding Concepts.** This section gives you the opportunity to measure your progress at mastering the material in the chapter by asking you to write about specific concepts. The exercises follow the sequence of material in the textbook.
- **Applying Strategies and Concepts.** Learning about adjustment requires that you develop critical thinking skills and the ability to apply concepts to your own adjustment as well as the adjustment of others. This section asks you to think about important issues raised by the chapter.
- **Answers to Chapter Questions.** This section at the end of each chapter lists the answers to the questions in the Guided Review, Practice Test A, Identifying Concepts, and Practice Test B.

The textbook also includes many learning aids. In addition, a CD and a Web site provide not only additional practice tests but also video clips, self-assessments, and other material to enrich your understanding. Be sure to read the Preface of the textbook to learn about these aids.

With a little effort on your part, you can gain significant understanding of the field of human adjustment and its applications to your own life and the world around you.

STUDY SKILLS

Adjustment is an exciting and useful area of study, but there is so much to learn that at times it can seem overwhelming. The most important point in studying is to *be prepared*. If you are prepared to take lecture notes, read and study your textbook, and prepare properly for tests, you will have no difficulty in mastering the material.

Taking Notes in the Classroom

The first step is to make sure you are prepared for class by reading the assignment, reviewing your notes, and generally feeling comfortable about attending class. Your task in the classroom is to practice active listening. Have all of your needed materials ready, and be relaxed enough so that you can focus on the lecture. Avoid distractions. If you are obliged to be absent from class, make arrangements to obtain notes from another student.

Many students have difficulty deciding what notes to take. Although there are individual differences, certain signals often act as guides to what the instructor considers important. He or she will often pause, repeat major points, and write key concepts on the board. Make sure that the important concepts expressed by your instructor are recorded in your notebook.

It is important to have a system of note taking that works for you. One effective method is to use a series of outlines to record the main ideas and important details. Make sure that your notebook is large and that you have enough paper. Consider leaving space in your notebook to include notes from your textbook. One system is to write lecture notes on the right-hand pages and notes from the textbook on the left-hand pages. Then you have all of the information for any one topic together. Remember that the notes you take from the classroom provide a structure for learning and let you know which topics your instructor considers important.

Studying Your Textbook

Reading and studying your textbook is the core of a good study program. *Human Adjustment* is organized so that it is easy to read and study. Here are several ideas about study skills in general.

The best-known study technique is probably SQ5R. Originated by Francis Robinson and expanded by Walter Pauk, it has proven extremely effective. The steps to the SQ5R study technique are as follows:

1. Survey. Always get the overall picture. When studying a chapter, glance at the chapter outline, skim the pages noting the major sections, and look over the chapter review.

2. Question. As you are examining the chapter, ask yourself questions about the content. The Learning Goals in your textbook provide a basic set of questions for the major sections of each chapter.

3. Read. Read for a purpose (to answer your questions). Read carefully and completely

(including tables and illustrations). Concentrate on getting the main ideas and the important details.

4. Record. Record the main ideas in each section. This encourages you to read actively to identify the important ideas. You can underline key words, write important points in the margin, or write a summary in your notebook. Keep your writing brief; focus on the really important ideas. Writing helps you remember and keeps you alert as you study. Keep topics organized, and include the main ideas and important details you want to remember. Use the notes as one way to review.

5. Recite. Recitation is an important step. Try to recall the main ideas and important details. The Review and Reflect sections in your textbook provide a structure for doing this. Can you answer the questions without referring back to the text? You can use the Reach Your Learning Goals section at the end of each chapter in the textbook as well as this study guide to check your answers. If you have any weak spots, now is the time to correct them.

6. Review. People easily forget what they learn if they do not review. Review shortly after first studying and several times before taking the test. This is an excellent opportunity to use this study guide, which was prepared to help you assess your understanding and guide your review of material.

7. Reflect. It is important to reflect on the main ideas that you have learned. This step allows you to think critically about the important issues raised in the chapter. Take some time to organize the information you have recently learned. Develop examples and applications of the major principles, and evaluate the various theories and viewpoints. This helps you remember and use the information.

Using the Study Guide

Each chapter in this study guide has nine sections to help you learn the material in the textbook. Following is my advice for making the most of the study guide when studying each chapter:

1. Before reading the textbook, examine the Chapter Outline to preview the topics. Note that the headings come from the textbook. You can also use the Chapter Outline when you don't have your textbook with you or during review sessions when you want to quickly go over the material you have already learned. You might want to write notes in the margin and to mark the points in the outline that are emphasized in class.

2. Read the Learning Goals before reading the textbook chapter. Refer to the Learning Goals at the beginning of every study session to orient you toward your study objectives.

3. After you have read the textbook chapter (and ideally have taken notes from it), work on the Guided Review. This section consists of completion statements that cover the main points of the chapter. It is the most detailed studying task in each chapter and will help you master the detailed information that you need to know for tests. Note that the Guided Review is organized by the Learning Goals. You might want to complete sections of the Guided Review as the information is covered in class. If there are items that you cannot complete, make note of them and restudy those sections of the textbook. Answers to the Guided Review are provided at the end of each study guide chapter.

4. The Key Terms for the chapter are listed next. Space is provided for you to write a brief definition in your own words. To ensure that you understand the material, putting the definition in your own words is better than repeating the definition in the textbook. Also, make sure you give an example or application of each term; this will help you retain the concept and prepare you to use the term. You are encouraged to mark the study guide to indicate your progress. For example, you might put "?" if you are not sure of the term, "X" if you cannot define it, and "!" when you have learned it. Defining key terms is also a useful exercise during study sessions. And you can probably find a friend to ask you to define terms as another form of assessment.

5. Practice Test A provides feedback on your mastery of the chapter so far. These multiple-choice tests are especially useful if your instructor includes multiple-choice questions on tests, but they provide an excellent source of feedback about your knowledge whatever testing format is used. Of course, your instructor will use different questions on a test, but these will help prepare you. The answers are given at the end of the study guide chapter.

6. Now you are ready to review the concepts presented in the textbook. Use the Identifying Concepts exercise to ensure that you remember the theories, people, and concepts included in the

chapter. For each item, you should write the correct term. Answers are included at the end of the study guide chapter.

7. If you understand an idea, you should be able to write about it, and it helps to have practice doing so. The Understanding Concepts activity gives you that practice and also helps prepare you for short-answer and essay questions on tests. If you have difficulty with a question, restudy the material in that section of the chapter.

8. The Applying Concepts and Strategies section gives you the chance to practice critical thinking skills and to focus on the strategies and applications discussed in the textbook. Many of the questions in this section do not have a simple answer. Some questions focus on your personal adjustment and ask you to apply concepts and strategies to your own life. Other questions ask you to consider broad philosophical or social issues. These questions are designed to help you learn to think critically, to apply concepts and information, and to use the material in the textbook to improve your own life.

9. The last activity in each chapter is Practice Test B, another multiple-choice test. Here is one additional opportunity to measure your understanding of the chapter.

10. When you have completed all of the chapter's activities, you might want to read the Chapter Outline again as a review of the chapter.

Managing Your Study Time

Do you always ends up cramming the night before a test or typing your report just hours before the deadline? One of the hardest tasks is to manage your time effectively.

It is useful to plot out a typical week's schedule so that you can see how your time is spent. Mark the hours that you will be in class (class attendance is significantly related to grade performance), and mark the time needed for other necessary activities—for sleep, meals, household and family responsibilities, exercise and leisure activities, employment hours, commuting time, and other built-in activities.

Do you have any time left for studying? Ideally, you should have more studying time than classroom time; a common guideline is 2 hours of studying per hour of class time. Figure out which hours are good ones for you to study, and pencil them in. Are there other activities that you need to switch, reduce, or eliminate for a while so that you can do your best as a student? Try to figure out a practical schedule.

Keep in mind that there is an unlimited amount that you could learn about and think about in every college course; therefore, it is important that you establish priorities for studying. Analyze which aspects of each course are most important to spend time on.

Are you putting off studying or reading a certain textbook or getting started on a term paper? Do you spend your time calling yourself lazy and stupid? Are there projects that you aren't starting because you fear that you cannot do them well? Or do you delay tasks because you aren't quite certain what is expected of you? The number-one cause of procrastination is perfectionism. You may want to do such a good job on a task that it becomes forbidding to get started. You must break through that roadblock and just get started. Remind yourself that no one is perfect and that you just need to begin and can make revisions later. It is helpful to break down a big test or project into more manageable, less threatening components.

Almost as important as when to study is where to study. If you are going to do some of your studying on campus, explore the campus for the best studying location. In your living space, explore which areas are best for serious studying. You may do best when studying at a desk or study table. Or you may do better in a soft chair that you come to associate only with studying. Some people can study in bed, but others would tend to fall asleep while studying. Some students do well studying at a kitchen table, but here environmental cues may lead to an increase in eating! If possible, choose an area in which studying will be the only major activity done in that place. In that way, you will develop environmental cues that will help you become a more efficient student. Also provide yourself with the best lighting, sound, and temperature.

Preparing for and Taking Tests

The best way to prepare for a test is through regular review and self-testing by using this study guide. Review your lecture notes regularly, glance at the Chapter Outline before you begin a study session, and examine the Learning Goals to prepare your study time. Keep up to date on all of your assignments, and manage your time so you have opportunities for study.

Make sure you have a positive attitude about tests, and prepare carefully for them. Try to relax when taking tests, and work as carefully as possible. If you use the *Study Guide* to help prepare yourself, you should not have any great difficulties on test days.

There are two general types of tests. The first type is the objective test (such as multiple choice or completion). When you take an objective test, first survey the test to determine the number of questions and the grading system. As you go through the questions, answer the easy questions first in order to build confidence and perhaps obtain needed information for other questions. Read the entire question carefully. Especially on multiple-choice questions, carefully consider each option. Think of multiple-choice questions as a series of true/false questions. If you don't know an answer and there is no penalty for guessing, then guess. If later you think another answer is better, then change it. Use any time left in the period to go over your answers and make sure you have marked the answers you intended.

The second type of test is the short-answer or essay test. This type of question is represented by the Key Terms, Understanding Concepts, and Applying Concepts and Strategies sections in this study guide. You need to plan your time and read directions carefully. You are being asked in each question to do a specific task, and it is important to follow directions exactly. For example, you may be asked to compare, define, describe, discuss, explain, state, or summarize. Each request requires a different response. On essay tests, organization counts, as do grammar and spelling. Give an example wherever you can to show you that understand the application of the concept. Use any extra time to go over your answers and elaborate as necessary.

Many students experience test anxiety, which has three components. The physiological component includes bodily reactions to stress, such as increased heart rate and breathing, nausea, headache, and sweating. The emotional component includes feelings of fear, panic, and anxiety. And the cognitive component includes worry, and problems with thinking and memory.

To deal with the physiological components of test anxiety, learn to relax. One suggestion is to develop an anxiety hierarchy and practice systematic desensitization (which is explained in Chapter 15, Therapies). To deal with the cognitive and emotional components of anxiety, work on cognitive restructuring (discussed in Chapter 5, Coping). Modify your negative thoughts into positive ones. For instance, rather than thinking "I will never pass" before the exam, think "I will do my best"; rather than thinking "I am stupid" during the exam, think "I am prepared"; rather than thinking "I know I flunked" after the exam, think "It could have been worse." If you properly prepare for a test, you will feel more relaxed and you will be able to do your best.

CHAPTER **1**   **ADJUSTING TO LIFE**

Chapter Outline

I. EXPLORING ADJUSTMENT

A. What Is Adjustment?

Adjustment is the psychological process of adapting to, coping with, and managing the problems, challenges, and demands of everyday life.

B. Contexts, Diversity, and Adjustment

Contexts refer to the historical, economic, social, and cultural factors that influence us.

1. ECOLOGICAL THEORY

Urie Bronfenbrenner's ecological theory explores how people are influenced by five contexts: the microsystem, mesosystem, exosystem, macrosystem, and chronosystem.

2. CONTEXTS AND EXPERIENCE

Your experience of the systems described by ecological theory depends partly on your sociocultural context—on your culture, ethnicity, and gender.

C. Thinking Critically about Adjustment

- Advice about adjustment should be met with critical thinking, which is the process of thinking reflectively and evaluating evidence.
- Curiosity, intellectual precision, and skepticism stimulate critical thinking.
- In examining evidence, a critical thinker asks, What is the source of the evidence? How strongly does the evidence support a position? Is there disconfirming evidence? Are there other possible factors and explanations?

ADJUSTMENT STRATEGIES *Involving*

Critical Thinking

1. Describe and interpret behavior carefully.
2. Identify values and challenge assumptions.
3. Examine the influence of context and culture.

4. Seek multiple points of view and alternative explanations.
5. Appreciate individual and group differences.
6. Engage in self-reflection to improve self-knowledge.

II. SUBJECTIVE WELL-BEING AND ADJUSTMENT

Subjective well-being refers to how people evaluate their lives in terms of their happiness and life satisfaction

A. Are Rich People Happier?

- Money does not make people happy.
- Having enough money for life's necessities is important to happiness.

B. Who Is Happy?

- Happy people have good social relationships, are mentally healthy, and are likely to show many other positive characteristics.
- Research indicates that there is little or no link between subjective well-being and age, gender, level of education, or parenthood.
- Most people are slightly happy.

ADJUSTMENT STRATEGIES *for*

Happiness and Life Satisfaction

1. Reflect on your responses to the self-assessment in the textbook.
2. Recognize that no single factor produces a happy person; multiple factors are at work.
3. Develop good social relationships.
4. Learn how to cope effectively with stress.
5. Involve yourself in activities that you enjoy and value.
6. Develop purposefulness and incorporate spirituality into your life.

III. THE SCIENTIFIC APPROACH TO ADJUSTMENT

A. Psychology and Adjustment

- Psychology is the scientific study of behavior and mental processes.
- Because it is a science, psychology tests assumptions and gathers evidence to support explanations of behavior. It adopts scientific attitudes toward information and uses scientific methods when conducting research.

B. Adopting a Scientific Attitude

Taking a scientific attitude means thinking critically and being objective.

C. Using the Scientific Method

- Theories help organize and connect observations and research.
- Testing hypotheses is at the heart of the scientific method, which is essentially a four-step process:
    1. CONCEPTUALIZE A PROBLEM
    2. COLLECT RESEARCH INFORMATION

3. ANALYZE DATA

4. DRAW CONCLUSIONS

ADJUSTMENT STRATEGIES *for*

Writing to Improve Your Health*

1. Write about issues that currently preoccupy you.

2. Just start and keep writing.

3. Write when you feel prepared to become emotionally involved with the writing.

4. Keep the writing to yourself.

5. Do not expect writing to be a cure-all or to have instant effects.

*Based on J. W. Pennebaker, Opening Up: The Healing Power of Expressing Emotions, Rev. ed. (New York: Guilford Press, 1997).

D. Experimental and Correlational Research

1. EXPERIMENTAL RESEARCH

- An experiment is a carefully regulated procedure in which one or more factors believed to influence the behavior being studied are manipulated while other factors are held constant.

- Experiments demonstrate cause and effect.

- Key elements of an experiment are independent and dependent variables and control and experimental groups.

2. CORRELATIONAL RESEARCH

- Some hypotheses cannot be tested through experiments.

- In correlational research the goal is to describe the strength of the relationship between two or more events or characteristics.

- Correlation does not equal causation.

E. Being a Wise Consumer of Information about Research

- Reports on research in the popular media may emphasize sensationalist findings, overgeneralize results, or mislead in other ways.

- Individuals should take responsibility for evaluating reports on research.

ADJUSTMENT STRATEGIES *for*

Understanding Adjustment Research

1. Distinguish between group results and individual needs.

2. Don't overgeneralize from a small sample.

3. Look for answers beyond a single study.

4. Don't attribute causes where none have been found.

5. Evaluate the source of the information.

IV. RESOURCES FOR IMPROVING ADJUSTMENT

A. Mental Health Professionals

Mental health professionals who can help individuals adjust include clinical psychologists, counselors, and psychiatrists.

B. National Support Groups

- National support groups offer education and support for people with a particular problem.

- The quality of a support group may vary considerably from one locale to another.

C. Self-Help Books

High-quality self-help books can be as effective as therapist-administered treatment, but in many cases they should not be used as a substitute for professional help.

ADJUSTMENT STRATEGIES *for*

Selecting a Self-Help Book

1. Select a book that makes realistic recommendations, not grandiose claims.
2. Examine the evidence reported in the book.
3. Select a self-help book that recognizes that a problem is caused by a number of factors and has alternative solutions.
4. A self-help book that focuses on a particular problem is better than one that offers a general approach to solving all of your problems.
5. Don't be conned by psychobabble or slick writing.
6. Check out the author's educational credentials.
7. Be wary of authors who complain about or reject the conventional knowledge of mental health experts.

D. The Internet

Web sites exist for every conceivable topic related to adjustment, but many are inadequate in terms of accuracy and practicality.

ADJUSTMENT STRATEGIES *for*

Finding the Best Information on the Internet

1. In many instances, the adjustment strategies for evaluating self-help books also apply to Web sites.
2. Evaluate the credibility of the Web site.
3. Avoid Web sites that are purely commercial, such as those selling a particular book, seminar, drug, treatment center, or private clinical practice.
4. Be wary about information from blogs, listserves, mailing lists, bulletin boards, and chat rooms.
5. Guard your privacy.
6. Block "cookies."
7. Don't consider the Internet a substitute for professional help.

Learning Goals

After reading and studying this chapter, you should be able to

1. Identify some key concepts that provide a foundation for understanding adjustment.
   a. Define adjustment.
   b. Outline keys aspects of the contexts that influence adjustment.
   c. Explain the key characteristics of critical thinking.

2. Define subjective well-being and describe the factors related to it.
   a. Describe the relationship between wealth and happiness.
   b. Outline factors that are linked to subjective well-being.

3. **Characterize the scientific foundations of the study of adjustment.**
   a. Define psychology.
   b. Describe scientific attitudes toward information.
   c. Explain what theory, hypothesis, and the scientific method are.
   d. Describe experimental and correlational research and the differences between them.
   e. List guidelines for being a wise consumer of information about research.

4. **Discuss resources for improving adjustment and cautions in their use.**
   a. Identify key types of professionals who can help people adjust more effectively.
   b. Describe national support groups and their role in adjustment.
   c. Identify guidelines for evaluating and using self-help books.
   d. Identify guidelines for evaluating and using Web sites that discuss adjustment.

Guided Review

After you have read this chapter in the textbook, complete these statements. Topics are discussed in the same order as in the chapter. Answers are provided at the end of the study guide chapter.

Learning Goal 1: Identify some key concepts that provide a foundation for understanding adjustment

Goal 1a: Define adjustment

1. The psychological process of adapting to, coping with, and managing the problems, challenges, and demands of everyday life is _____.

2. The small everyday events to which we adjust are called _____.

Goal 1b: Outline keys aspects of the contexts that influence adjustment

3. _____ refers to the historical, economic, social, and cultural factors that people must adjust to.

4. _____ _____ holds that people are influenced by five environmental systems.

5. The five systems described by Bronfenbrenner are the microsystem, mesosystem, exosystem, macrosystem, and _____.

6. _____ refers to the behavior patterns, beliefs, and all other products of a group of people that are passed on from generation to generation.

7. _____ is rooted in cultural heritage, nationality, race, religion, and language.

8. Sex refers to the biological dimension of being female or male whereas _____ refers to the sociocultural dimension of being female or male.

Goal 1c: Explain the key characteristics of critical thinking

9. Critical thinkers show _____, a reluctance to believe claims until they examine the evidence.

10. Critical thinkers question the _____ of evidence, checking for bias.

11. Critical thinkers look for additional factors and _____ _____ when they are presented with a claim about the cause of some behavior.

12. Critical thinkers examine the influence of _____ when they try to understand a particular behavior.

Learning Goal 2: Define subjective well-being and describe the factors related to it

13. _____ _____ refers to how people evaluate their happiness and satisfaction with life.

Goal 2a: Describe the relationship between wealth and happiness

14. Extremely wealthy people are _____ happier than people who can buy what they need.

15. Individuals who strive the most for wealth tend to have _____ subjective well-being than those who do not strive for wealth.

Goal 2b: Outline factors that are linked to subjective well-being

16. Happy people tend to have good _____ _____, to be mentally healthy and altruistic, and to have high levels of creativity, self-esteem, optimism, extraversion, and self-control.

17. Research indicates that _____, gender, level of education, and parenthood are not linked to happiness.

18. Satisfaction with one's health has a moderate link to satisfaction with life, and physical attractiveness has a _____ _____ link with subjective well-being.

Learning Goal 3: Characterize the scientific foundations of the study of adjustment

Goal 3a: Define psychology

19. The scientific study of behavior and mental processes is _____.

20. We can observe behavior but we _____ mental processes and feelings.

21. Because it is a science, psychologists adopt scientific attitudes toward information and use the _____ _____ when they conduct research.

Goal 3b: Describe scientific attitudes toward information

22. Adopting a scientific attitude means thinking _____.

23. Adopting a scientific attitude also requires trying to be _____.

Goal 3c: Explain what theory, hypothesis, and the scientific method are

24. A _____ is a broad idea or set of closely related ideas that attempts to explain observations.

25. A _____ is a testable prediction.

26. The _____ _____ is a four-step process in which a problem is conceptualized, data are collected, data are analyzed, and conclusions are drawn.

Goal 3d: Describe experimental research and correlational research and the differences between them

27. _____ are carefully regulated procedures in which certain factors are manipulated while others are held constant.

28. In experiments _____ variables are manipulated and the effects on _____ variables are measured.

29. A _____ _____ serves as a baseline for measuring the effect of manipulating the independent variable.

30. In an experiment people should be placed in experimental or control groups through _____ _____.

31. In _____ _____ the goal is to describe the strength of the relationship between two or more events or characteristics.

32. Correlational research cannot establish _____.

Goal 3e: List guidelines for being a wise consumer of information about research.

33. Most research focuses on _____, not individuals.

34. Wise consumers of research do not _____ from a small sample; they do not expect to find answers from a single study; and they evaluate the source of information.

35. When two or more factors are simply correlated with each other, _____ interpretations are not justified.

Learning Goal 4: Discuss resources for improving adjustment and pitfalls to avoid in using them

Goal 4a: Identify key types of professionals who can help people adjust more effectively

36. _____ and _____ psychology is the specialization that focuses on evaluating and treating people who have psychological problems.

37. _____ is the branch of medicine that specializes in abnormal behavior and psychotherapy.

Goal 4b: Describe national support groups and their role in adjustment

38. National support groups offer _____ and support for people with a particular problem.

39. The typical leader of a national support group is a _____.

Goal 4c: Identify guidelines for evaluating and using self-help books

40. In selecting self-help books it is best to _____ books that rely on anecdotes.

41. In selecting self-help books it is best to select books that focus on a particular problem and that recognize that a problem has _____ _____.

42. Vague but fashionable language about psychological problems is called _____.

Goal 4d: Identify guidelines for evaluating and using Web sites that discuss adjustment

43. When using Web sites on adjustment, it is important to evaluate their credibility and avoid sites that are _____.

44. Wise users of Web sites guard their privacy, block cookies, and do not treat the sites as substitutes for _____ _____.

Key Terms

Briefly define each key term and provide an example or application.

1. adjustment

2. contexts

3. ecological theory

4. cross-cultural studies

5. ethnicity

6. gender

7. critical thinking

8. subjective well-being

9. psychology

10. behavior

11. inferences

12. mental processes

13. scientific method

14. theory

15. hypothesis

16. experiment

17. independent variable

18. dependent variable

19. experimental group

20. control group

21. random assignment

22. correlational research

23. clinical and counseling psychology

24. psychiatry

25. bibliotherapy

Practice Test A

Answer these multiple-choice questions to assess your understanding of the chapter. Answers are provided at the end of the study guide chapter.

___ 1. The psychological process of adapting to, coping with, and managing the problems, challenges, and demands of everyday life is called
a. pseudopsychology.
b. ethnicity.
c. adjustment.
d. psychology.

___ 2. Losing your car keys, being caught in a long waiting line, and not being able to reach a friend by phone are examples of
a. hassles.
b. cultural bias.
c. status quo.
d. irritability.

___ 3. According to Bronfenbrenner's ecological theory, a parent's experience at work
a. is outside the environmental systems that affect a child's adjustment.
b. is part of the exosystem that may affect a child's adjustment.
c. is not likely to be relevant to a child's adjustment.
d. is part of the microsystem crucial to a child's adjustment.

___ 4. Race is a classification of people that
a. is synonymous with ethnicity.
b. has nothing to do with ethnicity.
c. is based on analysis of the human genome.
d. is based on real or imagined physical characteristics.

___ 5. Sex refers to the ____ dimension of being female or male whereas gender refers to the ____ dimension of being female or male.
a. genetic; hormonal
b. sociocultural; biological
c. environmental; genetic
d. biological; sociocultural

___ 6. Suppose you argued with your friend and when asked about it said, "Sam's really defensive." Your statement is
a. a behavioral description.
b. an inference.
c. a statement of fact.
d. a description of context.

___ 7. Subjective well-being refers to
a. a person's mood.
b. an expert's measurement of a person's average mood.
c. a person's evaluation of his or her own life in terms of happiness and life satisfaction.
d. an expert's analysis of a person's satisfaction with life.

___ 8. Profiles of very happy people consistently show that
a. they have good social relationships.
b. happiness decreases with age.
c. happiness and education are inversely related.
d. happiness and income are inversely related.

___ 9. Psychology is the study of
a. phenomena that can be directly observed and measured.
b. behavior and its consequences.
c. behavior and mental processes.
d. human adjustment.

___ 10. Science is characterized by
a. the subject matter examined.
b. an absence of speculation and theory.
c. the methods used to study a problem.
d. precision and certainty.

___ 11. Experimental research
a. allows researchers to address questions about causation.
b. provides information only about the strength of the relationships between events or characteristics.
c. involves manipulation of dependent variables and measurement of the effect on independent variables.
d. requires that researchers establish at least two carefully selected control groups.

___ 12. Which of the following is necessary in order to conclusively answer a research question?
a. multiple studies with common results
b. an experimental study
c. a case study with a large sample size
d. a correlational study

___ 13. Unlike clinical and counseling psychologists, psychiatrists
a. deal only with serious mental disorders.
b. work with people whose psychological problems are not serious.
c. are physicians who specialize in psychopathology.
d. offer psychotherapy.

___ 14. Bibliotherapy refers to
a. use of self-help books.
b. books about therapy.
c. corrections to books about adjustment.
d. none of the above.

_____ 15. Information on blogs, Internet bulletin boards, and chat rooms devoted to adjustment
a. is carefully edited and checked by the webmaster.
b. is posted only if it comes from a recognized expert.
c. may be posted by anyone and may include gossip and superstition.
d. is more reliable than information on other Web sites.

Identifying Concepts

Answers are provided at the end of the study guide chapter.

1. CONTEXT OF ADJUSTMENT   Identify the aspect of the context defined by each statement:

a. The immediate setting in which a person lives and the people with whom that person interacts directly

b. The influence that a social setting in which a person does not have an active role exerts on his or her experiences in an immediate context

c. The sociohistorical circumstances and patterning of events over a person's lifetime

d. A composite of characteristics that may include a person's cultural heritage, nationality, race, language, and religion

e. Sociocultural dimension of being male or female

2. SCIENTIFIC APPROACH   Identify the aspect of scientific research illustrated by each of the following statements about Pennebaker and Beal's research:

a. Expressing emotions can eliminate those emotions.

b. If people write about their negative emotions and the situations that caused them, their stress will decrease and they will be healthier.

c. One group of participants was told to write about an upsetting experience and how they felt about it; a second group was told to write about a topic unrelated to an emotional event.

d. Pennebaker and Beal recorded the number of visits that their participants made to the student health center before, during, and after the study.

Understanding Concepts

Complete these exercises to develop your understanding of important ideas in this chapter.

1. List five everyday hassles.

2. Why is it important to include sociocultural contexts in the study of adjustment?

3. What are five question that a critical thinker asks about evidence?

4. Why is it important to use verbs when describing behavior?

5. Give an example of how your behavior changes depending on the context.

6. Why is it important to seek multiple viewpoints on a subject? Give an example.

7. The textbook cites a research finding that people who rate themselves high in positive emotions over time have good social relationships. Does this research indicate causation or correlation? Explain.

8. What are the advantages and disadvantages of including mental processes in the science of psychology?

9. Suppose a friend told you that because she just read a report that a survey of 15 people found that people who drink two glasses of red wine a day experience less stress, she plans to start drinking red wine. What are three problems with the friend's interpretation of the survey results?

10. Compare and contrast psychology and astrology.

Applying Concepts and Strategies

Complete these exercises to develop your ability to apply this chapter's material to your life and the world. Your responses will differ from those of other students in the class, and it is helpful to share your ideas with other students.

1. What are the most common hassles that you face each week? Pick the two that bother you the most. How do you handle them?

2. Look at Figure 1.1 in the textbook or at the description of the environmental systems described by Bronfenbrenner. For each type of system, describe one way in which it is affecting your life.

3. Think about the important contexts in your life. Which ones have helped you the most? Which ones cause you the most difficulty?

4. One adjustment strategy involving critical thinking is to describe and interpret behavior carefully. How could applying this strategy help you in your everyday life? Describe one interaction with other people in which applying this strategy might help you adjust more effectively.

5. How can you get beyond your perspective to see another's? What are four or five specific steps that you might take to do so?

6. How can you enhance your own self-knowledge? The "Application Strategies Involving Critical Thinking" section in the textbook includes two steps that you might take. Try to describe three or four other possible steps to take to improve your self-knowledge.

7. Review this week's newspapers or news magazines (in print or online) and find reports about psychological studies. Do you see any shortcomings in the reports, such as overgeneralizing from small samples or using correlational findings to talk about cause and effect?

8. Go to a library or a bookstore and look at the variety of self-help books that are available. Locate a couple of books that you would like to read, and explain your choices.

Practice Test B

Answer these multiple-choice test questions to help you assess your understanding of the textbook chapter. Answers are provided at the end of the study guide chapter.

___ 1. Marianna is a white evangelical Protestant immigrant from Russia who speaks Russian. This is a summary of Marianna's
a. ethnicity.
b. culture.
c. microsystem.
d. mesosystem.

___ 2. The behavior patterns and beliefs of a particular group that are passed on from generation to generation constitute the group's
a. ethnicity.
b. gender.
c. culture.
d. sociodemography.

___ 3. A survey examined beliefs about telekinesis and telepathy among college students in the United States, Sweden, Ecuador, Japan, India, and Senegal. This is an example of
a. channeling.
b. an experiment.
c. a cross-cultural study.
d. none of the above.

___ 4. When Ann watches a new TV commercial, she withholds her opinion until she has had a chance to investigate the claims. She is showing
a. cultural context.
b. cultural bias.
c. withdrawal.
d. skepticism.

_____ 5. Tom always asks other people how they would solve a particular problem. What critical thinking strategy is he using?
a. Describing behavior carefully
b. Identifying values
c. Examining context and culture
d. Seeking multiple points of view

_____ 6. Studies of the relationship between wealth and happiness find that people who receive a windfall such as a large inheritance typically
a. are overwhelmed and miserable.
b. are much happier than other people.
c. are elated in the short term and moderately happier than other people over the long term.
d. are elated in the short term but are no happier than other people over the long term.

_____ 7. Studies of the relationship between wealth and happiness indicate that
a. wealth has no relationship to happiness.
b. having enough money to buy life's necessities is important to happiness.
c. happiness increases as wealth rises.
d. happiness decreases as wealth increases.

_____ 8. People who strive for intimacy and personal growth report
a. lower subjective well-being than those who seek money in order to gain power.
b. lower subjective well-being than those who strive mostly for wealth.
c. higher subjective well-being than those who strive mostly for wealth.
d. about the same subjective well-being as those who strive mostly for wealth.

_____ 9. On average, most people are
a. very happy.
b. mostly happy.
c. slightly happy.
d. rarely happy.

_____ 10. Feeling good as you think about your new friend is an example of a
a. behavior.
b. mental process.
c. context.
d. inference.

_____ 11. A correlation between two factors allows the researcher to conclude
a. that one factor is causing the other.
b. that some third factor is causing them both.
c. that neither factor is causing the other.
d. none of the above.

_____ 12. Men who have committed sexual assaults against women report drinking more alcohol than nonassaultive men. Which of the following is a reasonable conclusion?
a. Drinking causes men to assault women.
b. The tendency to assault women causes men to drink.
c. Society promotes drinking, which leads men to assault women.
d. Drinking and being assaultive are related.

Answers to Chapter Questions

Guided Review

1. adjustment
2. hassles
3. context
4. ecological theory
5. chronosystem
6. culture
7. ethnicity
8. gender
9. skepticism
10. source
11. alternative explanations
12. context
13. subjective well-being
14. not
15. lower
16. social relationships
17. age
18. small positive
19. psychology
20. infer
21. scientific method
22. critically
23. objective
24. theory
25. hypothesis
26. scientific method
27. experiments
28. independent; dependent
29. control group
30. random assignment
31. correlational research
32. causation
33. groups
34. generalize
35. causal
36. clinical; counseling
37. psychiatry
38. education
39. member (*or* nonprofessional)
40. avoid
41. alternative solutions (*or* multiple causes)
42. psychobabble
43. commercial
44. professional help

Practice Test A

1. c
2. a
3. b
4. d
5. d
6. b
7. c
8. a
9. c
10. c
11. a
12. a
13. c
14. a
15. c

Identifying Concepts

1. Context of Adjustment
   a. microsystem
   b. exosystem
   c. chronosystem
   d. ethnicity
   e. gender
2. Scientific Approach
   a. theory
   b. hypothesis
   c. independent variable
   d. dependent variable

Practice Test B

1. a
2. c
3. c
4. d
5. d
6. d
7. b
8. c
9. c
10. b
11. d
12. d

CHAPTER **2**   # PERSONALITY

Chapter Outline

I. WHAT IS PERSONALITY?

- Personality is a pattern of enduring and distinctive thoughts, emotions, and behaviors that characterizes the way an individual adapts to the world.
- The psychodynamic, behavioral and social cognitive, humanistic, and trait perspectives help us understand personality; parts of these perspectives are complementary rather than contradictory.

II. PSYCHODYNAMIC PERSPECTIVES

Psychodynamic perspectives view personality as being primarily unconscious and developing in stages.

A. Freud's Psychoanalytic Theory

Sigmund Freud created psychoanalysis, which is based on the idea that the unconscious holds the key to understanding personality.

   1. PERSONALITY STRUCTURES

- According to Freud, personality consists of three structures: the id, the ego, and the superego.
- The id is unconscious and consists of instincts, which are the individual's reservoir of psychic energy. It is ruled by the pleasure principle, always seeking pleasure and avoiding pain.
- The ego is partly conscious and is the structure of personality that deals with the demands of reality. It operates according to the reality principle, checking the demands of the id against what is possible.
- The superego is the structure of personality that takes into account whether something is right or wrong.

   2. DEFENSE MECHANISMS

- Defense mechanisms are unconscious methods of dealing with conflict. They reduce anxiety by distorting reality.
- Repression, the most pervasive defense mechanism, keeps unacceptable impulses out of awareness and pushes traumatic memories into the unconscious.
- Other defense mechanisms include sublimation, denial, rationalization, displacement, projection, reaction formation, and regression.

3. PERSONALITY DEVELOPMENT
   - Freud believed that personality is the result of experiences early in life.
   - According to Freud, personality develops through five stages, each of which is defined by the part of the body that is the center of pleasure.
   - Freud's five stages of personality development are the oral, anal, phallic, latency, and genital stages.
   - At each of Freud's stages, the demands of reality conflict with the needs of the pleasure center. If needs are either under- or overgratified, the individual becomes fixated at that stage of personality development.

B. Psychoanalytic Revisionists

Some theorists who followed Freud's core ideas disagreed with his emphasis on sexuality, early experience, and the unconscious and with his slight attention to sociocultural factors.

1. HORNEY'S SOCIOCULTURAL THEORY
   - Karen Horney argued that observable data were needed to support Freud's hypotheses and that sociocultural influences on personality must be considered.
   - According to Horney, the need for security—not sex or aggression—is our prime motive and a key difference among people is the extent to which they tend to move toward, away from, or against other people.

2. JUNG'S ANALYTICAL THEORY
   - Carl Jung believed that all people share a collective unconscious, which he saw as the deepest layer of the unconscious.
   - Archetypes are ideas and images that express the collective unconscious.

3. ADLER'S INDIVIDUAL PSYCHOLOGY
   - Alfred Adler argued that the conscious mind and social factors play a larger role in shaping personality than Freud realized.
   - According to Adler's individual psychology, people are motivated by purposes and goals and create their own lives as they strive for superiority.
   - Overcompensation is the individual's attempt to deny reality or to conceal a weakness. It may take the form of either an inferiority complex or a superiority complex.

ADJUSTMENT STRATEGIES *Based on*

Psychodynamic Approaches

1. Think about your experiences as a child and how you act today.
2. Recognize that you have unconscious feelings, drives, and desires that you may not easily identify.
3. Examine your thoughts, feelings, and behaviors to determine the extent that you are using defense mechanisms.
4. Evaluate the extent to which your security needs are being met.
5. Examine whether you have feelings of superiority or inferiority and discover areas of life in which you can excel.

C. Evaluating Psychodynamic Perspectives

- Psychodynamic theorists share a belief that current and early experiences shape personality, that personality develops through a series of stages, that people give meaning to their experiences in a way that shapes personality, that unconscious motives lie behind behavior, and that conflicts between our inner world and reality create anxiety.

- From a psychodynamic perspective insight into our unconscious and an ability to deal with reality without overreliance on defense mechanisms are at the core of effective adjustment.
- Prominent criticisms of the psychodynamic perspective include the claim that its main concepts are difficult to test; that it presents an overly pessimistic view of people; that it overemphasizes biology, the unconscious, and sexuality; and that it has a male, Western bias.

III. BEHAVIORAL AND SOCIAL COGNITIVE PERSPECTIVES

According to behavioral and social cognitive perspectives, personality can be understood by examining the environment, experience, and behavior and analyzing how people learn to behave in certain ways.

A. Classical Conditioning

- Russian physiologist Ivan Pavlov discovered classical conditioning.
- In classical conditioning a previously neutral stimulus, called the conditioned stimulus (CS), is associated with a stimulus (the unconditioned stimulus, or UCS) that automatically elicits a response, called the unconditioned response (UCR). As a result of this association, the conditioned stimulus comes to evoke a response (called the conditioned response, or CR) that is similar to the unconditioned response.
- Classical conditioning is thought to play an important role in the learning of fears and in the development of stress-related health problems.

B. Skinner's Behaviorism

B. F. Skinner developed the concept of operant conditioning, which is a form of learning in which the consequences of a behavior change the frequency of that behavior.

1. REINFORCEMENT AND EXTINCTION
   - Reinforcement increases the probability that a behavior will occur again.
   - Extinction occurs when reinforcement ceases and the frequency of a behavior therefore decreases.

2. PUNISHMENT
   Punishment decreases the likelihood that a behavior will occur.

3. APPLYING SKINNER'S APPROACH TO PERSONALITY
   - According to Skinner, personality is nothing more than an individual's behavior, which is determined by the external environment.
   - Skinner and other behaviorists conclude that personality is learned, that it changes depending on the situations that an individual experiences, and that personality therefore can be changed by rearranging the situations that an individual experiences.

C. Social Cognitive Theory

Albert Bandura and Walter Mischel are the pioneers of social cognitive theory, which holds that behavior, the environment, and cognitive factors all influence personality.

1. OBSERVATIONAL LEARNING
   - People learn not only through classical and operant conditioning but also through observational learning, which is learning that occurs when a person observes and then repeats someone else's behavior.
   - Observational learning requires the cognitive processes of attention and retention as well as production and reinforcement.

2. RECIPROCAL DETERMINISM
   According to Bandura, the relationships among behavior, the environment, and cognitive factors are characterized by reciprocal determinism; that is, each influences and is influenced by the others.

3. PERSONAL CONTROL
   - Social cognitive theorists hold that people can regulate their own behavior and that adjustment can be measured by people's belief in their capacity to exercise some control.

- Three aspects of personal control are delay of gratification, self-efficacy, and internal locus of control.

ADJUSTMENT STRATEGIES *for*

Increasing Your Self-Efficacy*

1. Select something you expect to be able to do.
2. Distinguish between past performance and your present project.
3. Pay close attention to your successes.
4. Keep written records so that you will be aware of your successes.
5. List the specific kinds of situations in which you expect to have the most difficulty and the least difficulty.

*Based on Watson, D. L. & Tharp, R. G. (2002). Self-directed behavior (8th ed.). (Belmont, CA: Wadsworth).

ADJUSTMENT STRATEGIES *Based on*

Behavioral and Social Cognitive Perspectives

1. Recognize the extent to which reinforcement and punishment influence your behavior.
2. Examine the extent to which you use reinforcement and punishment when interacting with others.
3. Use your ability to learn through observation.
4. If you don't have a mentor, consider obtaining one.
5. Evaluate the extent to which you are good at delaying gratification.
6. Examine whether you have an internal or an external locus of control.

D. Evaluating the Behavioral and Social Cognitive Perspectives

- The behavioral and social cognitive perspectives have fostered a scientific approach to adjustment.
- Critics of these perspectives object that they give too little attention to the enduring aspects of personality and to biological influences and that they are mechanistic.

IV. HUMANISTIC PERSPECTIVES

The humanistic perspective holds that each person has a capacity for growth and the freedom to choose his or her own destiny, and it emphasizes the positive qualities of the human personality.

A. Rogers's Approach

Carl Rogers argued that each person has an innate tendency to become a fully functioning person—that is, one who takes a positive approach to life, is open to experience, and has harmonious relationships with others.

1. THE SELF
   - According to Rogers, the self emerges as a result of an individual's experiences with the world.
   - In Rogers's view, the constraints and criticisms that individuals experience condition them to distort and devalue their true selves and create conflict between their real and ideal selves.

2. UNCONDITIONAL POSITIVE REGARD, EMPATHY, AND GENUINENESS
   Rogers proposed that unconditional positive regard, empathy, and genuineness are the key ingredients of good relationships and key methods for helping people develop a positive self-concept.

ADJUSTMENT STRATEGIES *for*

Becoming a Fully Functioning Person

1. Take a positive approach to life and believe in your capacity for personal growth.

2. Be open to experience.

3. Don't be overly defensive.

4. Develop a more positive self-concept.

5. Have harmonious relationships with others.

B. Maslow's Approach

- Abraham Maslow argued that people must satisfy their basic needs before they will be motivated to satisfy higher needs.

- According to Maslow, people satisfy their needs in the following order: physiological, safety, love and belongingness, esteem, and self-actualization.

ADJUSTMENT STRATEGIES *for*

Becoming Self-actualized

1. Be motivated to change.

2. Be responsible.

3. Evaluate your motives.

4. Examine your positive emotional experiences.

5. Have a mission in life.

6. Monitor your progress.

C. Evaluating Humanistic Perspectives

- Humanistic perspectives have brought attention to the importance of how people perceive themselves and the world as well as the significance of conscious experience and the positive qualities of human personality.

- Critics of the humanistic perspective object that it is very difficult to test, that it is overly optimistic, and that it encourages self-absorption.

V. TRAIT PERSPECTIVES

A. Trait Theories

According to trait theories, personality consists of broad, enduring dispositions that are reflected in how people behave.

1. EYSENCK'S DIMENSIONS OF PERSONALITY

   Hans Eysenck proposed that traits arise from the interaction of three dimensions of personality: introversion-extraversion, stable-unstable (or neuroticism), and psychoticism.

2. THE BIG FIVE PERSONALITY FACTORS

   Research by Costa and McCrae provided the foundation for the view that personality can be captured by five "supertraits": openness, conscientiousness, extraversion, agreeableness, and neuroticism (or emotional stability).

B. Traits, Situations, and Culture

Walter Mischel argued that rather than consisting of broad internal traits that are consistent, personality often changes with the situation.

1. TRAIT-SITUATION INTERACTION

   The ability of a trait to predict behavior varies and depends on the trait, the person, and the situation.

2. CULTURE AND PERSONALITY

   • The broad cultural context as well as the immediate situation influences personality.

   • Cultures may be broadly classified according to the extent to which they encourage the traits of individualism or collectivism.

ADJUSTMENT STRATEGIES *for*

Interacting with People from Individualist and Collectivist Cultures*

For those from collectivist cultures who are interacting with someone from an individualist culture,

1. compliment the individual more than you are used to in your collectivist culture.
2. expect the person to be more competitive than people in your collectivist culture.
3. feel free to talk about your accomplishments.
4. expect that a person from an individualist culture will not be as attached to his or her family and extended family as you are.
5. do not expect the person to give a high priority to consensus.

For those from individualist cultures interacting with someone from a collectivist culture,

1. pay attention to the person's group memberships.
2. do not provoke competitive situations.
3. if you must criticize the collectivist, do so only in private.
4. cultivate long-term relationships.

*Based on H. C. Triandis, R. Brislin, & C. Hui, "Cross-cultural Training across the Individualism Divide," *International Journal of Intercultural Relations, 12* (1988): 269–288.

C. Evaluating Trait Perspectives

• Identifying a person's traits does tell us something important about that person, and traits have been linked to various aspects of adjustment.

• Understanding personality requires going beyond traits and also considering situations and their interactions with traits.

VI. PERSONALITY ASSESSMENT

A. Types of Assessment

Assessments of personality vary from tests designed by quacks to scientific measures that are reliable and valid.

B. Projective Tests

Projective tests of personality are based on the assumption that a person's responses to ambiguous stimuli will reflect his or her feelings, needs, and attitudes.

1. **RORSCHACH INKBLOT TEST**
    - People taking a Rorschach test are asked to describe what they see in each of a series of inkblots.
    - The Rorschach does not meet standards of reliability and validity, but many clinicians claim it is a valuable tool.

2. **OTHER PROJECTIVE TESTS**
    - The Thematic Apperception (TAT) is a popular projective test in which people are asked to tell a story about each of a series of pictures.
    - The TAT and other projective tests have been criticized for having low reliability and validity.

C. Self-report Tests
- On self-report tests people are asked whether items describe their personality or not.
- Items are included on empirically keyed self-report tests if they have been shown to predict some independent criterion.
    1. **MINNESOTA MULTIPHASIC PERSONALITY INVENTORY (MMPI)**

    The most widely used empirically keyed personality test is the MMPI.

    2. **ASSESSMENT OF THE BIG FIVE FACTORS**

    The Neuroticism Extraversion Openness Personality Inventory and the Hogan Personality Inventory are used to assess the big five factors.

D. Behavioral and Cognitive Assessment
- Behavioral assessments are based on direct observations of a person's behavior.
- Cognitive assessments aim to discover what thoughts underlie behavior.

Learning Goals

After reading and studying this chapter, you should be able to

1. **Define personality and identify major issues in the study of personality.**

2. **Summarize the psychodynamic perspectives.**
    a. Identify key concepts of Freud's theory.
    b. Explain key ways in which Jung, Adler, and Horney disagreed with Freud.
    c. Identify strengths and weaknesses of the psychodynamic perspectives.

3. **Explain the behavioral and social cognitive perspectives.**
    a. Describe classical conditioning.
    b. Outline key elements of Skinner's behaviorism.
    c. Explain the social cognitive view of personality.
    d. Identify strengths and weaknesses of the behavioral and social cognitive perspectives.

4. **Describe the humanistic perspectives.**
    a. Describe key elements in Rogers's theory.
    b. Outline Maslow's explanation of human behavior.
    c. Identify strengths and weaknesses of the humanistic perspectives.

5. **Discuss the trait perspectives.**
    a. Describe major trait theories.
    b. Discuss the roles of traits and situations in personality.
    c. Identify strengths and weaknesses of the trait perspectives.

6. **Characterize the main methods of personality assessment.**
   a. Describe key characteristics of assessments of personality.
   b. Discuss projective tests.
   c. Describe self-report tests.
   d. Describe how behavioral and cognitive assessments differ from projective and self-report tests.

Guided Review

After you have read this chapter in the textbook, complete these statements. Topics are discussed in the same order as in the chapter. Answers are provided at the end of the study guide chapter.

Learning Goal 1: Define personality and identify major issues in the study of personality

1. Psychologists define _____ as a pattern of enduring, distinctive thoughts, emotions, and behaviors that characterizes the way an individual adapts to the world.

2. The major perspectives on personality offer differing views of the characteristics that are key to adjustment and give different emphases to the roles played in personality by _____ and learned characteristics, by consciousness and the _____, and by internal and external factors.

Learning Goal 2: Summarize the psychodynamic perspectives

Goal 2a: Identify key concepts of Freud's theory

3. According to Freud's psychoanalytic theory, the _____ holds the key to understanding personality.

4. The _____ is the personality structure that consists of instincts and is guided by the pleasure principle.

5. The _____ is the personality structure that is guided by the reality principle.

6. The personality structure that deals with morals is the _____.

7. _____ _____ are unconscious methods by which the ego distorts reality to protect itself from anxiety.

8. The basic defense mechanism that keeps threatening impulses and memories unconscious is

   _____.

9. Freud believed that people go through five stages of development, each of which is characterized by a different focus of pleasure: the _____, _____, _____, latency, and genital stages.

10. During the phallic stage, boys experience the _____ complex, developing an intense desire to replace their fathers in order to enjoy their mothers' love.

11. Either undergratification or overgratification may lead to _____ at a particular stage of development.

Goal 2b: Explain key ways in which Jung, Adler, and Horney disagreed with Freud

12. Compared with Freud, Karen Horney placed less emphasis on biological factors and more emphasis on _____ factors.

13. For Horney, people are primarily motivated by the need for _____.

14. According to Jung, the _____ _____ is the impersonal, deepest layer of the unconscious shared by all human beings.

15. The collective unconscious is reflected through emotion-laden ideas and images called _____.

16. Adler's theory, called _____ psychology, emphasizes each person's uniqueness and holds that people strive for superiority.

17. According to Adler, _____ factors are more important than sexual motivation in shaping personality.

18. The attempt to overcome imagined or real inferiorities or weaknesses by developing one's abilities is called _____, which Adler believed was a normal process.

Goal 2c: Identify strengths and weaknesses of the psychodynamic perspectives

19. Important contributions of psychodynamic perspectives include their attention to early experiences, to conflict and anxiety, and to the _____.

20. Critics claim that psychodynamic perspectives offer an overly _____ view of human nature, that its concepts are difficult to test, and that many of these perspectives have a male, Western bias.

Learning Goal 3: Explain the behavioral and social cognitive perspectives

21. The behavioral and social cognitive perspectives analyze personality by examining how people _____ to behave.

22. Pioneers of the behavioral and social cognitive perspectives discovered three types of learning: classical conditioning, _____ _____, and observational learning.

Goal 3a: Describe classical conditioning

23. Classical conditioning associates a new stimulus with a stimulus (called the unconditioned stimulus) that automatically elicits an unlearned response (called the _____ _____).

24. As a result of its association with the unconditioned stimulus, the conditioned stimulus evokes the _____ _____, which is a response similar to the unconditioned response elicited by the unconditioned stimulus.

Goal 3b: Outline key elements of Skinner's behaviorism

25. Operant conditioning is a form of learning in which the _____ of a behavior change the probability that the behavior will occur.

26. Reinforcement increases the probability that a behavior will occur again; extinction occurs when a behavior is no longer _____.

27. According to Skinner, your behavior is your personality, behavior is learned, and behavior is determined by the _____.

Goal 3c: Explain the social cognitive view of personality

28. Social cognitive theory stresses that personality depends not just on behavior and the environment but also on _____ factors.

29. Albert Bandura demonstrated that people learn not only through operant and classical conditioning but also as a result of _____ _____.

30. According to Bandura, personality depends on behavior, the environment, and cognitive factors and the relationship among these three is characterized by _____ _____.

31. In Bandura's view, adjustment can be measured by people's belief that they can exercise some _____.

32. Three aspects of personal control are _____ _____ _____, self-efficacy, and locus of control.

Goal 3d: Identify strengths and weaknesses of the behavioral and social cognitive perspectives.

33. The behavioral and social cognitive perspectives provides strategies and techniques for improving adjustment, but critics argue that these perspectives ignore the role of biology in personality and that they are _____.

Learning Goal 4: Describe the humanistic perspectives

Goal 4a: Describe key elements in Rogers's theory

34. Rogers believed that each person has an innate tendency to try to become a _____ _____ person.

35. According to Rogers, the greater the discrepancy between the _____ self, which is the self developed from our experiences, and the _____ self, the more maladjusted we are.

36. Rogers proposed three keys to helping people develop a positive self-concept: _____ _____ _____, empathy, and genuineness.

Goal 4b: Outline Maslow's explanation of human behavior

37. Maslow proposed that people are motivated by a hierarchy of needs in which the first needs that must be satisfied are physiological needs followed by _____, love and belongingness, _____, and finally _____, which is the need to develop one's full potential as a human being.

38. According to Maslow, most people stop maturing after they have developed a high level of _____.

Goal 4c: Identify strengths and weaknesses of the humanistic perspectives

39. The humanistic perspectives highlight the whole person and the _____ aspects of human nature, but they are difficult to test, may be overly optimistic, and may encourage narcissism.

Learning Goal 5: Discuss the trait perspectives

Goal 5a: Describe major trait theories

40. The father of trait theory, _____ _____, believed that each individual has a unique set of personality traits.

41. Eysenck found that the interaction of three dimensions of personality—_____, _____, and psychoticism—produces personality traits.

42. Much recent research has focused on the big five factors of personality, or supertraits—_____, _____, _____, agreeableness, and neuroticism.

Goal 5b: Discuss the roles of traits and situations in personality

43. A trait is most likely to predict a person's behavior if it is a very specific trait, if that person tends to display that trait consistently, and if _____ influences are not powerful.

44. People in Eastern cultures are more likely than people in Western cultures to display _____, which is a tendency to value group goals over personal goals.

Goal 5c: Identify strengths and weaknesses of the trait perspectives

45. Trait perspectives have produced research that sheds light on characteristics that are tied to adjustment, but _____ as well as traits must be considered in order to understand personality.

Learning Goal 6: Characterize the main methods of personality assessment

Goal 6a: Describe key characteristics of assessments of personality

46. A measure of personality is _____ if results of the test are consistent over time and in different situations.

47. A measure of personality is _____ if it measures what it claims to measure.

Goal 6b: Discuss projective tests

48. The _____ _____ test, which uses an individual's perceptions of inkblots to assess his or her personality, does not meet criteria of reliability and validity but is still used because many clinicians believe it provides insights about a person's unconscious.

49. The Thematic Apperception Test is a popular _____ test in which an individual is asked to tell a story about a series of pictures.

Goal 6c: Describe self-report tests

50. On the MMPI, NEO-PI-R, and other _____ tests, test takers indicate whether or not the items describe their personalities or behaviors.

51. On the MMPI and other _____ _____ tests, test takers cannot tell from the subject of a test item just what that item is measuring.

Goal 6d: Describe how behavioral and cognitive assessments differ from projective and self-report tests

52. Behavioral assessments, unlike projective and self-report tests, do not aim to remove the influence of the _____ on personality.

53. Cognitive assessments of personality try to discover the _____ that underlie behavior.

Key Terms

Briefly define each key term and provide an example or application.

1. personality

2. psychodynamic perspectives

3. id

4. ego

5. superego

6. defense mechanisms

7. Oedipus complex

8. collective unconscious

9. archetype

10. individual psychology

11. classical conditioning

12. operant conditioning

13. reinforcement

14. extinction

15. punishment

16. social cognitive theory

17. observational learning

18. reciprocal determinism

19. self-efficacy

20. locus of control

21. humanistic perspectives

22. unconditional positive regard

23. hierarchy of needs

24. self-actualization

25. trait theories

26. big five factors of personality

27. individualism

28. collectivism

29. projective test

30. Rorschach inkblot test

31. Thematic Apperception Test (TAT)

32. self-report tests

33. empirically keyed test

34. Minnesota Multiphasic Personality Inventory (MMPI)

Practice Test A

Answer these multiple-choice questions to assess your understanding of the chapter. Answers are provided at the end of the study guide chapter.

____ 1. Psychologists use the word *personality* to refer to
a. a person's ability to adapt in the world.
b. the social and community aspects of a person.
c. the distinctive aspects of a person.
d. the adaptive and successful characteristics of a person.

____ 2. Which theory emphasizes unconscious processes?
a. Psychodynamic
b. Behavioral
c. Humanistic
d. Trait

____ 3. According to Freud, the struggle between meeting one's needs and caring for others is resolved by
a. the id.
b. the ego.
c. the superego.
d. fixations.

____ 4. When a person reverts to an earlier stage of development to resolve unconscious conflicts, the person is using the defense mechanism of
a. regression.
b. rationalization.
c. repression.
d. displacement.

____ 5. According to Karen Horney, the primary force motivating people is
a. a striving for superiority.
b. anatomy, which is destiny.
c. a need for security.
d. the collective unconscious.

____ 6. Which psychodynamic theorist referred to the inferiority complex?
a. Freud
b. Jung
c. Adler
d. Horney

____ 7. Which of the following is true about classical conditioning?
a. Many fears may be learned through classical conditioning.
b. Classical conditioning results from observation.
c. Classical conditioning demonstrates the power of punishment.
d. Classical conditioning demonstrates that attention and conscious memory are necessary if learning is to occur.

____ 8. A behavior that increases in frequency after it is followed by removal of an aversive stimulus has been
a. positively reinforced.
b. negatively reinforced.
c. punished.
d. extinguished.

____ 9. Skinner's approach to personality relies on the idea that
a. behaviors are learned through observation.
b. punishment is more powerful than rewards.
c. personality is behavior and behavior is learned.
d. personality is innate.

____ 10. Another name for observational learning is
a. modeling.
b. classical conditioning.
c. trial and error learning.
d. reciprocal determinism.

____ 11. The belief that you can master a situation is known as
a. self-esteem.
b. locus of control.
c. self-efficacy.
d. self-concept.

____ 12. Carl Rogers believed that
a. the criticisms and constraints that children receive from their parents provide the foundation for healthy adjustment.
b. the criticisms and constraints that children receive from their parents create negative self-perceptions and lead to distortions of their true selves.
c. the criticisms and constraints that children receive from their parents teach self-efficacy.
d. the criticisms and constraints that children receive from their parents foster identification.

____ 13. The humanistic perspectives emphasize the role of
a. the experimental approach to personality.
b. conscious experience.
c. the unconscious.
d. biological factors.

____ 14. Researchers have found that the big five factors of personality
a. show up in assessments of personality in diverse countries.
b. show up in assessments of personality only in Western countries.
c. show up in assessments of personality only in Eastern countries.
d. show up in assessments of personality only among children.

___ 15. The MMPI is useful for
a. diagnosing serious mental disorders.
b. assessing problems such as anger.
c. assessing the careers most appropriate for individuals.
d. all of the above.

Identifying Concepts

Answers are provided at the end of the study guide chapter.

1. DEFENSE MECHANISMS   Identify the defense mechanism illustrated in each example.

a.   Although Lynda never cleans her dorm room, she complains to her parents about her messy roommate.

b.   Hank hates animals but becomes a compassionate zookeeper.

c.   Sue runs home to her mother every time she fights with her husband.

d.   Tom said he did poorly on his exam because of the electrical storm.

2. PEOPLE IN PERSONALITY   For each statement, identify the person whose contribution to psychology is described.

a.   Proposed stages of personality development based on centers of pleasure

b.   Proposed that security, not sex or aggression, is the most important motive

c.   Developed the concept of self-efficacy

d.   Argued that unconditional positive regard is important

e.   Proposed situationism

3. ASSESSMENTS OF PERSONALITY   Identify the type of personality assessment in each example.

a.   You are asked to look at a series of pictures and make up a story about what is going on in each of them.

b.   You are asked to read a series of descriptions and then rate how accurately each description fits you.

c.   You are asked to say the first thing you think of after each of a series of words is read to you.

d.   You are asked to answer a series of questions about what you remember about a serious argument with a close friend or romantic partner on the day after the argument.

Understanding Concepts

Complete these exercises to develop your understanding of important ideas in this chapter.

1. Provide an example of each component in the definition of personality given in the textbook.

2. Discuss the differences between the id and the ego.

3. Explain how Freud's psychoanalytic theory is male-biased.

4. Summarize how Karen Horney, Carl Jung, and Alfred Adler revised Freud's ideas.

5. Describe key differences between classical conditioning and operant conditioning.

6. List and discuss the processes necessary for observational learning to occur.

7. Discuss how delay of gratification, self-efficacy, and an internal locus of control contribute to personal control.

8. Discuss the characteristics of humanistic perspectives that led Maslow to label them a "third force" in psychology.

9. Compare Rogers's fully functioning person with Maslow's self-actualizing person.

10. Discuss the relationship between traits and situations.

11. Contrast individualism and collectivism.

12. Discuss the weaknesses of personality assessments based on face validity.

Applying Concepts and Strategies

Complete these exercises to develop your ability to apply this chapter's material to your life and the world. Your responses will differ from those of other students in the class, and it is helpful to share your ideas with other students.

1. Write a brief description of your own personality. Do you tend to think in terms of the psychodynamic, behavioral, humanistic, or trait approach? Which perspective do you use the least? Why?

2. Suppose you read a case study in which an individual is said to have a very strong superego but a weak id and a weak ego. How would you expect that individual to behave in everyday life? What strengths and what problems do you think that person might display?

3. Describe examples, from your own life if possible, of projection and reaction formation.

4. Assess your use of the three strategies described by Horney: moving toward people, moving away from people, and moving against people. Which of these strategies do you use most? Least? Do you rely on just one or two of these strategies, or do you balance use of the three strategies? Design a course of action that would increase your balance.

5. Provide an example of how classical conditioning influences personality.

6. Select a behavior and describe how it might be influenced by reinforcement.

7. Select one characteristic of your personality. Now list three or four of your behaviors that illustrate this characteristic. Analyze whether these behaviors reflect classical conditioning, operant conditioning, or observational learning.

8. Suppose that you find yourself doing very poorly in school this semester. Every week you resolved to complete the required reading for your courses, but every week you ended up spending only a couple of hours reading and fell farther and farther behind. You had plenty of additional time but always put off the reading in favor of doing something, almost anything, else. Take a social cognitive approach to this problem and describe two steps you might take to increases the chance that you will spend at least five hours a week reading for your courses. Then describe two steps you might take if you adopt a behavioral approach to the problem.

9. List 15 things you did during the past week. Now classify these actions according to which of the needs in Maslow's hierarchy motivated them. Which needs seem to motivate most of your behavior? How does the answer compare with your ideas about what goals are most important to you?

10. Review the description of your personality that you wrote in Exercise 1. Pick a trait that you included in the description and describe five specific times in the last month when you displayed this trait. Can you describe five times when you displayed the trait's opposite? How would you evaluate your consistency on this trait and the effect of situations on your consistency?

Practice Test B

Answer these multiple-choice test questions to help you assess your understanding of the textbook chapter. Answers are provided at the end of the study guide chapter.

___ 1. According to Freud, reasoning, problem solving, and decision making are functions of
a. the id.
b. the unconscious.
c. the ego.
d. the superego.

___ 2. Defense mechanisms
a. function to reduce anxiety.
b. are always unhealthy.
c. are all based on reaction formation.
d. ease social conflicts.

___ 3. Jung believed that the collective unconscious reflects
a. each person's unique history and needs.
b. the shared past of all people.
c. the ego's attempts to constrain the id.
d. the ego's attempts to constrain the superego.

___ 4. When stirring patriotic music is played during a political candidate's commercial, the ad maker probably hopes that the music will serve as
a. an unconditioned stimulus.
b. a conditioned response.
c. an archetype.
d. an unconditioned response.

___ 5. A parent who spanks a son for being disobedient may hope to decrease the boy's disobedience through _____ but may also increase the boy's violent behavior as a result of _____.
a. negative reinforcement; punishment
b. punishment; observational learning
c. negative reinforcement; punishment
d. extinction; negative reinforcement

___ 6. Belief in your ability to exercise control over yourself and events around you is key to adjustment according to
a. psychodynamic theorists.
b. behaviorists.
c. social cognitive theorists.
d. humanistic theorists.

___ 7. People who assume that their own actions are responsible for what happens to them have
a. a superority complex.
b. an inferiority complex.
c. an external locus of control.
d. an internal locus of control.

___ 8. Research has tied an external locus of control with a tendency to
a. know about health-related issues.
b. exercise regularly.
c. conform.
d. use efficient problem-solving strategies.

___ 9. Research regarding Maslow's hierarchy of needs
a. has confirmed the broad outlines of his hierarchy.
b. has not confirmed that the hierarchy actually governs behavior.
c. indicates that esteem needs must be fulfilled before belongingness needs will motivate behavior.
d. indicates that esteem needs must be fulfilled before security needs will motivate behavior.

___ 10. Research regarding the big five factors of personality suggests
a. that more specific traits are better predictors of behavior.
b. that these supertraits are found around the world.
c. that there may be additional supertraits.
d. all of the above.

___ 11. Personality traits have their greatest influence on behavior when
a. people are with others.
b. situational influences are minimal.
c. a person is provided with unconditional positive regard.
d. situational influences are at their peak.

___ 12. Most psychologists in the field of personality today
a. are interactionists.
b. combine psychodynamic and humanistic perspectives.
c. are situationists.
d. are Jungians.

___ 13. People who score high on the conscientiousness dimension tend to
a. have irrational ideas.
b. be productive.
c. have difficulty controlling their impulses.
d. have unhappy marriages.

___ 14. The MMPI
a. is based on face validity.
b. is designed to measure the big five factors of personality.
c. includes validity scales to determine whether the test-taker is being defensive, deceptive, or evasive.
d. includes only clinical scales.

Answers to Chapter Questions

Guided Review

1. personality
2. innate; unconscious
3. unconscious
4. id
5. ego
6. superego
7. defense mechanisms
8. repression
9. oral; anal; phallic
10. Oedipal
11. fixation
12. sociocultural
13. security
14. collective unconscious
15. archetypes
16. individual
17. social
18. compensation
19. unconscious
20. pessimistic (or negative)
21. learn
22. operant conditioning
23. unconditioned response
24. conditioned response
25. consequences
26. reinforced
27. environment
28. cognitive (person)
29. observational learning
30. reciprocal determinism
31. control
32. delay of gratification
33. reductionist (or mechanistic)
34. fully functioning
35. real; ideal
36. unconditional positive regard
37. safety; esteem; self-actualization
38. esteem
39. positive
40. Gordon Allport
41. introversion-extraversion; stable-unstable (neuroticism)
42. openness; conscientiousness, extraversion
43. situational
44. collectivism
45. situations
46. reliable
47. valid
48. Rorschach inkblot
49. projective
50. self-report
51. empirically keyed
52. situation
53. thoughts

Practice Test A

1. c
2. a
3. b
4. a
5. c
6. c
7. a
8. b
9. c
10. a
11. c
12. b
13. b
14. a
15. d

Identifying Concepts

1. DEFENSE MECHANISMS
   a. projection
   b. reaction formation
   c. regression
   d. rationalization
2. PEOPLE IN PERSONALITY
   a. Freud
   b. Horney
   c. Bandura
   d. Rogers
   e. Mischel
3. ASSESSMENTS OF PERSONALITY
   a. projective
   b. self-report
   c. projective
   d. cognitive assessment

Practice Test B

1. c
2. a
3. b
4. a
5. b
6. c
7. d
8. c
9. b
10. d
11. b
12. a
13. b
14. c

CHAPTER **3**   # THE SELF, IDENTITY, AND VALUES

Chapter Outline

I. THE SELF

A. Self-Concept
- Self-concept is an individual's overall thoughts and feelings about his or her abilities, personality, and other attributes.
- Some representations of the self are based on one's own viewpoint; others are based on the viewpoints of other people.
  1. SELF-CONGRUENCE AND SELF-DISCREPANCY
     - The self-concept includes representations of the actual self, the ideal self, and the ought self, among other representations.
     - Discrepancies among these selves create problems, which are described by the self-discrepancy theory of E. Tory Higgins.
  2. POSSIBLE SELVES

     People also have conceptions of their hoped-for possible selves and their dreaded possible selves.
  3. THE SELF IN SOCIOCULTURAL CONTEXT
     - Selves emerge as individuals adapt to their cultural environments.
     - Individualist cultures tend to favor possible selves that emphasize the distinctiveness of the individual, individualism, and assertive self-management.
     - Collectivist cultures tend to favor possible selves that strengthen groups.

B. Self-Esteem
- Self-esteem refers to a person's overall evaluation of his or her self-worth or self-image, an evaluation that does not necessarily match reality.
  1. VARIATIONS IN SELF-ESTEEM
     - People have both a general level of self-esteem and fluctuating degrees of self-esteem related to specific domains of life.
     - Most research finds that self-esteem tends to be stable at least across a month or so, but it can change, especially in response to transitions.

- Variations in self-esteem have been linked with many aspects of adjustment, but much of the research is correlational.

ADJUSTMENT STRATEGIES *for*
Increasing Self-Esteem

1. Identify your sources of self-esteem and the causes of low self-esteem.
2. Face a problem and try to cope with it.
3. Seek emotional support.
4. Take responsibility for your self-esteem.
5. Look for opportunities to achieve.
6. Explore resources to improve your self-understanding.

---

2. THE DARK SIDE OF HIGH SELF-ESTEEM: NARCISSISSM

Narcissists are excessively self-centered and self-congratulatory.

II. IDENTITY

Identity refers to an integrated sense of the self in which different parts come together in a unified whole.

A. Erikson's Ideas on Identity

- Erik Erikson proposed the most comprehensive theory of how identity is formed.
- According to Erikson, questions about identity become especially important in the fifth of Erikson's eight developmental stages, the identity versus identity confusion stage.

1. THE ROLE OF EXPERIMENTATION

The psychosocial moratorium that occurs during the adolescent and emerging adulthood years fosters the search for an identity.

2. IDENTITY OVER THE LIFE SPAN

- Identity development begins during infancy and continues throughout life, but identity development during adolescence and emerging adulthood (from age 18 to 25) is especially critical.
- An identity is formed in bits and pieces, and it may change during adulthood.

B. The Four Statuses of Identity

- According to James Marcia, a individual's status on the path of identity development is defined by the extent to which that individual has experienced an identity crisis and the extent to which he or she has made a commitment to an identity.
- Marcia has described four identity statuses: identity diffusion, identity foreclosure, identity moratorium, and identity achievement.

C. Developmental Changes in Identity

- The timing of identity development may be different for different aspects of identity, such as vocational identity, political identity, and so forth.
- Individuals become more certain of their identity as they move from early to middle adulthood, but they may continue to explore new alternatives as their lives change.

D. Ethnic Identity

Ethnic identity is a sense of membership in an ethnic group, along with attitudes and feelings related to that membership.

1. CONTEXTS AND VARIATIONS IN ETHNIC IDENTITY
   - Ethnic identity tends to be stronger among members of minority groups than among members of mainstream groups.
   - Characteristics of ethnic identity are greatly affected by an individual's context—such as how long an immigrant's family has been in this country and the characteristics of a person's neighborhood.
2. HELMS'S MODEL OF ETHNIC IDENTITY DEVELOPMENT

   Janet Helms has proposed that ethnic identity develops in four stages: pre-encounter, encounter, immersion/emersion, and internalization/commitment.

E. Gender and Identity

Gender differences in identity development have faded as women have developed a stronger interest in careers.

III. VALUES

A. Exploring Values

Individuals might not be aware of their values until they experience a clash between values.

ADJUSTMENT STRATEGIES *for*

Clarifying Your Values*

1. Imagine attending your own funeral and hearing people speak about you.
2. Make a dream list by asking yourself what you would do if you had unlimited time and resources.
3. Take the self-assessment of values in the textbook, review your five most important values, and compare them with the dream list.
4. Take one minute to examine how your values relate to four basic areas of self-fulfillment: physical needs, social needs, mental needs, and spiritual needs.

*Based on S. R. Covey, *The Seven Habits of Highly Effective People* (New York: Simon & Schuster, 1989) and S. R. Covey, A. R. Merrill, & R. R. Merrill, *First Things First* (New York: Simon & Schuster, 1994).

B. College Students' Values
- Compared with U.S. students 30 years ago, college students today show less interest in the well-being of others and in developing a meaningful philosophy of life and more interest in being well off financially.
- Community service brings benefits not only to the recipients of the service but also to the volunteers.

C. Meaning in Life

The search for meaning in life may fulfill a need for purpose, for values, for a sense of efficacy, and for self-worth.

D. Sociocultural Perspectives on Values

Individualist cultures may encourage excessive concern with a search for self-fulfillment, identity, and a positive self-image.

IV. RELIGION

A. The Scope of Religion in People's Lives
- The role of religion in people's lives varies greatly with nationality, gender, and age.
- Commitment to particular religious denominations and institutions is declining in the United States.

B. Religion and Health
   Religious activity has a positive link with various measures of physical health.

C. Religious Coping
   Religion can help people cope with stress.

Learning Goals

After reading and studying this chapter, you should be able to

1. **Discuss self-concept and self-esteem.**
   a. Define *self-concept* and describe its components.
   b. Describe self-esteem, its characteristics, and strategies for enhancing it.

2. **Describe what identity is and how it is formed.**
   a. Explain Erikson's ideas about identity.
   b. Describe the four identity statuses.
   c. Outline how identity changes over the lifetime.
   d. Describe key aspects of ethnic identity.
   e. Discuss gender differences in the development of identity.

3. **Summarize some important aspects of values.**
   a. Explain what values are and why it is important to clarify your own values.
   b. Describe the values of U.S. college students and the benefits of service learning.
   c. Discuss the search for meaning in life.
   d. Describe some negative consequences of pursuing the values emphasized by individualist cultures.

4. **Characterize the role of religion in people's lives.**
   a. Describe variations in the role of religion in people's lives.
   b. Discuss research on links between religion and health.
   c. Outline how religion might help people cope with stress.

Guided Review

After you have read this chapter in the textbook, complete these statements. Topics are discussed in the same order as in the chapter. Answers are provided at the end of the study guide chapter.

Learning Goal 1: Discuss self-concept and self-esteem

Goal 1a: Define self-concept *and describe its components*

1. A _____ consists of a person's overall perceptions, thoughts, and feelings about his or her characteristics, including perceptions of these characteristics from different viewpoints.

2. Our representations of ourselves include not only an _____ self, which represents the characteristics we believe we actually possess, but also an _____ self and an _____ self.

3. According to self-discrepancy theory, discrepancies between the actual and ideal selves lead to dejection-related emotions such as _____ or _____.

4. Self-discrepancy theory also predicts that discrepancies between the actual self and ought self lead to agitated emotions such as _____ or _____.

5. Other components of the self-concept are _____ _____, or conceptions of what we might become.

6. Possible selves provide frameworks for _____.

7. According to Hazel Markus and her colleagues, _____ cultures encourage the development of possible selves that highlight a person's distinctiveness whereas _____ cultures encourage the development of possible selves that are defined in terms of their relationship with others.

Goal 1b: Describe self-esteem, its characteristics, and strategies for enhancing it

8. The overall evaluation of one's self-worth or self-image is called _____.

9. Along with a general level of self-esteem, people may have fluctuating levels of self-esteem regarding various domains such as _____, _____, _____, and _____.

10. Changes in self-esteem are most likely during _____.

11. There are _____ correlations between school performance and self-esteem.

12. High self-esteem is linked with happiness and with a tendency to _____ _____.

13. Strategies for increasing self-esteem include identifying sources of high or low self-esteem, trying to cope with a problem rather than avoiding it; seeking _____ _____, and looking for opportunities to _____.

14. _____ appear to have excessive esteem for themselves and little if any empathy for others.

Learning Goal 2: Describe what identity is and how it is formed

15. _____, which is an integrated sense of self, is a self-portrait composed of many parts, such as a career identity, a religious identity, a political identity, and so on.

Goal 2a: Explain Erikson's ideas about identity

16. Questions about who we are become central during what Erikson called the _____ versus _____ _____ stage.

17. Erikson believed that people who do not successfully resolve the identity crisis suffer _____ _____ and either withdraw from others or lose their identity in the crowd.

18. The gap between childhood security and adult autonomy, known as the _____ _____, gives youth a "selective permissiveness" that facilitates the search for an identity.

19. Identity formation begins during _____, but in adolescence and emerging adulthood a person's development is advanced enough for the person to synthesize earlier identities and construct a path toward maturity.

Goal 2b: Describe the four identity statuses

20. According to Marcia, a person's identity status is based on the existence and extent of _____, which is the exploration of alternative roles and personalities, and of _____, or personal investment in an identity.

21. Identity _____ is the identity status of individuals who have not yet experienced an identity crisis and have not made any identity commitments.

22. Identity _____ is the status of individuals who have made a commitment but have not experienced a crisis.

23. Identity _____ is the status of individuals who are in crisis but have not made a commitment.

24. Individuals who have undergone a crisis and have made a commitment are in the status called identity _____.

Goal 2c: Outline how identity changes over the lifetime

25. Compared with college freshmen, more college seniors are in the status called identity _____.

26. Identity _____ is the process of refining and enhancing the identity choices made earlier.

27. Many individuals who develop positive identities follow "_____" cycles, which they may repeat throughout their lives.

Goal 2d: Describe key aspects of ethnic identity

28. Ethnic identity includes a sense of membership in an _____ _____.

29. Erikson believed that throughout history the struggle of minorities to maintain a _____ identity within the larger culture has fueled the creation of churches, empires, and revolutions.

30. For second-generation immigrants, ethnic identity is likely to be linked to retention of their ethnic group's _____ and _____ _____.

31. The extent to which descendants of immigrants retain ethnic identities may be affected by broad social factors such as media images and _____.

32. For minority youth in poor urban neighborhoods, _____ _____ may be especially good at building ethnic pride.

33. According to Helms's model of ethnic identity development, minority individuals prefer the dominant society's values during the _____ stage.

34. According to Helms, the move to the _____ stage of ethnic identity is usually gradual and often is triggered by some event that tells individuals that they will never belong to the mainstream culture.

35. Helms's stage 3 of ethnic identity development begins with _____ in the minority culture and is followed by discontent with rigid attitudes.

36. In Helms's stage 4 of ethnic identity development, _____/_____, individuals integrate their personal and cultural identities.

Goal 2e: Discuss gender differences in the development of identity

37. In the 1960s and 1970s, _____ concerns were more central to male than to female identity, but gender differences in identity have faded.

Learning Goal 3: Summarize some important aspects of values

Goal 3a: Explain what values are and why it is important to clarify your own values

38. Values are _____ that reflect what matters most to us.

39. A _____ _____ is a clash between values that encourage opposing actions.

40. Clarifying your values increases the chances that you will make good choices about your _____ and about how you spend your time.

Goal 3b: Describe the values of U.S. college students and the benefits of service learning

41. In a 2003 survey, almost _____ of U.S. college freshmen cited financial well-being as a very important reason for attending college.

42. Service learning takes education out into the _____ and helps adolescents become less self-centered.

43. Researchers have found increased motivation and improved _____ among young people who perform community service.

Goal 3c: Discuss the search for meaning in life

44. Viktor Frankl emphasized that the _____ of life adds meaning to it.

45. Roy Baumeister tied the search for meaning to needs for _____, for values, for a sense of efficacy, and for _____.

Goal 3d: Describe some negative consequences of pursuing the values emphasized by individualist cultures

46. Baumeister argues that the individualist culture of the United States leads Americans to place such a high priority on their identity and self-image that they become too _____, too motivated for change, and overly stressed.

47. _____ _____, which is a therapy based on Zen Buddhism, counters self-absorption by providing exercises that train people to live in the present moment and to do constructive work with full attention.

Learning Goal 4: Characterize the role of religion in people's lives
Goal 4a: Describe variations in the role of religion in people's lives

48. Religious interest _____ if it is measured by asking people whether they attend religious services rather than by asking whether they pray.

49. Religious interest tends to be _____ among women than among men.

Goal 4b: Discuss research on links between religion and health

50. Among people in the religious mainstream researchers generally find a _____ or neutral link between religion and physical health.

51. Research has linked religious commitment or participation with moderate blood pressure and with _____ _____.

52. Positive connections between participation in religious organizations and physical health might reflect a healthier life style or the benefit of _____ _____ provided by religious activity.

Goal 4c: Outline how religion might help people cope with stress

53. Religion may help people cope with stress by helping them find meaning or comfort, by providing a way to achieve a sense of mastery and control, by fostering _____ _____ and identity, and by helping them to give up old objects of value and find new sources of significance.

Key Terms

Briefly define each key term and provide an example or application.

1. self-concept

2. actual self

3. ideal self

4. ought self

5. self-discrepancy theory

6. possible selves

7. self-esteem

8. narcissism

9. identity

10. identity versus identity confusion stage

11. psychological moratorium

12. identity diffusion

13. identity foreclosure

14. identity moratorium

15. identity achievement

16. ethnic identity

17. values

18. values conflict

19. service learning

20. morita therapy

Practice Test A

Answer these multiple-choice questions to assess your understanding of the chapter. Answers are provided at the end of the study guide chapter.

____ 1. Your perception of your characteristics, of how others view you, and of the characteristics you would like to possess are part of your
a. actual self.
b. self-concept.
c. self-discrepancy.
d. ought self.

____ 2. Steven would like to be more musical and creative than he has been. This is an example of his
a. ideal self.
b. real self.
c. actual self.
d. ought self.

____ 3. A person is likely to experience guilt, fear, or anxiety as a result of
a. discrepancies between ought and ideal selves.
b. discrepancies between real and actual selves.
c. discrepancies between actual and ideal selves.
d. discrepancies between ought and actual selves.

____ 4. Conceptions of what you might become are your
a. actual self.
b. possible self.
c. interpersonal self.
d. collective self.

____ 5. According to a recent study, self-esteem
a. tends to rise during adolescence and decline in adulthood.
b. tends to remain stable throughout life.
c. tends to decline during adolescence and then rise in adulthood.
d. tends to decline throughout life.

____ 6. If your self-esteem is low, you might improve it by
a. determining the specific sources of your low self-esteem.
b. finding a straightforward skill that you can master.
c. taking advantage of opportunities to be in situations that will give you emotional support or social approval.
d. doing all of the above.

_____ 7. If Raymond has a narcissistic personality, he is likely to
a. think often about his relationships with others.
b. have a grandiose view of his abilities.
c. have a clear view of his actual self.
d. have deep respect for other people.

_____ 8. Questions about identity
a. become a common concern during adolescence.
b. arise for the first time during adolescence.
c. are settled for better or worse during adolescence.
d. are ignored until adolescence passes.

_____ 9. The opportunity to try out different roles and aspects of the personality is offered by
a. the second of Erikson's developmental stages.
b. the preencounter stage.
c. psychosocial moratoriums.
d. psychosexual fixations.

_____ 10. Identity formation usually
a. occurs as a result of a crisis.
b. occurs after a flash of heightened awareness and insight.
c. occurs as a result of great emotional turmoil.
d. occurs gradually, in bits and pieces.

_____ 11. David is in his fourth year of college, has declared a major, and belongs to several social clubs and honor societies. Which is the most likely status of David's identity?
a. identity diffusion
b. identity foreclosure
c. identity moratorium
d. identity achievement

_____ 12. .Ethnic identity
a. exists only among minority groups.
b. tends to be stronger among members of minority groups than among other people.
c. is almost never retained by second-generation immigrants.
d. causes antisocial behavior among adolescents.

_____ 13. Standards that are applied to determine the worth of things are
a. values.
b. metrics.
c. needs.
d. none of the above.

_____ 14. According to Baumeister, the stress felt by many Americans is in part because of
a. overemphasis on living in the present moment.
b. excessive attention to the meaning of life.
c. giving such a high priority to the social good.
d. giving such a high priority to self-fulfillment and personal identity.

_____ 15. Morita therapy
a. is designed to help teenagers overcome identity crises.
b. is designed to improve self-esteem.
c. provides exercises that decrease egocentrism and self-consciousness.
d. provides exercises for dealing with value conflicts.

Identifying Concepts

Answers are provided at the end of the study guide chapter.

1. IDENTITY STATUS. Identify the status described in each statement:

a. Linda has wanted to be a nurse for as long as she can remember.

b. Karen has changed her major four times and still is not certain what she wants to do.

c. Hank spent time exploring alternatives before selecting his major.

2. STUDENTS OF SELF AND IDENTITY Identify the person whose contribution is described in each of the following statements.

a. Developed a model of ethnic identity development

b. Proposed four statuses of identity

c. Developed self-discrepancy theory

d. Explored cultural differences in construction of the self

e. Developed the most comprehensive theory of how identity is formed

Understanding Concepts

Complete these exercises to develop your understanding of important ideas in this chapter.

1. According to self-discrepancy theory, what are the effects of specific types of discrepancies between the various selves? Explain why these effects are expected.

2. What functions are served by dreaded and hoped-for possible selves?

3. Compare and contrast self-esteem and self-efficacy. Which would you expect to do a better job of predicting whether people would bother to vote?

4. How does a psychosocial moratorium contribute to the development of identity?

5. Compare and contrast the main features of each of Marcia's four identity statuses.

6. Describe the stages in Helms's model of ethnic identity development.

7. Summarize the advantages of volunteering to provide services such as tutoring or helping older adults.

8. How, according to Baumeister, does the emphasis on individuality in the United States lead to excessive self-criticism and stress?

9. Summarize the possible explanations for the finding that religious participation is linked to a longer life.

10. Summarize five ways in which religious activity can help people cope with stress.

Applying Concepts and Strategies

Complete these exercises to develop your ability to apply this chapter's material to your life and the world. Your responses will differ from those of other students in the class, and it is helpful to share your ideas with other students.

1. Compare and contrast the roles of your actual self, ideal self, and ought self in your life.

2. How do you think your family members and social networks have influenced your actual self, ideal self, and ought self?

3. How do schools influence the possible selves of students? Did your grade school or high school influence your possible selves? If so, describe that influence and how the curriculum or teaching methods contributed to it. Would you change the curriculum or teaching methods to alter that influence?

4. Select two or three television shows that you know well. Describe how they might affect viewers' actual, ideal, ought, and possible selves. Have they affected your self-understanding?

5. Describe your experience with Marcia's identity statuses: identity diffusion, identity foreclosure, identity moratorium, and identity achievement. How did your gender and your ethnic identity influence your identity development?

6. In what ways do you think youth gangs might be related to identity development?

7. List four values that you think are among the dominant values of your city. Describe the evidence for these values. Do you share these values? Why or why not? Describe several ways in which what you do with your time demonstrates either that you share or that you disagree with one of these values.

Practice Test B

Answer these multiple-choice test questions to help you assess your understanding of the textbook chapter. Answers are provided at the end of the study guide chapter.

___ 1. Your self-concept is influenced by
a. your personal reflections.
b. your experiences.
c. your sociocultural context.
d. all of the above.

___ 2. Joseph feels that he should volunteer time at a nursing home. This is an example of his
a. actual self.
b. ought self.
c. ideal self.
d. real self.

___ 3. A person is likely to experience disappointment, shame, or sadness when there are
a. discrepancies between ought and ideal selves.
b. discrepancies between real and actual selves.
c. discrepancies between actual and ideal selves.
d. discrepancies between actual and ought selves.

___ 4. Discrepancies between different viewpoints of the self or different domains of the self are most likely to produce the emotions predicted by self-discrepancy theory when
a. you are aware of the discrepancy.
b. the discrepancy is important to you.
c. the discrepancy is real, not imagined.
d. all of the above are true.

___ 5. Representations of what a person might become, would like to become, and is afraid of becoming are known as
a. possible selves.
b. probable selves.
c. self-discrepancies.
d. levels of unconsciousness.

___ 6. Having dreaded possible selves as well as hoped-for possible selves
a. is unhealthy, producing paralyzing conflict.
b. creates low self-esteem.
c. is healthy, helping us work toward goals and define what is to be avoided.
d. discourages personal growth.

___ 7. Cultures that encourage people to define their possible selves in ways that strengthen their groups are most likely to be found in
a. Western countries.
b. industrialized countries.
c. nonreligious countries.
d. non-Western countries.

___ 8. People who have high self-esteem
a. rank themselves positively in all domains.
b. are perceiving themselves accurately.
c. may still have varying levels of self-esteem regarding specific domains.
d. are narcissistic.

___ 9. Researchers have found that job performance by adults
a. is sometimes related to self-esteem.
b. depends on self-esteem.
c. is not affected by self-esteem.
d. has no influence on self-esteem.

___ 10. Which of the following is true about individuals with high self-esteem?
a. They are more likely than people with low self-esteem to take initiative.
b. They are prone to both prosocial and antisocial actions.
c. They are more likely than people with low self-esteem to experiment with sex.
d. All of the above.

___ 11. Identity foreclosure occurs when a person
a. has experienced an identity crisis and made an identity commitment.
b. is experiencing an identity crisis and has not yet made an identity commitment.
c. has made an identity commitment but has not experienced an identity crisis.
d. has neither made an identity commitment nor experienced a crisis.

___ 12. The idea that the most important identity changes take place in emerging adulthood rather than during adolescence
a. has been refuted by most research.
b. is refuted by research showing that many adolescents are identity diffused.
c. has not been tested by research.
d. is supported by research showing that the number of individuals with identity-achieved status continues to increase during the last few years of college.

___ 13. Research indicates that a positive ethnic identity among African-American and Latino adolescents is linked to
a. academic problems.
b. low self-esteem.
c. positive engagement with school.
d. truancy.

___ 14. The sequence of stages in Helms's model of ethnic identity development
a. has not been tested by research.
b. has been confirmed by many studies.
c. describes only a minority of adolescents according to research studies.
d. applies only to older adults according to research studies.

Answers to Chapter Questions

Guided Review

1. self-concept
2. actual; ideal; ought
3. sadness; disappointment (*or* shame)
4. anxiety; fear (*or* guilt)
5. possible selves
6. self-evaluation (*or* determining meaning)
7. individualist; collectivist
8. self-esteem
9. school; work; relationships; sexuality (*or* athletics, and so on)
10. transitions
11. modest
12. take initiative
13. emotional support; achieve (*or* improve your self-understanding)
14. narcissists
15. identity
16. identy; identity confusion
17. identity confusion
18. psychosocial moratorium
19. infancy
20. crisis; commitment
21. diffusion
22. foreclosure
23. moratorium
24. achievement
25. achievement
26. consolidation
27. MAMA
28. ethnic group
29. separate
30. language; social networks
31. discrimination
32. youth (*or* community) organizations
33. pre-encounter
34. encounter
35. immersion
36. internalization/commitment
37. vocational (*or* career)
38. standards
39. value conflict
40. goals
41. three fourths
42. community
43. self-esteem (*or* grades *or* motivation)
44. finiteness
45. purpose; self-worth
46. self-critical
47. morita therapy
48. drops
49. higher
50. positive
51. longer life
52. social connections
53. social solidarity

Practice Test A

1. b
2. a
3. d
4. b
5. c
6. d
7. b
8. a
9. c
10. d
11. d
12. b
13. a
14. d
15. c

Identifying Concepts

1. IDENTITY STATUSES
   a. identity foreclosure
   b. identity moratorium
   c. identity achievement
2. STUDENTS OF SELF AND IDENTITY
   a.. Helms
   b. Marcia
   c. Higgins
   d. Markus
   e. Erikson

Practice Test B

1. d
2. b
3. c
4. d
5. a
6. c
7. d
8. c
9. a
10. d
11. c
12. d
13. c
14. a

Chapter Outline

I. WHAT IS STRESS?

A. Definitions of Stress
- Stress is the response to stressors, which are threatening circumstances and events that tax an individual's coping abilities.
- Stressors may be acute or chronic, physical, emotional, or psychosocial.

B. General Adaptation Syndrome
- According to Hans Selye, stressors produce a series of physiological reactions that eventually lead to loss of appetite, muscular weakness, and decreased interest in the world.
- The general adaptation syndrome (GAS) is Selye's term for the body's reaction to stressors that persist, a reaction that has three stages.
    1. ALARM

        During the brief alarm stage the release of cortisol and the arousal of the sympathetic nervous system mobilize the body's resources for action.
    2. RESISTANCE

        The resistance stage of the GAS is marked by physiological changes that help the body protect itself from injury and infection.
    3. EXHAUSTION

        If the stressor persists and the body enters the exhaustion stage, physiological reactions that were helpful in the short term may begin to cause irreversible damage.

C. Cognitive Appraisal
- Reactions to potential stressors vary from one individual to another.
- Whether an event is stressful depends to some degree on an individual's cognitive appraisal, which takes place in two steps: an interpretation of the event and an evaluation of one's ability to cope with it.

II. STRESS AND ILLNESS

A. Stress and the Immune System
- The immune system recognizes and destroys foreign materials such as bacteria, viruses, and tumors, thus defending the body against disease.
- Psychoneuroimmunology examines connections among psychological factors, the nervous system, and the immune system.
- Research indicates that both acute and chronic stressors alter the functioning of the immune system.

B. Stress and Cardiovascular Disease
- Chronic stress is associated with high blood pressure, heart disease, and early death.
- Stress can affect the development and course of cardiovascular disease both directly and indirectly.

C. Stress and Cancer
- Cancer may influence a person's quality of life and health-related behaviors in ways that create stress.
- The stress created by cancer may compromise the immune system, damaging the body's ability to resist cancer.

III. SOURCES AND MEDIATORS OF STRESS

A. Environmental Factors
Cataclysmic events such as war, fire, and the death of a loved one are important stressors, but so are many everyday situations.

1. LIFE EVENTS AND DAILY HASSLES
- When several stressors are simultaneously experienced, their effects may be compounded.
- Holmes and Rahe devised the Social Readjustment Rating Scale to measure the possible effect of clusters of life events—such as changing jobs, getting married, getting divorced—but total scores on the scale do not reliably predict future health.
- An alternative approach measures daily hassles and daily uplifts, but such assessments also fail to accurately predict future health.

2. CONFLICT
- Conflict occurs whenever we must decide between incompatible options, and it acts as a potential stressor.
- Major types of conflict are approach/approach, avoidance/avoidance, and approach/avoidance.

3. OVERLOAD
Stimuli can overwhelm our ability to cope with them, producing overload, which can lead to burnout, a state of physical and emotional exhaustion.

ADJUSTMENT STRATEGIES *for*

Avoiding Burnout*

1. Take an inventory of the stressors in your life.
2. Pare down your commitments.
3. Pamper yourself.
4. Recognize when to seek outside help.

* Based on M. C. Stoppler, *Stress Management* (2003), http://stress.about.com.

B. Personality Factors

Certain personality characteristics help or hinder people to cope with stressors and make them more or less vulnerable to illness.

1. TYPE A/TYPE B BEHAVIOR PATTERNS

   Excessive competitiveness, impatience, hostility, and being hard-driven are part of the Type A behavior pattern.

2. HOSTILE AND ANGRY PEOPLE
   - Hostility is the component of the Type A behavior pattern that has been most consistently linked with coronary problems.
   - Some people are hot reactors: their physiological reactions to stressors are intense.
   - Contrary to the catharsis hypothesis, acting out your anger does not reduce anger in the long term.

ADJUSTMENT STRATEGIES *for*

Reducing Anger

1. Wait.
2. Relax.
3. Change the way you think.
4. Solve problems.
5. Help others.
6. Change your perspective.
7. Join or form a self-help group.
8. Seek counseling.

---

3. HARDINESS
   - Research indicates that a hardy personality can provide a buffer against stress.
   - Hardiness is a personality style characterized by a sense of commitment, a sense of control, and a tendency to perceive problems as challenges.

4. PERSONAL CONTROL
   - Self-efficacy and an internal locus of control are two components of personal control.
   - The perception as well as the reality of personal control can buffer the effect of stressors.

C. Work-Related Factors

Lack of control, overload, and jobs that do not meet expectations are important sources of stress on the job.

D. Sociocultural Factors

Sociocultural factors influence what stressors we encounter, how we perceive them, and how we confront them.

1. GENDER

   Although females show the same immediate physiological responses to acute stress that males do, other factors may make aggressive responses to stressors less likely in females than in males.

2. ACCULTURATIVE STRESS
   - The negative consequences of contact between distinctive cultural groups is called acculturative stress.
   - People may try to adapt to cultural conflict through assimilation, integration, separation, or marginalization.

3. POVERTY

- A disproportionate number of people in U.S. minority groups are poor and thus face stressors as a result of both acculturative stress and poverty.
- Poverty may bring many chronic stressors such as inadequate housing, vulnerability to crime, and economic uncertainty.

IV. POST-TRAUMATIC STRESS DISORDER

Post-traumatic stress disorder (PTSD) is a psychological disorder that may develop after exposure to a traumatic event.

A. Symptoms and Developmental Course of PTSD

- Symptoms of PTSD may include flashbacks, constricted ability to feel emotions, excessive arousal, difficulties with memory and concentration, feelings of apprehension, and impulsive outbursts.
- For PTSD to be diagnosed, the symptoms must be severe and endure for more than a month.
- Most people who experience traumatic events do not develop PTSD.

B. Stressful Events and PTSD

Various highly stressful events can trigger PTSD, including the following:

1. COMBAT AND WAR-RELATED TRAUMA

2. ABUSE

3. NATURAL AND UNNATURAL DISASTERS

ADJUSTMENT STRATEGIES *for*

Coping with a Terrorist Attack*

1. Identify your feelings.
2. Remember past coping successes.
3. Talk with others about your fears.
4. Try to maintain your routines.
5. Think positively.
6. Understand that terrorist attacks create fear and uncertainty.
7. If you are having trouble coping, consider seeing a mental health professional.

*Based on American Psychological Association, *Coping with Terrorism* (Washington, DC: APA, 2003).

Learning Goals

After reading and studying this chapter, you should be able to

1. **Explain what stress is and describe its main components.**
   a. Define stress.
   b. Outline the reactions that constitute the general adaptation syndrome.
   c. Explain how cognitive appraisal influences the response to stressors.

2. **Discuss links between stress and illness.**
   a. Discuss what psychoneuroimmunology has revealed about the link between stress and the immune system.
   b. Outline the links between stress and cardiovascular disease.
   c. Describe the relationship between cancer and stress.

3. **Identify key sources and buffers of stress.**
   a. Describe major environmental sources of stress.
   b. Discuss the role that personality characteristics can play in decreasing or increasing vulnerability to stress.
   c. Outline characteristics that can make a job stressful.
   d. Discuss how gender, conflict between cultures, and poverty are related to stress.

4. **Characterize post-traumatic stress disorder.**
   a. Describe the symptoms and typical course of PTSD.
   b. Outline the types of events that can trigger PTSD.

Guided Review

After you have read this chapter in the textbook, complete these statements. Topics are discussed in the same order as in the chapter. Answers are provided at the end of the study guide chapter.

Learning Goal 1: Explain what stress is and describe its main components
Goal 1a: Define stress

1. _____ is the response of individuals to the circumstances and events that threaten them and tax their coping abilities.

2. _____ are threatening aspects of the environment that induce stress reactions.

Goal 1b: Outline the reactions that constitute the general adaptation syndrome

3. _____, founder of stress research, defined stress as the wear and tear on the body due to the demands placed on it.

4. The _____ _____ _____ describes the common effects on the body if stressors persist, and it consists of the three stages of alarm, resistance, and exhaustion.

5. During the _____ stage, which is essentially the same as the fight-or-flight response, the body mobilizes its resources.

6. Physiological changes during the alarm stage involve two pathways: the _____- _____ pathway and the sympathetic nervous system pathway.

7. Signals along the two pathways during the arousal stage result in the release of _____, norepinephrine, and epinephrine.

8. As a result of the signals transmitted during the alarm stage, _____ _____, _____ _____, and attention all increase.

9. During the _____ stage of the GAS, activity of the endocrine and sympathetic nervous systems remains elevated.

10. Activity during the resistance stage includes the release of hormones that reduce _____.

11. If stressors persist too long, the body's reactions become so damaging that the individual moves into the _____ stage, which may bring irreversible damage to the body and even death.

Goal 1c: Explain how cognitive appraisal influences the response to stressors

12. _____ _____ is Lazarus's term for a two-step process in which individuals interpret events in their lives as harmful, threatening, or challenging and determine whether they can cope with the events.

13. According to Lazarus, in _____ appraisal individuals interpret whether an event involves harm that has already occurred, a threat of some future danger, or a challenge to be overcome.

14. During _____ appraisal individuals evaluate their resources and determine how to use them to cope with an event.

Learning Goal 2: Discuss links between stress and illness

Goal 2a: Discuss what psychoneuroimmunology has revealed about the link between stress and the immune system

15. During the alarm and exhaustion stages of the GAS, the _____ system functions poorly, making the body vulnerable to disease.

16. Psychoneuroimmunology is the field that explores connections among psychological factors (such as emotions), the _____ system, and the _____ system.

17. The immune system helps keep us healthy by recognizing and combating _____, _____, and other foreign bodies.

18. The basic machinery of the immune system consists of _____ _____ _____, which are released from organs of the lymph system located throughout the body.

19. The release of _____-_____ _____ from the hypothalamus starts the chain of reactions that signals the adrenal gland to produce cortisol in response to stressors.

20. The presence of both acute and chronic stressors has been linked to _____ _____ of the immune system.

21. Having good social relationships has been linked with increased levels of a type of white blood cells called _____ cells.

Goal 2b: Outline the links between stress and cardiovascular disease

22. Chronic stress is associated with high _____ _____, heart disease, and early death.

23. Stress can affect the development of heart disease directly, by altering _____ processes, and indirectly, by affecting the frequency of smoking, overeating, and exercise.

Goal 2c: Describe the relationship between cancer and stress

24. Being diagnosed with cancer and receiving treatments for cancer can increase _____, which in turn can suppress the body's ability to fight off disease.

25. Diminished activity of _____ cells occurs in cancer patients, and low activity of these cells is linked with the development of additional malignancies.

Learning Goal 3: Identify key sources and buffers of stress

Goal 3a: Describe major environmental sources of stress

26. Cataclysmic events such as _____, _____, and _____ constitute one type of stressor, but everyday hassles are another environmental source of stress.

27. The _____ _____ _____ was developed by Holmes and Rahe to measure the cumulative effect of clusters of life events, but by itself it cannot accurately predict future health.

28. Yet another source of stress is _____, which occurs when one must decide between incompatible stimuli.

29. In the least stressful type of conflict, an _____/_____ conflict, the individual must choose between two attractive stimuli or circumstances.

30. In an _____/_____ conflict the individual must choose between two unattractive options.

31. In an _____/_____ conflict the individual faces one stimulus or circumstance that has both positive and negative characteristics; vacillation is a frequent response.

32. A gradual accumulation of everyday stresses may cause _____, which is a state of exhaustion marked by chronic fatigue and a feeling of hopelessness.

Goal 3b: Discuss the role that personality characteristics can play in decreasing or increasing vulnerability to stress

33. Decades ago, cardiologists Friedman and Rosenman suggested that men who developed coronary disease tended to display what was called the _____ _____ behavior pattern, characterized by traits such as excessive competitiveness, impatience, and hostility.

34. Further research showed that the component of Type A behavior most consistently associated with coronary problems is _____.

35. People who are outwardly hostile or who turn anger inward are more likely than less angry people to

_____ _____ _____.

36. Research suggests that the _____ hypothesis regarding anger is incorrect, and acting angrily does not have any long-term power to reduce anger.

37. Two first steps for reducing anger are simply to _____ and _____ if you find yourself becoming angry.

38. Stress may be buffered by a _____ personality, which is characterized by a sense of commitment, a sense of control, and a tendency to perceive problems as challenges.

39. Two components of a sense of control are _____ and an _____ locus of control.

Goal 3c: Outline characteristics that can make a job stressful

40. Workplace stress is likely to be high when people have little _____ over the workplace, when they experience overload, and when their jobs do not meet their expectations.

41. Work-related stress is likely to be high under conditions of _____ autonomy and _____ external control.

42. One recent study found that the employees most likely to experience stress are those who feel they are not up to the job despite having _____ over their job responsibilities.

Goal 3d: Discuss how gender, conflict between cultures, and poverty are related to stress

43. Sociocultural factors influence stress by affecting which _____ individuals are likely to encounter as well as how they perceive and believe they should confront them.

44. Some theorists argue that women are more likely to respond to stressors with a _____-and-_____ response instead of the fight-or-flight response.

45. Research indicates that the _____ _____ _____ to acute stressors by men and women are the same.

46. Aggression in women seems to be more _____ than aggression in men.

47. The negative consequences that result from contact between two distinctive cultural groups is called _____ _____.

48. People from a minority culture may adapt to the dominant culture through _____, _____, _____, or marginalization.

49. Female-headed families and people from minority groups are more likely than others to face additional stress from _____.

50. Potent stressors in the lives of the poor include inadequate _____, increased vulnerability to _____, economic uncertainty, and other conditions that create a sense of powerlessness.

Learning Goal 4: Characterize post-traumatic stress disorder

51. _____ _____ _____ is a psychological disorder that develops through exposure to a traumatic event.

Goal 4a: Describe the symptoms and typical course of PTSD

52. Symptoms of PTSD vary but may include _____, constricted ability to feel emotions, excessive arousal, difficulties with _____ and concentration, apprehension, and impulsive outbursts of behavior.

53. Many people exposed to a traumatic event display some symptoms of PTSD after the event, but PTSD is only diagnosed if symptoms are _____ and last for at least a month.

54. Symptoms of PTSD may appear immediately after the trauma, or they may not appear until _____ later.

55. Typically, people who suffer from PTSD experience some periods of _____.

Goal 4b: Outline the types of events that can trigger PTSD

56. PTSD may be triggered by highly stressful circumstances and events such as war, abuse, or _____ such as earthquakes and plane crashes.

Key Terms

Briefly define each key term and provide an example or application.

1. stress

2. stressors

3. general adaptation syndrome (GAS)

4. cognitive appraisal

5. psychoneuroimmunology

6. approach/approach conflict

7. avoidance/avoidance conflict

8. approach/avoidance conflict

9. burnout

10. Type A behavior pattern

11. Type B behavior pattern

12. catharsis

13. hardiness

14. acculturative stress

15. post-traumatic stress disorder (PTSD)

Practice Test A

Answer these multiple-choice questions to assess your understanding of the chapter. Answers are provided at the end of the study guide chapter.

____ 1. Stress refers to the response to
a. threatening circumstances.
b. events that tax an individual's ability to cope.
c. physical or emotional threats.
d. any of the above.

___ 2. According to Selye, stressors eventually produce
a. muscular weakness.
b. decreased interest in the world.
c. loss of appetite.
d. all of the above.

___ 3. The general adaptation syndrome (GAS) is
a. the set of symptoms associated with post-traumatic stress syndrome.
b. the initial reaction to a stressor.
c. Selye's term for the set of effects on the body when stressors persist.
d. the response of the immune system when a stressor first appears.

___ 4. The alarm stage is
a. the brief first stage of the GAS.
b. the extended response of the sympathetic nervous system to a stressor.
c. the second stage of the GAS.
d. the final stage of the GAS.

___ 5. Which of the following statements about cortisol is true?
a. It is a steroid released by the adrenal glands.
b. It helps get "fuel" to the muscles for increased activity.
c. At high levels it suppresses the immune system.
d. All of the above are true.

___ 6. The alarm stage of the GAS
a. produces hormones that inflame the muscles.
b. damages the adrenal glands.
c. mobilizes the body's resources.
d. decreases vigilance.

___ 7. The circulation of high levels of hormones that reduce inflammation is characteristic of
a. the alarm stage of the GAS.
b. the resistance stage of the GAS.
c. the exhaustion stage of the GAS.
d. none of the above.

___ 8. During the exhaustion stage of the GAS
a. hormonal activity returns to pre–alarm stage levels.
b. functioning of the immune system returns to pre–alarm stage levels.
c. activity of NK-cells returns to pre–alarm stage levels.
d. responses that were helpful in the short term may cause irreversible damage.

___ 9. Two people might respond to a stressor in different ways because of differing
a. cognitive appraisals.
b. personality characteristics.
c. sociocultural characteristics.
d. all of the above.

___ 10. Lazarus's term for individuals' interpretation of events as harmful, threatening, or challenging and their determination of whether they can cope with the events is
a. fight-or-flight response.
b. tend-and-befriend response.
c. catharsis.
d. cognitive appraisal.

___ 11. The scientific field that explores connections among psychological factors, the nervous system, and the immune system is
a. psychoneuroimmunology.
b. endocrinology.
c. psychiatry.
d. oncology.

___ 12. Research to date has shown that
a. stress may activate dormant viruses that diminish the individual's ability to cope with disease.
b. acute but not chronic stressors are linked to a decline in activity of the immune system.
c. acute and chronic stressors are linked to changes in the functioning of the immune system.
d. stress is tied to an increase in the activity of NK-cells.

___ 13. Research by Cohen and his colleagues suggests
a. that interpersonal but not work-related stress influences the immune system.
b. that stress-triggered changes in the immune system and hormones might increase vulnerability to infection.
c. that stress directly promotes disease-producing processes.
d. none of the above.

___ 14. The Social Readjustment Rating Scale
a. produces a measure of life events that a person has experienced in the past year.
b. often fails to predict future health problems.
c. includes positive as well as negative events but ignores the tension of daily hassles.
d. does all of the above.

___ 15. A personality style that is characterized by impatience, hostility, and excessive competitiveness is known as the
a. Type C behavior pattern.
b. Type B behavior pattern.
c. Type A behavior pattern.
d. hardy personality.

___ 16. Research consistently links an increased risk of coronary problems with
a. the Type B behavior pattern.
b. the hardy personality type.
c. a hostile personality.
d. an external locus of control.

___ 17. Research indicates that acting angrily
a. has a cathartic event.
b. reduces anger in the long term.
c. increases anger in the short term but eventually reduces it.
d. does not reduce anger in the long term.

___ 18. Research on the hardy personality type indicates that
a. hardiness does not influence the effects of stressors.
b. hardiness may provide a buffer against stress.
c. personality characteristics do not influence the effects of stressors.
d. hardiness increases vulnerability to stress.

_____ 19. Members of an ethnic minority may
a. avoid acculturative stress through assimilation.
b. minimize acculturative stress if they can choose features from both the minority and the dominant cultures.
c. avoid acculturative stress through marginalization.
d. minimize acculturative stress through marginalization.

_____ 20. Post-traumatic stress disorder is
a. the set of physiological reactions that occurs immediately after a traumatic event.
b. a psychological disorder that develops through exposure to a traumatic event.
c. a medical condition that occurs immediately after a traumatic event.
d. the set of psychological reactions that occurs immediately after a traumatic event.

Identifying Concepts

Answers are provided at the end of the study guide chapter.

1. HARDINESS   Identify the characteristic of hardiness that is illustrated by each statement.

a. Mimi is a take-charge person.

b. Jen is excited about the expanded responsibilities at work.

c. Dick is devoted to helping his colleagues.

2. IMPORTANT PEOPLE IN RESEARCH ON STRESS Identify the person whose contribution to stress research is described by each statement.

a. Developed theory of GAS

b. Proposed Type A behavior pattern

c. Proposed concept of cognitive appraisal

Understanding Concepts

Complete these exercises to develop your understanding of important ideas in this chapter.

1. Identify the three stages of Selye's general adaptation syndrome.

2. Discuss the links between stress and illness.

3. Describe the scale designed by Holmes and Rahe, what it aims to measure, and whether it is successful.

4. Summarize the weaknesses of attempts to predict health by adding up a person's self-report of daily hassles.

5. Describe the three major types of conflict.

6. What conditions increase the chances that a person will experience burnout?

7. Compare the psychoanalytic catharsis hypothesis and the social learning theory view of catharsis.

8. Describe the hardy personality and discuss its role as a stress buffer.

9. Discuss ways in which poverty may increase powerlessness and thus vulnerability to stress.

10. Describe the symptoms of PTSD.

Applying Concepts and Strategies

Complete these exercises to develop your ability to apply this chapter's material to your life and the world. Your responses will differ from those of other students in the class, and it is helpful to share your ideas with other students.

1. Think back over the last month and describe three stressors that you faced. In each case, what was your primary appraisal of the stressor? Your secondary appraisal? Did you experience stress?

2. Complete Self-Assessment 4.1: How Vulnerable Am I? and evaluate the results. How vulnerable are you? What could you do to reduce your vulnerability?

3. Some people bounce a check and become completely stressed out about it. Other people bounce a check and don't worry about it. What factors might explain such vast differences in responding to potentially stressful events?

4. One strategy mentioned in the textbook for reducing anger is to change the way you think. Recall the last two times you got angry. What specific steps could you have taken to change the way you thought about the incident? What are other strategies for reducing anger?

5. Do you think that you have a hardy personality? Why or why not?

6. How might assimilation be stressful for a first-generation immigrant?

7. Imagine that you are homeless for one day. What new stressors do you think you would experience? What would you be able to do to buffer their effect?

Practice Test B

Answer these multiple-choice test questions to help you assess your understanding of the textbook chapter. Answers are provided at the end of the study guide chapter.

____ 1. Selye concluded that stressors of different types produce
a. the same physical reactions and eventually similar symptoms.
b. unique physical reactions.
c. a few basic types of physical reactions.
d. varied physical reactions depending on how the events are interpreted.

___ 2. The alarm stage of the GAS
a. appears only in men.
b. is essentially the same as the fight-or-flight response described by Cannon.
c. is essentially the same as the first step of the process of cognitive appraisal.
d. appears only when the stressor is a threat to survival.

___ 3. During the alarm stage signals that travel through the neuroendocrine-immune pathway
a. decrease the levels of cortisol in the body.
b. decrease the levels of epinephrine in the body.
c. increase the levels of cortisol in the body.
d. shut down the immune system.

___ 4. The neuroendocrine-immune pathway
a. goes through the hypothalamus and the sympathetic nervous system.
b. goes through the hypothalamus and the parasympathetic nervous system.
c. goes through the hypothalamus and the pituitary gland to the adrenal glands.
d. goes through the pituitary to the thalamus.

___ 5. During the alarm stage the signals that pass through the sympathetic nervous system
a. result in the release of epinephrine and norepinephrine.
b. result in a decrease in levels of epinephrine and norepinephrine.
c. increase blood pressure and decrease heart rate.
d. decrease the levels of cortisol.

___ 6. Lauren thinks of an upcoming job evaluation as a challenge; Joe thinks of it as a threat to his future with his company. According to Lazarus, their reactions are examples of
a. secondary appraisal.
b. exhaustion stage.
c. primary appraisal.
d. burnout.

___ 7. Lauren decides that she should prepare for her evaluation by reviewing the events of the last few months before she comes to work in the morning; Joe decides that he should call in sick and hope that the evaluation is forgotten. According to Lazarus, their reactions are examples of
a. secondary appraisal.
b. exhaustion stage.
c. primary appraisal.
d. burnout.

___ 8. The chain of reactions that signals the adrenal gland to produce cortisol
a. begins with the release of NK-cells from the pituitary.
b. begins with the release of corticotrophin-releasing hormone (CRH) by the hypothalamus.
c. ends with the release of NK-cells from the pituitary.
d. ends with the release of CRH by the hypothalamus.

___ 9. Research by Cohen and his colleagues found that
a. stress had no effect on the probability that adults exposed to a virus would catch a cold.
b. positive ties with family and friends had no effect on the probability that adults exposed to a virus would catch a cold.
c. adults who faced interpersonal or work-related stress for at least a month were more likely than people who experienced less stress to catch a cold after exposure to viruses.
d. interpersonal but not work-related stress influenced the probability that adults would catch a cold.

___ 10. Research on possible links between chronic stress and cardiovascular disease indicates that
a. stress influences the risk of cardiovascular disease only indirectly, by influencing health-related behavior.
b. stress cannot affect the physiological processes that underly the development and course of cardiovascular disease.
c. stress influences the risk of cardiovascular disease both directly, through its effect on physiological processes, and indirectly.
d. reactions to physical stressors but not psychological stressors may influence the processes that underly cardiovascular disease.

___ 11. Research on stress and cancer indicates that
a. stress causes cancer through both its direct physiological effects and its indirect effects on behavior.
b. stress has no effect on the development or course of cancer.
c. stressors initiate biological changes that inhibit cellular immune responses that in turn affect the development and course of cancer.
d. none of above is true.

___ 12. A study that compared nations that had fought and nations that remained at peace in wars since 1900 found
a. no difference in rates of violence after the war.
b. that postwar rates of crime were lower in nations that had fought.
c. that postwar rates of homicide were lower in nations that had fought.
d. that postwar rates of homicide were higher in nations that had fought.

___ 13. Research comparing male and females responses to acute stressors shows that
a. the fight-or-flight response occurs only in males.
b. females are likely to display a tend-or-befriend response.
c. males are likely to display a tend-or-befriend response.
d. immediate hormonal and sympathetic nervous system responses are the same in males and females.

___ 14. The symptoms of PTSD
a. appear immediately after a traumatic event.
b. appear within a month after a traumatic event.
c. might not appear until years after a traumatic event.
d. do not appear until a month after a traumatic event.

___ 15. The chances that a person will develop PTSD appear to
a. depend entirely on the nature of a traumatic event.
b. increase if the person chose to be exposed to the event.
c. decrease if the person had some preparation for the traumatic event or some autonomy during the event.
d. increase if the person had decision-making authority during the traumatic event.

Answers to Chapter Questions

Guided Review
1. stress
2. stressors
3. Selye
4. general adaptation syndrome (GAS)
5. alarm
6. neuroendocrine-immune
7. cortisol
8. blood pressure; heart rate
9. resistance
10. inflammation
11. exhaustion
12. cognitive appraisal
13. primary

14. secondary
15. immune
16. nervous; immune
17. bacteria; viruses
18. white blood cells
19. corticotrophin-releasing hormone
20. poorer functioning
21. NK-
22. blood pressure
23. physiological
24. stress
25. NK-
26. war; fire; accidents
27. Social Readjustment Rating Scale
28. conflict
29. approach/approach
30. avoidance/avoidance
31. approach/avoidance
32. burnout
33. Type A
34. hostility
35. develop heart disease
36. catharsis
37. wait; relax
38. hardy
39. self-efficacy; internal
40. control
41. low; high
42. control
43. stressors
44. tend; befriend
45. immediate physiological responses
46. cerebral
47. acculturative stress
48. assimilation; integration; separation
49. poverty
50. housing; crime
51. post-traumatic stress disorder
52. flashbacks; memory
53. severe
54. years
55. remission
56. disasters

Practice Test A
1. d
2. d

3. c
4. a
5. d
6. c
7. b
8. d
9. d
10. d
11. a
12. c
13. b
14. d
15. c
16. c
17. d
18. b
19. b
20. b

Identifying Concepts
1. HARDINESS
   a. control
   b. challenge
   c. commitment
2. IMPORTANT PEOPLE
   a. Selye
   b. Friedman and Rosenman
   c. Lazarus

Practice Test B
1. a
2. b
3. c
4. c
5. a
6. c
7. a
8. b
9. c
10. c
11. c
12. d
13. d
14. c
15. c

CHAPTER 5

COPING

Chapter Outline

I. EXPLORING COPING

A. What Is Coping?

Coping is the process of managing taxing circumstances, expending effort to solve life's problems, and seeking to master or reduce stress.

B. Classifications of Coping

Several ways of classifying coping strategies have been influential.

1. PROBLEM-FOCUSED AND EMOTION-FOCUSED COPING

    • Problem-focused coping is the strategy of facing and trying to solve problems.

    • Emotion-focused coping is the strategy of responding to problems emotionally, especially by using defensive mechanisms.

2. MEANING-MAKING COPING

    Meaning-making coping draws on beliefs, values, and goals to modify the meaning of a stressful situation.

3. ACTIVE-COGNITIVE, ACTIVE-BEHAVIORAL, AND AVOIDANCE STRATEGIES

    • Active-cognitive strategies are coping responses in which individuals actively think about a situation in an effort to adjust more effectively.

    • Active-behavioral strategies are coping responses in which individuals take some action to improve their situation.

    • Avoidance coping strategies are responses that aim to keep stressful circumstances out of awareness.

C. Coping and Contexts

The effectiveness of a particular coping strategy depends in part on the demands and resources of the environment.

II. STRATEGIES FOR COPING

A. Think Positively and Optimistically

- Thinking positively and avoiding negative thoughts is almost always a good coping strategy.
- A positive mood improves our ability to process information and enhances self-esteem.

  1. COGNITIVE RESTRUCTURING AND POSITIVE SELF-TALK
     - Cognitive restructuring is the process of replacing thoughts that maintain a problem.
     - One tool used in cognitive restructuring is self-talk, the statements we make to ourselves when we think about something.

ADJUSTMENT STRATEGIES *for*

Self-Talk

1. Fine tune your self-talk.
2. Use uncomfortable emotions as a cue to listen to your self-talk.
3. Assess your self-talk during difficult situations.
4. Compare your self-talk predictions with what actually took place.
5. Enlist someone's help in identifying ways in which your self-talk is distorted.
6. Find out which self-statements help you to cope effectively.

---

  2. POSITIVE SELF-ILLUSIONS

     Having positive illusions about ourselves can help us cope with the world, although imagining negative outcomes can help us prepare for problems.

  3. DEVELOPING AN OPTIMISTIC OUTLOOK
     - Being optimistic often helps coping.
     - Seligman treats optimism as a tendency to explain bad events as the result of external, unstable, and specific causes; others define optimism as the expectation that good thing are more likely to happen than bad things.
     - Research indicates that compared with pessimists, optimists tend to be physically and mentally healthier and to function more effectively.

ADJUSTMENT STRATEGIES *for*

Becoming More Optimistic*

1. Identify your thoughts and feelings after an unpleasant event.
2. Identify your pattern of thinking about unpleasant events.
3. Distract yourself from pessimistic thoughts.
4. Dispute your pessimistic thoughts.

* Based on M. E. P. Seligman, *Learned Optimism* (New York: Knopf, 1990).

B. Increase Self-Control

A belief that we have control of ourselves and our circumstances has three key components—an internal locus of control, a strong sense of self-efficacy, and the ability to delay gratification—and each increases the chances that we will deal with problems effectively.

   1. THOUGHT STOPPING

Thought stopping is the self-control strategy in which a person says "Stop!" when an unwanted thought occurs and immediately replaces it with a more pleasant thought.

   2. EMPOWERMENT

To empower is to help individuals develop skills they need to control their own lives.

C. Seek Social Support

Social support is feedback from others that one is loved, esteemed, and part of a network of communication and mutual obligation.

D. Use Proactive Coping

Proactive coping aims to eliminate, offset, or reduce the impact of potential stressors before they occur.

E. Engage in Enjoyable Activities and Use Humor

- Enjoyable activities and humor can make people less inhibited and therefore able to cope more effectively.
- Enjoyable activities lead to positive emotions, which in turn aid coping.
- Positive humor dampens stress and strengthens the immune system.

F. Use Multiple Coping Strategies

Using several coping strategies is likely to be more effective than relying on just one strategy.

III. COPING WITH EMOTIONS

A. Emotional Approach Coping

- Emotional approach coping is the strategy of actively processing and expressing emotion.
- Research suggests that emotional approach coping might be adaptive in the short term but leads to rumination in the long term.

B. Regulation of Emotion

- Two widely used strategies for dampening the impact of emotions are reappraisal, which consists of changing how you think about a situation, and suppression, which means inhibiting the outward signs of emotion.
- Reappraisal is a more effective strategy for regulating emotion than suppression.

C. Emotional Intelligence

Emotional intelligence—the ability to perceive, express, understand, and regulate emotion—helps people cope with stress.

D. Coping and Positive Emotion

Positive emotions enhance the ability to deal with problems and have beneficial physical effects that may dampen the effect of stressors.

IV. STRESS MANAGEMENT

A. Exploring Stress Management

- Stress management programs teach individuals how to appraise stressful events, how to develop skills for coping with stress, and how to apply these skills.
- Meditation, relaxation, and biofeedback are three techniques that often are taught in stress management programs.

B. Meditation and Relaxation

- Meditation is a system of mental exercises that usually aim either to empty the mind or to increase concentration.
- Meditation and relaxation procedures can help people reduce headaches, hypertension, anxiety, and insomnia.

ADJUSTMENT STRATEGIES *for*

Meditation

1. Find a quiet place to sit.
2. Pay attention to your breathing.
3. Repeat a single word silently to yourself.
4. Practice meditation regularly.

C. Biofeedback

- Biofeedback is a process that allows people to learn to control physiological responses that are normally involuntary, such as blood pressure and muscular tension.
- Biofeedback can help people reduce the intensity of migraine headaches and chronic pain.

Learning Goals

After reading and studying this chapter, you should be able to

1. **Describe what coping is, types of coping, and the role of contexts in coping.**
   a. Define coping.
   b. Outline major types of coping strategies.
   c. Explain the relationship between contexts and coping.

2. **Discuss individual coping strategies.**
   a. Outline techniques for teaching yourself to think positively.
   b. Identify ways to increase self-control.
   c. Discuss the relationship between social support and coping.

d. Describe proactive coping.
e. Explain how enjoyable activities and humor are related to coping.
f. Discuss the benefits of using multiple coping strategies.

3. **Summarize factors involved in coping with emotions.**
    a   Describe emotional approach coping and its effectiveness.
    b. Discuss strategies for regulating emotion and their effectiveness.
    c. Describe the components of emotional intelligence.
    d. Explain how positive emotions facilitate coping.

4. **Explain stress management.**
    a. Describe stress management programs.
    b. Discuss the use of meditation and relaxation for stress management.
    c. Discuss biofeedback and its effectiveness.

Guided Review

After you have read this chapter in the textbook, complete these statements. Topics are discussed in the same order as in the chapter. Answers are provided at the end of the study guide chapter.

Learning Goal 1: Describe what coping is, types of coping, and the role of contexts in coping

Goal 1a: Define coping

1. The process of managing taxing circumstances, expending effort to solve problems, and trying to master or reduce stress is called _____.

Goal 1b: Outline major types of coping strategies

2. One way of classifying coping strategies distinguishes _____-_____coping, which involves facing a problem and trying to solve it, and _____-_____ coping, which involves responding to stress in an emotional way.

3. Strategies that draw on beliefs, values, and goals to modify the meaning of a stressful situation are classified as _____-_____ coping.

4. Another way of classifying coping strategies categorizes them as active-cognitive, _____-_____, and avoidance.

5. _____-_____ strategies are coping responses in which individuals think about a situation in an effort to adjust more effectively.

6. Active-behavioral strategies are coping responses in which individuals take some _____ to deal with a situation.

7. _____ strategies are responses that keep stressful circumstances out of awareness.

Goal 1c: Explain the relationship between contexts and coping

8. Whether a coping strategy is effective depends in part on the demands and resources of the environment; in other words, on the _____.

Learning Goal 2:   Discuss individual coping strategies

Goal 2a: Outline techniques for teaching yourself to think positively

9. _____ _____ is almost always a good strategy for dealing with stress because a positive mood improves our ability to process information and enhances our self-esteem.

10. Three techniques to teach yourself to think positively are to learn to use _____ _____-_____, to maintain positive self-illusions, and to develop an _____ outlook.

11. _____ _____ is the process of replacing the thoughts, ideas, and beliefs that maintain a problem.

12. _____-_____ (also called self-statements) is the soundless mental speech we use when we think about something, plan, or solve problems.

13. Self-talk often becomes a _____-_____ _____.

14. Maintaining some positive illusions about oneself and the world is _____.

15. Happy people often have falsely _____ opinions about themsevles, give self-serving explanations of events, and have _____ beliefs about their ability to control the world around them.

16. The ideal orientation may be to have either mildly inflated positive illusions or a _____ orientation.

17. Although a negative outlook can increase the chances of feeling angry or guilty or inadequate, imagining _____ _____ brings the benefit of helping people prepare for stressful circumstances.

18. In Seligman's view, _____ explain bad events as the result of external, unstable, and specific causes, whereas _____ explain bad events as due to internal, stable, and global causes.

19. Seligman compared pessimism to _____ _____.

20. In Seligman's approach, optimism is much like _____-_____.

21. Another approach to optimism views it as the expectancy that _____ _____ are likely to occur in the future; thus _____ continue to believe that their goals can be attained.

22. Researchers have found that compared with pessimists, optimists tend to be _____ and to function more effectively.

Goal 2b: Identify ways to increase self-control

23. A belief that we have some control over ourselves and our circumstances enhances coping, and this belief in personal control has three main components: an _____ locus of control, a strong sense of _____-_____, and the ability to _____ _____.

24. Locus of control is linked with how people explain _____.

25. A strong sense of self-efficacy helps people set _____ _____ and to _____ in the face of difficulty.

26. Many individuals have difficulty maintaining a plan for coping because their problematic behavior provides _____ _____.

27. _____ _____ is a self-control strategy in which the individual says "Stop!" when an unwanted thought occurs and then replaces it immediately.

28. _____ means assisting individuals to develop skills they need to control their own lives.

Goal 2c: Discuss the relationship between social support and coping

29. _____ _____ is feedback from others that one is loved, esteemed, and part of a network of communication and mutual obligation.

30. The benefits of social support fall into three categories: _____ assistance, _____, and _____ support.

31. Researchers have found that _____ people and people with _____ _____ _____ tend to have less social support than people who do not have these problems.

32. People with _____ _____ _____ tend to live longer than people with fewer types of social relationships and to be less likely to catch cold when exposed to a virus.

Goal 2d: Describe proactive coping

33. Proactive coping refers to responses to _____ stressors.

34. Proactive coping may be either _____ or preventive.

35. Unlike reactive coping, proactive coping is future-oriented, manages _____ rather than risks, and is motivated by the perception of situations as challenging.

Goal 2e: Explain how enjoyable activities and humor are related to coping

36. Engaging in enjoyable activities and using humor can sometimes help individuals become less _____, thus helping them cope more effectively.

37. Recent research suggests that enjoyable activities and laughter are linked to strong responses of the _____ system.

38. Positive humor (not hostile sarcasm) dampens _____.

Goal 2f: Discuss the benefits of using multiple coping strategies

39. The combined effect of _____ _____ _____ may allow a person to cope successfully with stress.

Learning Goal 3: Summarize factors involved in coping with emotions

Goal 3a Describe emotional approach coping and its effectiveness

40. Over the long term, _____-_____ coping is usually a better strategy than emotion-focused coping, which is often linked with _____ levels of distress.

41. Emotion-focused coping may be effective in the _____ _____ or when combined with problem-focused coping.

42. Coping by actively processing and expressing emotion is called _____ _____ coping.

43. Research has documented _____ results for emotional approach coping.

44. Over the long term, emotional processing may turn into _____, which is the tendency to focus passively and repeatedly on negative emotions and their consequences.

Goal 3b: Discuss strategies for regulating emotion and their effectiveness

45. The process by which individuals influence which emotions they experience, when they experience them, and how they experience and express them is called _____ _____.

46. Gross argues that strategies for regulating emotion are more effective when they are used _____ rather than _____ in emotional experiences.

47. Two strategies for regulating emotion are _____ and _____; the first is more effective.

Goal 3c: Describe the components of emotional intelligence

48. _____ _____ is the ability to perceive, express, understand, and regulate emotion.

49. Goleman believes that being emotionally intelligent consists of developing emotional awareness, managing emotions, reading emotions, and _____ _____.

Goal 3d: Explain how positive emotions facilitate coping

50. Experiencing _____ _____ during stressful circumstances may improve the ability to deal with problems and with the physical effects of stressors.

51. _____ _____ improves a person's emotional state, and a person's emotional state influences the likelihood that _____ _____ will be provided.

Learning Goal 4: Explain stress management

Goal 4a: Describe stress management programs

52. Stress management programs teach individuals how to appraise stressful events, how to develop skills for coping with _____, and how to apply those skills.

53. Stress management programs come in many forms, including broad programs that teach a variety of techniques, programs that teach a specific technique such as _____ or _____ _____, and programs for people with a specific problem.

Goal 4b: Discuss the use of meditation and relaxation for stress management

54. Meditation is a system of mental exercises that help the individual attain physical or mental control for the sake of well-being or _____.

55. In the most popular form of meditation, _____ _____, participants focus their attention by repeating a mantra mentally or aloud.

56. Meditation creates a physiological states that resembles the transition from _____ to _____, but debate continues about whether meditation is more effective than relaxation in creating positive physiological effects.

Goal 4c: Discuss biofeedback and its effectiveness

57. In _____, an individual's muscular or visceral activities are monitored by instruments, and information from the instruments is fed back to the individual so that he or she can learn to control these activities.

58. Biofeedback can help people reduce the intensity of migraine headaches and chronic pain, but several studies have found that biofeedback offers no distinct advantage over _____ and _____ techniques.

Key Terms

Briefly define each key term and provide an example or application.

1. coping

2. problem-focused coping

3. emotion-focused coping

4. meaning-making coping

5. active-cognitive strategies

6. active-behavioral strategies

7. avoidance strategies

8. cognitive restructuring

9. self-talk

10. thought stopping

11. empowerment

12. social support

13. emotional approach coping

14. emotion regulation

15. emotional intelligence

16. stress-management programs

17. meditation

18. transcendental meditation (TM)

19. biofeedback

Practice Test A

Answer these multiple-choice questions to assess your understanding of the chapter. Answers are provided at the end of the study guide chapter.

___ 1. Coping is defined as
a. eliminating all stressors.
b. avoiding stressful events.
c. managing taxing circumstances.
d. developing supportive relationships.

___ 2. Richard Lazarus proposed classifying coping strategies into
a. meaning-making and avoidance coping.
b. avoidance and active coping.
c. problem-focused and emotion-focused coping.
d. active-behavioral and meaning-making coping.

___ 3. Positive appraisal is an example of meaning-making coping in which
a. you deny that a stressful event has happened.
b. you take positive action to solve a problem.
c. you reinterpret an event in a way that affirms your values, beliefs, and goals.
d. you replace negative thoughts with positive thoughts.

___ 4. The belief that we can control our environment, master a situation, and produce positive outcomes is called
a. narcissism.
b. self-esteem.
c. self-efficacy.
d. the coping illusion.

___ 5. The process of replacing thoughts, ideas, and beliefs that maintain a problem is called
a. cognitive restructuring.
b. thought stopping.
c. self-talk.
d. none of the above.

___ 6. Recent research has found increasing evidence that
a. seeing reality as accurately as possible is the surest path to health.
b. defensive pessimism is the surest path to health.
c. positive and negative outlooks on life are equally adaptive.
d. maintaining some positive illusions about oneself and the world is healthy.

___ 7. In Seligman's initial studies of learned helplessness,
a. people adjusted to their lack of control over their lives.
b. animals in an experiment became passive and unresponsive after experiencing shocks over which they had no control.
c. animals in an experiment learned to overcome prior helplessness and to control when they would be shocked.
d. people learned to overcome their prior lack of control over their lives.

___ 8. Research that compares optimists and pessimists has linked optimism with
a. better physical health.
b. more effective immune systems.
c. ability to avoid depression.
d. all of the above.

___ 9. Which of the following is not a benefit of social support?
a. Information
b. Tangible assistance
c. Emotional support
d. Structural change

___ 10. Using more than one coping strategy in a stressful situation is
a. less efficient than using just the right one.
b. often a waste of energy.
c. usually superior to using a single strategy.
d. not usually possible.

___ 11. The use of humor as a coping strategy has been linked to
a. decreased levels of S-IgA.
b. decreased NK-cell activity.
c. increased levels of an antibody believed to act against the common cold.
d. an inability to engage in problem-focused coping.

___ 12. Emotional approach coping refers to
a. the use of defensive mechanisms when faced with stressors.
b. the process of reacting to problems with emotional responses.
c. actively processing and expressing emotion.
d. efforts to maintain a positive mood in the face of stressors.

___ 13. Research indicates that experiencing positive emotions during stressful experiences
a. is extremely rare.
b. indicates mental instability.
c. distracts people from dealing with their problems.
d. is linked to using broad coping strategies, thinking about ways of dealing with the problem, and being objective.

___ 14. Stress management programs
a. usually involve sessions between a trainer and one individual.
b. deal only with the physical effects of stressors.
c. rarely help.
d. come in many forms.

___ 15. Om Mani Padme Hum is a
a. meditation master.
b. system of transcendental meditation.
c. mantra.
d. Zen Buddhist master.

___ 16. Biofeedback allows people to
a. improve thought stopping.
b. learn to control physiological responses that are normally involuntary.
c. learn to control negative thoughts.
d. improve cognitive restructuring.

Identifying Concepts

Answers are provided at the end of the study guide chapter.

1. TYPES OF COPING STRATEGIES   Identify the type of coping strategy illustrated by each statement.

a. George is failing his courses and has begun saying that he thinks school is a waste of time.

b. Rasheed's son was killed in the Iraq war, and Rasheed now says that Iraq would have destroyed the United States.

c. Jon was having trouble in class, so he went to a tutor.

d. Sallie did not receive a scholarship, and she logically analyzed her weaknesses.

e. Hank was depressed and started drinking to escape his problems.

2. INDIVIDUAL COPING STRATEGIES   Identify the specific strategy illustrated by each statement.

a. Each morning as he begins his training to try to qualify for a race, Russ says to himself, "This is going to be hard, but if I cut my time a little more today, I can make it."

b. Sara believes she is a slightly better tennis player than she is.

c. Tom listed five things he will do each weekday that should help him study more effectively.

d. Jill tells herself "Stop!" every time she thinks about her ex-boyfriend.

e. Juan has been feeling lonely and depressed since his girlfriend went overseas and this weekend went to a gym and to the church in his neighborhood.

Understanding Concepts

Complete these exercises to develop your understanding of important ideas in this chapter.

1. How do active-cognitive and active-behavioral coping strategies differ from defense mechanisms (see Chapter 2)?

2. Why is it healthy to have some positive self-illusions?

3. How can a negative outlook (or "just being realistic") create problems?

4. Summarize the benefits of optimistic thinking.

5. What are three components of a belief in personal control? What effect does each have on how a person handles problems?

6. List the five steps in the program described in the textbook for improving self-control.

7. Describe the major benefits of social support.

8. Define and describe what it means to actively process emotion.

9. List five components of proactive coping.

10. Describe two strategies for downregulating emotion.

11. List four components of emotional intelligence as described by Daniel Goleman.

12. Summarize the benefits of feeling positive emotions during a stressful experience.

13. What do stress management programs do?

14. Compare the relative effectiveness of meditation and relaxation training.

15. What is the goal of biofeedback?

Applying Concepts and Strategies

Complete these exercises to develop your ability to apply this chapter's material to your life and the world. Your responses will differ from those of other students in the class, and it is helpful to share your ideas with other students.

1. Caitlin is a full-time student with a part-time job as a waitress. Her earnings are not for luxuries; she needs a job to pay for food and other daily expenses. Last week she was told that the restaurant had to cut the number of waitresses and that her job would end in two weeks. She has not been able to find another job. Describe how she might apply each type of coping strategy discussed in the textbook. Which strategies do you think would be most effective?

2. Have you ever used meaning-making coping strategies? Describe a situation in which you have done so or a situation in which you think a meaning-making strategy would be your most effective strategy and then describe the strategy specifically.

3. Are you an optimist or a pessimist? Would you benefit from being more optimistic? How might you go about becoming more optimistic?

4. Create an example of a person whose life has set the stage for learned helplessness. Now imagine this person has lost his or her job and describe how learned helplessness might affect his or her response.

5. Choose three aspects of your life that you might want to change (such as your study habits, how you use your free time, how you react to disagreements, an unhealthy habit, your weight or fitness). Now apply the first step discussed in Adjustment Strategies for Improving Self-Control: For each of the three aspects of your life, describe the problem concretely and precisely so that if you wanted to, you could create a plan to deal with it.

6. Describe a situation in which a counselor might encourage a client to use thought stopping.

7. Describe an example of a program that empowers people.

8. When was the last time you sought social support? What benefits did you receive? Have you sometimes resisted seeking support when it might have helped you? If so, why?

9. Describe an example of anticipatory coping and an example of preventive coping.

10. Could you have put more humor and laughter into your life this week? How could you have done that, and what benefits might that have brought you?

11. Complete Self-Assessment 5.2: How Emotionally Intelligent Am I? How well did you score? Have you experienced a situation during the past year when greater emotional intelligence would have allowed you to cope better? Describe a social situation, real or fictional, in which either a better ability to manage emotions or a better ability to read emotions would have allowed you to improve your relationship with someone you care about.

Practice Test B

Answer these multiple-choice test questions to help you assess your understanding of the textbook chapter. Answers are provided at the end of the study guide chapter.

____ 1. Which of the following statements about emotion-focused coping is true?
a. In some circumstances emotion-focused coping is maladaptive.
b. Emotion-focused coping often relies on defensive mechanisms.
c. It is possible to successfully combine emotion-focused coping with problem-focused coping.
d. All of the above are true.

____ 2. Meaning-making coping is especially useful when you face
a. an acute stressor.
b. chronic stress that does not respond to problem-focused efforts.
c. daily hassles.
d. a very specific but complex problem.

____ 3. Active-cognitive and active-behavioral coping also may be categorized as
a. problem-focused coping.
b. emotion-focused coping.
c. meaning-based coping.
d. avoidance coping.

___ 4. The fact that a particular coping strategy may be effective in one situation but not another points to the importance of

a. emotion-focused coping.
b. thinking optimistically.
c. coping flexibility.
d. meaning-making coping.

___ 5. Because self-talk has a way of becoming a self-fulfilling prophecy, it is important to

a. meditate and avoid self-talk.
b. monitor your self-talk.
c. reduce your self-talk.
d. increase your self-talk.

___ 6. An absence of illusions

a. may thwart individuals from undertaking ambitious projects.
b. is necessary for effective adjustment.
c. is linked to mental health.
d. is correlated with many indicators of physical health.

___ 7. Defensive pessimism is sometimes useful in

a. motivating you to do everything you can to make things go smoothly.
b. helping you develop strategies for dealing with problems.
c. spurring constructive evaluation of negative possibilities.
d. motivating you to do all of the above.

___ 8. Community-based centers that assist persons in developing specific skills to regain control of their lives are an example of

a. meaning making.
b. empowerment.
c. cognitive restructuring.
d. emotional support.

___ 9. Using multiple coping strategies in a stressful situation

a. is likely to confuse the issue.
b. is ineffective.
c. can be superior to using a single strategy.
d. delays successful adjustment.

___ 10. For the most part, researchers have found that

a. emotion-focused coping and problem-focused coping are equally effective.
b. emotion-focused coping is linked with higher levels of distress.
c. emotion-focused coping is superior to problem-focused coping.
d. none of the above is true.

___ 11. In one study of emotional approach coping among women with breast cancer, over a three-month period

a. emotional expression was linked with decreased distress but emotional processing was linked with increased distress.
b. emotional expression and emotional processing were linked with increased distress.
c. emotional expression and emotional processing were linked with decreased distress.
d. emotional expression was linked with increased distress and emotional processing was linked with decreased distress.

____ 12. Rumination is

a. the inevitable result of stress.

b. related to increased symptoms of depression.

c. the result of avoidance strategies.

d. the result of meaning-making coping.

____ 13. Mindfulness mediation

a. is the most popular form of meditation in the United States.

b. involves maintaining a floating state of consciousness and focusing on whatever comes to mind at a particular moment.

c. does not influence symptoms of stress.

d. requires repeating a mantra.

____ 14. Researchers have found that the practice of meditation

a. activates brain processes involved in attention and control of the autonomic nervous system.

b. creates a state that shows qualities of both sleep and wakefulness but is distinct from both.

c. lowers oxygen consumption, slows heart rate, and produces regular and rhythmic patterns of brain activity.

d. does all of the above.

____ 15. Meditation and relaxation procedures

a. can help to reduce headaches, hypertension, anxiety, and insomnia.

b. can help to reduce psychological but not physiological symptoms of stress.

c. produce the same physiological changes as sleep.

d. are ineffective.

____ 16. Research indicates that biofeedback

a. is not effective in reducing chronic pain.

b. is far superior to meditation techniques.

c. is far superior to relaxation techniques.

d. might not offer advantages over meditation and relaxation techniques.

Answers to Chapter Questions

Guided Review

1. coping
2. problem-focused; emotion-focused
3. meaning-making
4. active-behavioral
5. active-cognitive
6. action
7. avoidance
8. context
9. thinking positively
10. positive self-talk; optimistic
11. cognitive restructuring
12. self-talk
13. self-fulfilling prophecy
14. healthy
15. high; exaggerated
16. realistic
17. negative consequences
18. optimists; pessimists
19. learned helplessness
20. self-efficacy
22. good things; optimists
22. healthier
23. internal; self-efficacy; delay gratification
24. setbacks
25. challenging goals; persist
26. immediate gratification
27. thought stopping
28. empowerment
29. social support
30. tangible; information; emotional
31. depressed; chronic fatigue syndrome
32. diverse social ties
33. potential
34. anticipatory
35. goals

36. inhibited
37. immune
38. stress
39. multiple coping strategies
40. problem-focused; increased
41. short term
42. emotional approach
43. mixed
44. rumination
45. emotional regulation
46. earlier; later
47. reappraisal; suppression
48. emotional intelligence
49. handling relationships
50. positive emotions
51. social support; social support
52. stress
53. relaxation; assertiveness training
54. enlightenment
55. transcendental meditation
56. sleep; wakefulness
57. biofeedback
58. meditation; relaxation

Practice Test A
1. c
2. c
3. c
4. c
5. a
6. d
7. b
8. d
9. d
10. c
11. c
12. c

13. d
14. d
15. c
16. b

Identifying Concepts
1. TYPES OF COPING STRATEGIES
   a. emotion-focused coping
   b. meaning-making coping
   c. active-behavioral strategy
   d. active-cognitive strategy
   e. avoidance coping strategy
2. INDIVIDUAL COPING STRATEGIES
   a. positive self-talk
   b. positive self-illusion
   c. improving self-control
   d. thought stopping
   e. seeking social support

Practice Test B
1. d
2. b
3. a
4. c
5. b
6. a
7. d
8. b
9. c
10. b
11. a
12. b
13. b
14. d
15. a
16. d

CHAPTER **6**   # SOCIAL THINKING, INFLUENCE, AND INTERGROUP RELATIONS

Chapter Outline

I. SOCIAL THINKING

Despite the uniqueness of each person, common principles govern how people identity the causes of behavior, form impressions of other people, and form impressions of the world.

A. Making Attributions

Attributions are thoughts about why people behave the way they do.

1. THE FUNDAMENTAL ATTRIBUTION ERROR

   The fundamental attribution error is the tendency for observers to overestimate the importance of a person's traits when they explain someone else's behavior and to underestimate the importance of the situation.

2. SELF-SERVING BIAS

   - When we explain our own behavior, we tend to take credit for successes and to blame failures on others or on the situation.

B. Forming Impressions

- First impressions tend to be lasting impressions in part because we pay more attention to what we learn first about a person than to later information and we interpet later information in light of existing impressions.

- We tend to take the information we have about a person and turn it into a unified whole, filling in the gaps.

1. STEREOTYPING AND ATTITUDES

   - To fill in gaps in our information about people, we rely on schemas and stereotypes.

   - Schemas are categories or frameworks that we use to simplify the world.

   - Stereotypes are generalizations about a group's characteristics.

   - Stereotypes may determine our attitudes, which are evaluations of people, objects, and ideas.

2. IMPRESSION MANAGEMENT

   Impression management, or self-presentation, is the process of acting in a way that presents a desired image.

3. SELF-MONITORING

Self-monitoring is paying attention to the impressions we make on others and fine-tuning our performance to optimize those impressions.

C. Changing Attitudes

Whether a message succeeds in changing attitudes depends on the following factors:

1. THE COMMUNICATOR (SOURCE)

The expertise and credibility of the source help determine whether a message is persuasive.

2. THE MESSAGE

- Whether a rational or an emotional message is more likely to be persuasive depends on many factors.

- The elaboration likelihood model explains the relation between emotional and rational appeals.

3. THE MEDIUM

4. THE TARGET

Age and attitude strength are two characteristics of the audience that influence whether a message succeeds in changing attitudes.

II. SOCIAL INFLUENCE

A. Conformity

Conformity is a change in a person's behavior to coincide more closely with the standards of a group.

1. ASCH'S CONFORMITY EXPERIMENT

In Solomon Asch's classic experiment in 1951, participants conformed to the incorrect opinion of the group 35 percent of the time.

2. FACTORS THAT CONTRIBUTE TO CONFORMITY

- For the most part, people conform either because they want to be liked (normative social influence) or because they want to be right (informational social influence).

- Other factors affecting whether a person will conform include whether the group is unanimous, whether the person has made a different prior commitment, and characteristics of the person, the group, and the culture.

B. Obedience

- Obedience is behavior that complies with the explicit demands of an individual with authority.

- Stanley Milgram conducted classic experiments on obedience in which most participants obeyed the demands of an authority figure even though they believed they were hurting another person.

ADJUSTMENT STRATEGIES *for*

Resisting an Unjust Request by a Person in a Position of Authority

1. Give the appearance of obeying but secretly do otherwise.
2. Publicly dissent but follow the order.
3. Disregard the order.
4. Challenge the authority.
5. Persuade a higher authority to intervene or organize a group of supporters.

C. Compliance

- Compliance is a change in behavior in response to a request.
- Robert Cialdini identified six conditions that foster compliance:
    1. RECIPROCATION
    2. COMMITMENT AND CONSISTENCY
    3. SOCIAL PROOF
    4. LIKING
    5. AUTHORITY
    6. SCARCITY

ADJUSTMENT STRATEGIES *for*

Resisting Persuasion and Compliance Tactics

1. Defend against reciprocity pressures.
2. Recognize and resist commitment and consistency pressures.
3. Reduce susceptibility to faulty social proof.
4. Reduce the unwanted influence of liking.
5. Defend against the detrimental effects of authority.
6. Combat scarcity pressures.

III. INTERGROUP RELATIONS

A. Groups and Their Functions

Groups satisfy our personal needs, reward us, provide information, raise our self-esteem, and give us an identity.

B. Group Identity: Us versus Them

- Unlike personal identity, social identity focuses on our commonalities with others.
- The various forms of social identity reflect different ways of connecting to groups and social categories.
    1. SOCIAL IDENTITY THEORY

        According to Henry Tajfel's social identity theory, we can improve our self-images by enhancing our social identity, which we can do either by favoring members of our in-group or by disparaging members of an out-group.

    2. ETHNOCENTRISM

        The tendency to favor one's own group and believe it is superior to other groups is called ethnocentrism .

    3. ETHNOCENTRISM AND THE SOCIAL SCIENCES

        Until recently, social scientists were mostly white males, and they displayed ethnocentrism by treating differences between minority and majority groups as deficits of minority groups.

C. Prejudice and Discrimination

- Prejudice is an unjustified negative attitude toward an individual based on the individual's membership in a group.
- Discrimination is an unjustified negative action toward an individual based on the individual's membership in a group.

1. **Sources of Prejudice**

   Sources of prejudice include personality characteristics, competition for scarce resources, efforts to enhance self-esteem, stereotypes, and cultural learning.

2. **Modern Racism**

   Overt prejudice and discrimination have largely been replaced in the United States by subtle expressions of racism.

D. Immigration

Immigrants may face not only prejudice and discrimination but also the stressors of language barriers, separation from support networks, and acculturative stress.

Adjustment Strategies *for*

International Students*

1. Show patience.
2. Have a support system.
3. Make new friends.
4. Share your culture.

* Based on J. W. Santrock and J. A. Halonen, *Your Guide to College Success, 3rd ed.* (Belmont, CA: Wadsworth, 2004).

E. Ways to Improve Interethnic Relations

Improving relations among people from differing ethnic backgrounds requires going beyond mere contact to task-oriented cooperation or intimate contact.

1. **Task-oriented Cooperation**

   Eliot Aronson's jigsaw classroom is an example of the kind of situation that can generate task-oriented cooperation among people of different ethnic backgrounds.

2. **Intimate Contact**

   Contact between people with different ethnic backgrounds can decrease prejudice if personal information and feelings are shared.

3. **Acknowledge Diversity**

   Recognizing and respecting differences is an important aspect of getting along with others in a diverse world.

Adjustment Strategies *for*

Improving Interethnic Relations

1. Participate in cooperative tasks.
2. Discuss personal worries, successes, failures, interests, and so on.
3. Pay attention to differences.
4. Imagine life from the other person's perspective.
5. Think reflectively.
6. Develop emotional intelligence.
7. Learn to communicate effectively.

Learning Goals

After reading and studying this chapter, you should be able to

1. **Describe how people think about the social world.**
   a. Define attributions and describe two common biases in how people make attributions.
   b. Outline factors that shape impressions of people.
   c. List key factors that determine whether people change their attitudes.

2. **Identify how people are influenced in social settings.**
   a. Outline the factors involved in conformity.
   b. Describe Milgram's studies of obedience.
   c. Outline six principles of persuasion and compliance.

3. **Discuss intergroup relations.**
   a. List the functions of groups.
   b. Describe how social identity leads to "we/they" thinking.
   c. Discuss the relationships among stereotypes, prejudice, and discrimination.
   d. Describe some of the special stressors faced by immigrants.
   e. Describe some effective strategies for improving interethnic relations.

Guided Review

After you have read this chapter in the textbook, complete these statements. Topics are discussed in the same order as in the chapter. Answers are provided at the end of the study guide chapter.

Learning Goal 1: Describe how people think about the social world

1. The field known as _____ _____ examines how people select, interpret, remember, and use social information.

Goal 1a: Define attributions and describe two common biases in how people make attributions

2. People's explanations about why people behave the way they do are called _____.

3. The _____ _____ _____ is the tendency of observers to overestimate the importance of a person's traits when they explain someone's behavior and to underestimate the importance of the situation.

4. When we explain our own behavior, we are a bit more likely to attribute it to the _____.

5. We also tend to exaggerate positive beliefs about ourselves with the help of _____-_____ _____, which is the tendency to attribute our successes to our own characteristics but to attribute our failures to external factors.

Goal 1b: Outline factors that shape impressions of people

6. First impressions tend to be _____ impressions in part because we pay more attention to what we first learn about a person than to later information and because we tend to interpret later information in light of existing impressions.

7. Whatever information we have about a person, we tend to _____ it and fill in the missing pieces.

8. We fill in incomplete impressions to create a unified whole by applying our existing _____, which often means using _____, which are generalizations about a group's characteristics.

9. _____ influence whether and how people apply stereotypes.

10. Evaluations of people, objects, and ideas are called _____.

11. The process of acting in a way that creates a desired impression is called _____ _____ or self-presentation.

12. To create a good impression, people use _____ _____, conform to _____ _____, show appreciation of others, and use behavioral matching.

13. Paying attention to the impressions you make on others and fine-tuning your performance is called _____-_____.

Goal 1c: List key factors that determine whether people change their attitudes

14. The effectiveness of attempts to persuade people to change their attitudes depends on characteristics of the source, the _____, the medium, and the audience.

15. Whether we are persuaded by someone who is attempting to change our attitudes depends in part on the communicator's _____ and _____.

16. The credibility of a source is influenced by the source's trustworthiness, power, attractiveness, _____, and similarity.

17. All other things being equal, the more _____ we are, the more we will change our attitudes.

18. The _____ _____ we are about the topic of a message, the more likely we are to respond to an emotional appeal.

19. Most people are persuaded only when _____ and _____ appeals go together.

20. The _____ _____ model attempts to explain the relation between emotional and rational appeals and proposes two routes for persuasion: a central route and a peripheral route.

21. Two characteristics of the audience that determine whether a message will be persuasive are _____ and _____ _____.

Learning Goal 2: Identify how people are influenced in social settings

22. Three important forms of social influence are conformity, obedience, and _____.

Goal 2a: Outline the factors involved in conformity

23. _____ is a change in a person's behavior so that it coincides more closely with a group standard.

24. In a 1951 experiment by _____ _____, participants gave obviously incorrect answers 35 percent of the time in order to conform to the answers given by other people.

25. One reason people conform is _____ social influence, which is the influence wielded by people because we want to have their approval or to avoid their disapproval.

26. A second reason people conform is _____ social influence, which is the influence wielded by people because we want to be right.

27. When a group's opinion is divided, individuals feel _____ pressure to conform.

28. If you do not have a prior commitment to a different idea or action, you are _____ likely to be influenced by the ideas or actions of others.

29. People with _____ self-esteem are more likely than other people to conform.

30. The chances that a person will conform with a group increase if members of the group are _____, attractive, or similar to the person.

31. Experiments indicate that rates of conformity tend to be _____ in individualistic than in collectivist cultures.

Goal 2b: Describe Milgram's studies of obedience

32. _____ is behavior that complies with the explicit demands of an individual in authority.

33. In a classic experiment by _____ _____ most participants were willing to deliver what they thought were powerful shocks to another person when told to do so by an authority figure.

34. In variations of his experiment Milgram found that disobedience increased when people saw other people _____, when the authority figure was not perceived to be _____, and when the authority figure was not close by.

Goal 2c: Outline six principles of persuasion and compliance

35. A change in behavior in response to a direct request is known as _____.

36. _____ _____ studied the tactics of those who make their living by gaining compliance with their requests and identified six basic principles of persuasion and compliance.

37. When salespeople give you something before asking you to buy a product, they are counting on the tendency to _____ to lead you to comply with their request.

38. Once people have made a commitment to do something, they become more likely to comply with a related request because most people prefer to be _____ in their behavior.

39. In order to decide whether to comply with a request, people look for _____ _____; in other words, they check what other people are doing.

40. People prefer to comply with a request when the person making the request is someone they know and _____.

41. Even symbols of _____ increase compliance.

42. The impression that an item is _____ increases the chances that people will comply with requests to buy it.

Learning Goal 3: Discuss intergroup relations

Goal 3a: List the functions of groups

43. Regardless of their size, groups may satisfy personal needs, provide rewards, serve as an important source of _____, raise our self-esteem, and give us an _____.

Goal 3b: Describe how social identity leads to "we/they" thinking

44. _____ _____ is the way you define yourself in terms of your group membership.

45. Unlike personal identity, which emphasizes each person's unique combination of characteristics, social identity focuses on our _____.

46. If we _____ with a group, we believe that we share numerous features with members of that group.

47. According to social identity theory, by favoring members of our in-group or disparaging members of an out-group, we enhance our social identity, improving our _____-_____.

48. _____ is the tendency to favor one's own group and believe it is superior to other groups.

Goal 3c: Discuss the relationships among stereotypes, prejudice, and discrimination.

49. Prejudice and discrimination both reflect and _____ antagonism between groups.

50. An unjustified negative attitude toward an individual based on an individual's membership in a group is called _____.

51. An unjustified negative action toward an individual based on an individual's membership in a group is called_____.

52. Theodor Adorno suggested that people with an _____ personality are more likely than other people to be prejudiced.

53. _____ over scarce resources may be one source of prejudice and discrimination.

54. Other sources of prejudice include the desire to enhance one's _____-_____, the tendency to apply _____, and the prejudice of others.

55. Subtle forms of racism are sometimes called _____ racism or _____ racism.

Goal 3d: Describe some of the special stressors faced by immigrants

56. Immigrants are more likely than long-time residents to experience stressors such as _____ _____, separation from support networks, and the dual struggle to preserve their _____ _____ and to acculturate.

Goal 3e: Describe some effective strategies for improving interethnic relations

57. Improving relations among people from different ethnic backgrounds requires, not just contact, but _____-_____ _____ or intimate contact.

58. One example of a situation that fosters task-oriented cooperation is the _____ _____ designed by Eliot Aronson.

Key Terms

Briefly define each key term and provide an example or application.

1. attribution

2. fundamental attribution error

3. stereotype

4. attitudes

5. impression management (self-presentation)

6. self-monitoring

7. elaboration likelihood model

8. conformity

9. normative social influence

10. informational social influence

11. obedience

12. door-in-the-face strategy

13. foot-in-the-door strategy

14. bystander effect

15. social identity

16. social identity theory

17. ethnocentrism

18. prejudice

19. discrimination

Practice Test A

Answer these multiple-choice questions to assess your understanding of the chapter. Answers are provided at the end of the study guide chapter.

____ 1. Attributions are
a. causal explanations of behavior.
b. predictions about social behavior.
c. observations of social behavior.
d. generalizations about the characteristics of a group.

____ 2. The fundamental attribution error is
a. the tendency for observers to overestimate the importance of the situation as an explanation for another person's behavior.
b. the tendency for actors to overestimate the importance of personality characteristics as an explanation for their own behavior.
c. the tendency for observers to overestimate the importance of personality characteristics and underestimate the importance of the situation as an explanation for another person's behavior.
d. the tendency for people to hold inflated views of their abilities.

____ 3. People maintain exaggerated positive views of themselves with the help of
a. the fundamental attribution error.
b. informational social influence.
c. the principles of compliance.
d. the self-serving bias.

____ 4. First impressions tend to be lasting impressions because we
a. pay more attention to what we learn first than to subsequent information.
b. tend to interpret later information in light of existing information.
c. organize impressions into a unified whole.
d. do all of the above.

____ 5. Generalizations about the characteristics of a group are known as
a. attitudes.
b. attributions.
c. stereotypes.
d. identities.

____ 6. Evaluations of people, objects, and ideas are known as
a. stereotypes.
b. prejudices.
c. attitudes.
d. attributions.

____ 7. Acting in a way that presents a desired image is called
a. self-monitoring.
b. compliance.
c. impression management.
d. obedience.

____ 8. When we pay attention to the impression we are making on others and fine-tune our presentation accordingly, we are engaged in
a. self-monitoring.
b. compliance.
c. persuasion.
d. none of the above.

____ 9. The less informed we are about the topic of a message,
a. the more likely we are to respond to an emotional appeal.
b. the less likely we are to respond to an emotional appeal.
c. the less likely we are to be persuaded.
d. the less importance we place on the source of the message.

___ 10. A change in a person's behavior to coincide more closely with a group's standard is called
a. compliance.
b. obedience.
c. conformity.
d. persuasion.

___ 11. In Solomon Asch's experiment, people who were asked to say which of three lines was the same length as another line
a. only rarely discounted their own opinion and went along with the incorrect answer given by other people in the group.
b. stuck with their own opinion unless the correct answer was unclear.
c. went along with incorrect answers given by other people in the group about 35 percent of the time.
d. went along with incorrect answers given by other people in the group about 80 percent of the time.

___ 12. In Milgram's experiments on obedience, when people thought that they were delivering shocks to another person,
a. about 10 percent continued to obey directions to give the highest level of shock.
b. almost 25 percent continued to obey directions to give the highest level of shock.
c. almost half continued to obey directions to give the highest level of shock.
d. almost two thirds continued to obey directions to give the highest level of shock.

___ 13. A change in behavior in response to a direct request is called
a. obedience.
b. conformity.
c. compliance.
d. impression management.

___ 14. If you are prejudiced,
a. you discriminate against a group of people.
b. you have a negative attitude about a person solely because the person is a member of a certain group.
c. you act against a person solely because the person is a member of a certain group.
d. you have an authoritarian personality.

___ 15. Contact can improve relations between people with different ethnic backgrounds if
a. the contact includes competition.
b. the people have extensive contact.
c. the people reveal personal information, sharing their worries, successes, and so on.
d. the contact occurs in a friendly, neutral setting.

Identifying Concepts

Answers are provided at the end of the study guide chapter.

1. ELEMENTS OF SOCIAL COGNITION   Identify the concept described in each statement:

a. A causal explanation for behavior

b. Generalization about a group's characteristics

c. Evaluation of people, objects, or ideas

d. Influence based on our desire to gain approval and to avoid disapproval

e. Influence based on our desire to be right

f. Definition of oneself in terms of group membership

2. IMPORTANT PEOPLE IN SOCIAL THINKING AND BEHAVIOR   Identify the person known for classic work related to each topic.

a. Conformity

b. Obedience

c. Principles of compliance and behavior

d. Authoritarian personality

Understanding Concepts

Complete these exercises to develop your understanding of important ideas in this chapter.

1. Summarize the differences between how people tend to explain their own behavior and how they explain the behavior of other people.

2. How does the way people form impressions of other people open the way to making errors about people?

3. What are two advantages of using stereotypes? What are two problems created by using stereotypes?

4. What are some useful strategies for impression management?

5. What characteristics make the source of a message credible and thus help the source change people's attitudes?

6. What are some advantages and disadvantages of conformity for the individual? For society?

7. Describe Milgram's classic experiment on obedience and his later findings on circumstances that encourage disobedience.

8. Describe the door-in-the-face strategy.

9. Describe the face-in-the-door strategy.

10. How are social identity and self-esteem linked according to Tajfel's social identity theory?

11. Summarize the possible sources of prejudice.

12. How does the jigsaw classroom encourage cooperation and a common goal?

Applying Concepts and Strategies

Complete these exercises to develop your ability to apply this chapter's material to your life and the world. Your responses will differ from those of other students in the class, and it is helpful to share your ideas with other students.

1. Think back to the last time you failed at something. Perhaps you did poorly on a test or you lost your temper with a friend. How did you explain your failure to yourself? Did your explanation show the self-serving bias? How does use of the self-serving bias help and harm efforts at adjustment?

2. Describe someone you met during the last month. Now list the basis for each characteristic you ascribed to that person. Were all of the characteristics based on observations, or did you "fill in the blanks" to unify your impressions of the person? Did you apply any stereotypes?

3. When was the last time you changed your mind about something? What persuaded you? Was your decision rational?

4. During recent political campaigns, commentators in the media have been fond of saying that voters are asking themselves whether a candidate is someone they would like to have a beer with or to have over for a backyard barbeque or whether a candidate is someone "like them." Do you think these are questions that voters should consider? How are these questions related to the principles of social influence discussed in the chapter? Why would someone that voters would like to have a beer with or that voters think is "like them" have an advantage in winning their vote?

5. You are on a committee that is recommending new training methods and procedures for guards at a camp where prisoners of war and suspected terrorists will be interrogated. Consider the research on conformity and obedience. Does it suggest any principles or guidelines that would affect your recommendations?

6. When have you regretted complying with someone's sales pitch or request? What could you have done to resist complying? List other strategies for resisting persuasion and compliance tactics.

7. Kay Deaux identified five types of social identity: ethnic and religious, political, vocations and avocations, personal relationships, and stigmatized groups. Which two types of social identity are most important to you? How would you describe your social identity?

8. Do you root for a sports team? If so, why? Does it affect you when the team wins or loses? How do your feelings for a sports team compare with your feelings about your city or country?

9. Suppose you're working with a community group in a neighborhood in which relations are tense between two ethnic groups. Devise a project analogous to the jigsaw classroom that might improve relations between the two groups. What are other strategies for improving interethnic relations?

Practice Test B

Answer these multiple-choice test questions to help you assess your understanding of the textbook chapter. Answers are provided at the end of the study guide chapter.

___ 1. The field that examines how people select, interpret, remember, and use information about the social world is called
a. social comparison.
b. social cognition.
c. clinical psychology.
d. applied psychology.

____ 2. When other people see your behavior, they have a natural tendency to explain it in terms of
a. your personality.
b. both your personality and the demands of the situation.
c. the demands of the situation.
d. none of the above.

____ 3. Self-serving bias is the tendency to
a. attribute other people's successes to external factors.
b. forget our failures.
c. attribute our successes to our own characteristics but our failures to external factors.
d. forget other people's successes.

____ 4. The tendency to apply negative stereotypes increases
a. when we are happy.
b. when we are angry.
c. if we tend to do a lot of self-monitoring.
d. if we are engaged in impression management.

____ 5. If you want to make a good impression in an interview, you should
a. smile.
b. maintain a neutral expression.
c. lean backward.
d. avoid eye contact.

____ 6. Conforming to situational norms, showing appreciation of others, and behavioral matching are techniques used in
a. changing attitudes.
b. impression management.
c. obtaining compliance.
d. self-monitoring.

____ 7. According to the elaboration likelihood model,
a. the central route to persuasion is the effective approach when people are not motivated to pay attention.
b. the peripheral route to persuasion is effective when people are not paying close attention to the message.
c. the attractiveness of the source is especially important when people are paying close attention to a message.
d. emotional appeals are not effective unless people are paying close attention to a message.

____ 8. Which of the following statements is true?
a. The age of the audience does not influence the chances that a message will be persuasive.
b. Older people are more likely to change their attitudes than younger people.
c. People with strong attitudes toward the subject are more likely to be persuaded than people with weakly held attitudes.
d. None of these statements is true.

____ 9. The tendency to conform increases
a. if members of the group are experts.
b. if people have low self-esteem.
c. if the group's opinion is unanimous.
d. under all of the above conditions.

___ 10. Milgram found that obedience
a. declined when people could see other people disobey the directions.
b. increased when the authority figure was not nearby.
c. was not affected by the legitimacy of the authority figure.
d. was not affected by the behavior of other people.

___ 11. The door-in-the-face strategy illustrates
a. the principle of reciprocity.
b. the principle of social proof.
c. the importance of authority.
d. the importance of scarcity.

___ 12. The foot-in-the-door strategy illustrates
a. the role of liking.
b. the role of commitment and consistency.
c. the importance of reciprocity.
d. the importance of social proof.

___ 13. In Tajfel's experiment,
a. the participants required large incentives in order to think of themselves as members of a group.
b. the participants demonstrated a reluctance to favor the out-group over the in-group.
c. the participants were easily led to think in terms of an in-group and to show intense favoritism toward the in-group.
d. the participants showed favoritism toward the in-group only if they knew the other members of the in-group.

___ 14. The characteristics of an authoritarian personality include
a. strict adherence to conventional ways of behaving and aggression against people who violate norms.
b. assertiveness and open-mindedness.
c. resistance to stereotypes but submission to authority figures.
d. rigid thinking and resistance to authority figures.

___ 15. Cooperative learning programs such as Aronson's jigsaw classroom
a. fail to improve relations among children.
b. improve social relationships but are not effective as an educational method.
c. are linked with decreased self-esteem and reduced motivation.
d. are linked with improved perceptions of different ethnic groups and improved academic performance.

Answers to Chapter Questions

Guided Review
1. social cognition
2. attributions
3. fundamental attribution error
4. situation
5. self-serving bias
6. lasting
7. unify
8. schemas; stereotypes
9. emotions
10. attitudes
11. impression management
12. nonverbal cues; situational norms
13. self-monitoring
14. message
15. expertise; credibility
16. likeability
17. frightened
18. less informed
19. rational; emotional
20. elaboration likelihood
21. age; attitude strength
22. compliance
23. conformity

24. Solomon Asch
25. normative
26. informational
27. less
28. more
29. low
30. experts
31. lower
32. obedience
33. Stanley Milgram
34. disobey; legitimate
35. compliance
36. Robert Cialdini
37. reciprocate
38. consistent
39. social proof
40. like
41. authority
42. scarce
43. information; identity
44. social identity
45. commonality
46. identify
47. self-image
48. ethnocentrism
49. perpetuate
50. prejudice
51. discrimination
52. authoritarian
53. competition
54. self-esteem; stereotypes
55. ambivalent; modern (*or* symbolic *or* aversive)
56. language barriers; ethnic identity
57. task-oriented cooperation
58. jigsaw classroom

Practice Test A
1. a
2. c
3. d
4. d

5. c
6. c
7. c
8. a
9. a
10. c
11. c
12. d
13. c
14. b
15. c

Identifying Concepts
1. ELEMENTS OF SOCIAL COGNITION
   a. attribution
   b. stereotype
   c. attitude
   d. normative social influence
   e. informational social influence
   f. social identity
2. PEOPLE IN SOCIAL THINKING AND BEHAVIOR
   a. Asch
   b. Milgram
   c. Cialdini
   d. Adorno

Practice Test B
1. b
2. a
3. c
4. b
5. a
6. b
7. b
8. d
9. d
10. a
11. a
12. b
13. c
14. a
15. d

CHAPTER 7

COMMUNICATING EFFECTIVELY

Chapter Outline

I. EXPLORING INTERPERSONAL COMMUNICATION

A. Building Blocks of Interpersonal Communication

The basic components of communication are the message, the channel, the processes of encoding and decoding, noise, and the relationship between the people who are communicating.

B. The Transactional Aspect of Communication

Interpersonal communication is an ongoing process in which messages flow back and forth between individuals who act as both senders and receivers, sometimes simultaneously.

C. Context

- The context influences the form and the content of communication.
- Important aspects of the context include the relationship between the people who are communicating and their sociocultural characteristics.

D. Defining Interpersonal Communication

Interpersonal communication is an ongoing transactional process that involves at least two individuals, each of whom acts as both sender and receiver, encoding and decoding messages, sometimes simultaneously.

II. VERBAL INTERPERSONAL COMMUNICATION

A. Speaking Skills

- To communicate effectively, you need to consider the background, needs, abilities, and other characteristics of your listeners.
- Communicating effectively requires selecting appropriate words, keeping in mind their connotative as well as denotative meanings.
- Messages are conveyed more effectively when spoken in a simple, concrete, and specific way.
- Verbal and nonverbal messages should be consistent.

B. Listening Skills

Hearing is a sensory process; listening is the psychological process of interpreting and understanding what is heard.

ADJUSTMENT STRATEGIES *for*

Becoming a Better Listener

1. Don't monopolize the conversation.
2. Pay careful attention to the person who is talking.
3. Practice reflective listening, restating the speaker's message.
4. Synthesize the themes and patterns that you hear.
5. Give feedback to the speaker.

C. Self-Disclosure

Self-disclosure is the communication of intimate details about ourselves.

1. THE JOHARI WINDOW
   - The Johari Window provides a framework for understanding the extent to which we and others are aware of information about ourselves.
   - The Johari Window divides information about ourselves into four categories: the open self, the hidden self, the blind self, and the unknown self.
2. SELF-DISCLOSURE IN RELATIONSHIPS
   - A series of low-risk self-disclosures may be enough to stimulate a relationship, but deep relationships usually demand risky self-disclosures.
   - Too much self-disclosure or disclosures too early in a relationship can damage a relationship; a moderate amount of self-disclosure often facilitates a relationship.

ADJUSTMENT STRATEGIES *for*

Increasing Self-Disclosure

1. Proceed gradually.
2. Recognize that people have different levels of intimacy needs.
3. Begin with facts.
4. When you are comfortable disclosing facts, include your thoughts, feelings, and needs.
5. Finally, risk talking about what your thoughts, feelings, and needs are right now.

D. Conflict and Assertiveness

- People deal with conflict in four basic ways: aggressively, manipulatively, passively, or assertively.
- Being assertive is the most effective way to handle conflict.

ADJUSTMENT STRATEGIES *for*

Becoming More Assertive*

1. Evaluate your rights.
2. Set a time for discussing what you want.
3. State the problem in terms of its consequences for you.

---

4. Describe the problem objectively.

5. Express your feelings about the situation.

6. Make your request in a straightforward way.

* Based on E. J. Bourne, *The Anxiety and Phobia Workbook, 2nd ed.* (Oakland, CA: New Harbinger, 1995).

E. Gender and Verbal Communication

Research confirms that there are gender differences in how people communicate.

1. RAPPORT TALK

- Rapport talk is conversation aimed at establishing connections and negotiating relationships, and women tend to enjoy rapport talk more than men do.

- Report talk is talk designed to give information, and men tend to prefer report talk to rapport talk.

2. SELF-DISCLOSURE

- Women tend to learn self-disclosure skills in same-sex friendships and to trust the relationship-enhancing qualities of self-disclosure.

- Men tend to associate self-disclosure with vulnerability and loss of control.

3. INTERRUPTIONS

Men are more likely than women to interrupt in a way that takes over a conversation.

F. Barriers to Effective Verbal Communication

Barriers to effective communication fall into three main categories: judging, proposing solutions, and avoiding the other person's concerns.

1. JUDGING

Judging may take the form of criticizing, name calling, labeling, and praising in a manipulative way.

2. PROPOSING SOLUTIONS

Proposing solutions may take the form of giving advice, questioning, ordering, threatening, and moralizing.

3. AVOIDING THE OTHER'S CONCERNS

Diversions and logical arguments are ways of avoiding the other person's concerns.

ADJUSTMENT STRATEGIES *for*

Effective Verbal Expression*

1. Be direct.

2. If you are hurt or angry, communicate immediately.

3. Be clear.

4. Do not disguise your intentions.

5. Be supportive.

* Based on Matthew McKay, Martha Davis, and Patrick Fannen, *Messages, 2nd ed.* (Oakland, CA: New Harbinger, 1995).

III. NONVERBAL INTERPERSONAL COMMUNICATION

Nonverbal communication refers to messages that are transmitted from one person to another by other than linguistic means, which includes body communication, spatial communication, and paralanguage.

A. Dimensions of Nonverbal Communication

1. CHARACTERISTICS OF NONVERBAL COMMUNICATION
   - Nonverbal communication is spontaneous and ambiguous.
   - Nonverbal leakage is the communication of true emotions through nonverbal channels even when the person tries to conceal the truth verbally.

2. DETECTING DECEPTION

   Researchers have identified certain nonverbal behaviors that people typically display when they are lying, but people are not very good at detecting deception unless they are trained to do so.

3. NONVERBAL COORDINATION

   Nonverbal behaviors usually occur in clusters.

4. CULTURE, ETHNICITY, AND NONVERBAL COMMUNICATION

   Cultures have different styles of nonverbal communication.

ADJUSTMENT STRATEGIES *for*

Improving Intercultural Communication*

1. Learn about the predominant tendencies in nonverbal communication in other cultures.
2. Recognize individual variations within a culture.
3. Practice intercultural communication.
4. Don't assume that yours is the best way to communicate.
5. Respect the choices of others.

* Based on Marcelle DuPraw and Marya Axner, *Toward a More Perfect Union in an Age of Diversity* (2003), http://www.wwcd.org/action/ampu/crosscult.html.

---

5. GENDER AND NONVERBAL COMMUNICATION

   There are gender differences in nonverbal communication.

B. Body Communication

1. GESTURES
   - A gesture is a motion of the limbs or body made to convey a message.
   - The meaning of a gesture may vary from culture to culture.

2. FACIAL EXPRESSIONS

   Although some facial expressions appear to be universal, the meanings of other facial expressions vary from culture to culture.

3. EYE COMMUNICATION

   In the United States eye contact is used to monitor feedback, signal a turn in the conversation, signal the nature of a relationship, and compensate for physical distance.

4. TOUCH COMMUNICATION
   - Touch is used to express sexuality, consolation, and dominance.
   - Touching patterns vary with gender and from one culture to another.

C. Spatial Communication

- Proxemics is the study of how people communicate through their use of space.
- The distances considered appropriate during different types of interactions vary from culture to culture.

D. Silence and Paralanguage

• Silence facilitates listening and helps set the pace of a conversation.

• Paralanguage refers to the nonlinguistic aspects of verbal expression, such as the rapidity, volume, and pitch of speech.

Learning Goals

After reading and studying this chapter, you should be able to

1. **Describe the basic aspects of interpersonal communication.**
   a. Outline the building blocks of interpersonal communication.
   b. Explain how interpersonal communication is transactional.
   c. Describe how context influences communication.
   d. Define interpersonal communication.

2. **Explain the keys to effective verbal interpersonal communication.**
   a. Outline guidelines for effective speaking.
   b. Outline guidelines for effective listening.
   c. Discuss self-disclosure and its role in relationships.
   d. Describe four ways of dealing with conflict in communications.
   e. Discuss differences in how men and women communicate.
   f. Describe key barriers to effective verbal communication.

3. **Describe the elements of nonverbal interpersonal communication.**
   a. Outline the characteristics and variations in nonverbal communication.
   b. Describe the different types of body communication.
   c. Discuss how space is used in nonverbal communication.
   d. Explain the use of silence and paralanguage in communication.

Guided Review

After you have read this chapter in the textbook, complete these statements. Topics are discussed in the same order as in the chapter. Answers are provided at the end of the study guide chapter.

Learning Goal 1: Describe the basic aspects of interpersonal communication

Goal 1a: Outline the building blocks of interpersonal communication

1. The _____ is the information delivered from a sender to a receiver.

2. The _____ of communication is the mode of delivery.

3. Communication requires both _____, which is the act of producing messages, and _____, which is the act of understanding messages.

4. _____ refers to factors that decrease the likelihood that a message will be accurately encoded or decoded.

5. In any communication there is some _____ between sender and receiver.

Goal 1b: Explain how interpersonal communication is transactional

6. Interpersonal communication is described as _____ because it is an ongoing process in which messages flow back and forth between the participants.

7. Participants in an interpersonal communication serve as both _____ and _____.

Goal 1c: Describe how context influences communication

8. Interpersonal communication always occurs in a _____ that influences the communication.

9. The _____ between the participants and their _____ characteristics are two important dimensions of the context of a communication.

10. When people from different _____ groups interact, they might follow different rules of communication.

Goal 1d: Define interpersonal communication

11. Interpersonal communication is an ongoing transactional process that involves at least two individuals, each of whom acts as both sender and receiver, _____ and _____ messages, sometimes simultaneously.

Learning Goal 2: Explain the keys to effective verbal interpersonal communication

Goal 2a: Outline guidelines for effective speaking

12. Which words are appropriate for your message depends in part on your _____.

13. The objective meaning of words is their _____ meaning, whereas the subjective meaning is their _____ meaning, which may vary considerably from person to person.

14. The more _____ a word, the more likely people are to agree on its meaning.

15. Messages are more likely to be effective when they are simple, concrete, and _____.

16. When your messages are abstract, general, or complex, it is best to include _____.

17. Good speakers also make their _____ and _____ messages consistent.

Goal 2b: Outline guidelines for effective listening

18. _____ is a physiological sensory process in which auditory sensations are received by the ears and transmitted to the brain.

19. _____ is the psychological process of interpreting and understanding what we hear.

20. A first step in effective listening is to avoid _____ the conversation.

21. _____ listening is a strategy in which the listener restates the speaker's message in a way that indicates acceptance and understanding.

22. Good listeners give _____ to a speaker quickly, honestly, clearly, and informatively.

Goal 2c: Discuss self-disclosure and its role in relationships

23. _____-_____ is the communication of intimate details about ourselves.

24. The _____ _____ provides a framework for understanding the extent to which we and others are aware of information about ourselves.

25. The Johari Window divides information about ourselves into four categories: the open self, the hidden self, the blind self, and the _____ self.

26. The _____ self consists of information about yourself that is known to you and to others whereas the hidden self consists of information about yourself that you are aware of but have not shared with others.

27. The _____ self consists of information that others know about you but that you do not; the hidden self consists of what no one, including you, knows about you.

28. A series of simple low-risk self-disclosures may be enough to stimulate a relationship, but deep relationships usually demand _____ _____-_____.

29. Privacy, a nonjudgmental ear, empathy, and a common bond all increase the chances that an individual will engage in _____-_____.

30. To increase self-disclosure in a relationship, it is usually best to proceed _____ and to begin with _____.

Goal 2d: Describe four ways of dealing with conflict in communications

31. People deal with conflict in four basic ways: aggressively, manipulatively, _____, and assertively.

32. In aggressive communication people communicate in hostile ways, whereas in manipulative communication they try to get what they want by making other people feel sorry for them or feel _____.

33. In passive communication people fail to say what they want or what they feel, whereas in _____ communication people express their views directly and openly.

Goal 2e: Discuss differences in how men and women communicate

34. Traditionally, women have been taught to be less _____ in their communications than men.

35. Deborah Tannen distinguishes _____ talk, which is conversation aimed at establishing connections and negotiating relationships, from _____ talk, which is talk designed to give information.

36. Women tend to enjoy _____ talk more than men do.

37. Females tend to learn _____-_____ skills in peer relationships and friendships with other females and to trust that _____-_____ enhances relationships.

38. Males tend to associate self-disclosure with _____ and loss of control.

Goal 2f: Describe key barriers to effective verbal communication

39. Barriers to interpersonal communication fall into three main categories: _____, proposing solutions, and avoiding the other's concerns.

40. _____ can be a barrier to interpersonal communication because it often implies a lack of confidence in the other person.

41. _____-_____ is a particularly harmful type of diversion that creates a barrier to communication by avoiding the other person's concerns.

42. Proposing _____ _____ may amount to avoiding the other person's concerns because it ignores the person's feelings.

Learning Goal 3: Describe the elements of nonverbal interpersonal communication

43. _____ _____ refers to messages that are transmitted by other than linguistic means.

Goal 3a: Outline the characteristics and variations in nonverbal communication

44. Nonverbal communication is spontaneous, often _____, and must be interpreted in context.

45. _____ _____ refers to the communication of true emotions through nonverbal channels even when the person tries to conceal the truth verbally.

46. Compared with people who are telling the truth, liars tend to blink more and have more dilated pupils; show more self-manipulating gestures; give shorter responses that are more _____, more _____, and more _____; speak in a more distancing way; speak in a higher pitch; and take more time to plan what they say.

47. Nonverbal behaviors usually come in _____.

48. Variations in how cultures or groups within a culture use specific elements of nonverbal communication combine to give them different _____ of communication.

49. _____ are more likely than _____ to be good at reading people's emotional cues, to smile, to cry when they see someone in distress, to look at their conversational partner, to sit quietly, and to have good posture.

Goal 3b: Describe the different types of body communication

50. Forms of body communication include _____, facial expressions, eye contact, and touch.

51. Touch may be used to express sexuality, consolation, or _____.

Goal 3c: Discuss how space is used in nonverbal communication

52. Edwin Hall identified four zones in which we interact: intimate distance, personal distance, social distance, and _____ distance.

53. How people use space communicates information about _____ and status, but standards for the use of space vary from culture to culture.

Goal 3d: Explain the use of silence and paralanguage in communication

54. As Goodman suggests, silences in a conversation act like _____ _____.

55. _____ refers to nonlinguistic aspects of verbal expression such as the rapidity, volume, and pitch of speech.

Key Terms

Briefly define each key term and provide an example or application.

1. message

2. channel

3. encoding

4. decoding

5. noise

6. transactional

7. interpersonal communication

8. denotation

9. connotation

10. hearing

11. listening

12. reflective listening

13. paraphrasing

14. self-disclosure

15. Johari Window

16. rapport talk

17. report talk

18. nonverbal communication

19. nonverbal leakage

20. gesture

21. proxemics

22. paralanguage

Practice Test A

Answer these multiple-choice questions to assess your understanding of the chapter. Answers are provided at the end of the study guide chapter.

___ 1. Hearing problems, poor vision, depression, and anxiety are examples of
a. channels of communication.
b. contexts of communication.
c. sources of noise.
d. paralanguage.

___ 2. In interpersonal communication, sending and receiving
a. are roles carried out by different people.
b. often occur simultaneously.
c. always occur sequentially.
d. always use different channels.

___ 3. If you don't think the labels "good" or "bad" apply to a word, then to you that word
a. has few connotations.
b. has many connotations.
c. lacks a clear denotative meaning.
d. has no denotative meaning.

___ 4. The more concrete a word is,
a. the larger the number of connotations.
b. the greater the opportunity for disagreement about its meaning.
c. the greater the chances that people will agree on its meaning.
d. the less effective it is.

___ 5. Good speakers tend to
a. look away from the listener.
b. use jargon.
c. use obscure words.
d. use verbal and nonverbal messages consistently.

___ 6. If you restate a speaker's message, you are applying the strategy of
a. risky self-disclosure.
b. passive communication.
c. reflective listening.
d. rapport talk.

___ 7. Which of the following is true about self-disclosure?
a. Engaging in self-disclosure early in a relationship is always beneficial.
b. A moderate amount of self-disclosure often facilitates a relationship.
c. People within one culture will have similar self-disclosure skills and needs.
d. A first step in self-disclosure is communicating what you are thinking and feeling and needing at that moment.

___ 8. Assertive communication
a. is abrasive and hostile.
b. was traditionally the typical communication style of U.S. women.
c. creates pity or guilt in the listener.
d. is the best way to deal with conflict.

_____ 9. Compared with men, women tend to self-disclose
a. more.
b. less.
c. equally.
d. about a narrower range of issues.

_____ 10. Proposing solutions
a. demonstrates that you are an effective listener.
b. usually deepens a relationship.
c. may be constructive but is often a barrier to effective communication.
d. is a key element of passive communication.

_____ 11. Which of the following is true about nonverbal behaviors?
a. Their meaning is universal.
b. They are always consistent with verbal behavior.
c. They occur spontaneously.
d. They always occur in the context of verbal behavior.

_____ 12. Making eye contact is generally considered
a. a sign of respect in cultures around the world.
b. rude by most African Americans.
c. a sign of respect by many Native Americans.
d. disrespectful by many Native Americans.

Identifying Concepts

Answers are provided at the end of the study guide chapter.

1. THE JOHARI WINDOW   Identify the area of the Johari Window illustrated by each of the following statements.

a. "Last night I had this dream about a trip to a really scary place."

b. "I'm a Methodist."

c. "If you can believe it, Sean told her that I interrupt people all the time!"

2. TYPES OF BODILY COMMUNICATION Identify the type of bodily communication illustrated in each example.

a. Giving the "ok" sign

b. Raising the eyebrows

c. Hugging someone

d. Looking during a conversation

Understanding Concepts

Complete these exercises to develop your understanding of important ideas in this chapter.

1. What are the components of interpersonal communication?

2. Give denotative and connotative meanings for the following words:

	Denotative meaning	Connotative meaning
animal		
woman		
feminine		
rule		
law		
life		

3. What are the characteristics of good speakers?

4. List strategies for effective listening.

5. How is the Johari Window useful in understanding your style of self-disclosure?

6. How does self-disclosure differ among men and women?

7. How does assertive communication differ from aggressive communication?

8. List barriers to effective verbal communication.

9. What are the main characteristics of nonverbal communication?

10. What is proxemics, and what are the four distances proposed by Hall?

Applying Concepts and Strategies

Complete these exercises to develop your ability to apply this chapter's material to your life and the world. Your responses will differ from those of other students in the class, and it is helpful to share your ideas with other students.

1. Analyze the main problems that occur in your important communications with others. What could you do to minimize these problems?

2. Review the section on listening skills and try to do your best listening for a few hours. What were the effects of practicing good listening skills? Did the speaker react to your efforts?

3. Discuss your approach to self-disclosure using the Johari Window. How risky is it for you to self-disclose early in a relationship? Are some thoughts so private that you would not disclose them?

4. Take and score the Self-Assessment on Argumentativeness. Do you tend to approach or avoid arguments? How does this affect your communication, your relationships, your peace of mind?

5. Think back over your recent conversations. Did you or the person you were talking with judge, provide solutions, or avoid the other's concern? What was the result? Which barrier occurred most often?

6. What did you learn from your family about using touch to communicate? Have you changed the way you use touch? How comfortable are you with touch?

7. How do you react to a roommate or to someone sitting next to you in the library or cafeteria? Are you very possessive of "your" space?

8. Experiment with using more silence in your communication. What are the results? How did you feel when remaining silent?

9. Many people do a large part of their communicating by phone. Does your paralanguage change when you talk on the phone instead of face to face? How does the absence of body communication affect your conversations?

10. When you communicate through e-mail, chat rooms, or on a blog, paralanguage as well as body language is missing. What is the result? How does communicating via the Internet compare with writing a letter, talking face to face, or talking on the phone?

Practice Test B

Answer these multiple-choice test questions to help you assess your understanding of the textbook chapter. Answers are provided at the end of the study guide chapter.

___ 1. The flowing process between sender and receiver is what makes communication
a. interpersonal.
b. transactional.
c. verbal.
d. intimate.

___ 2. A person's meaning is more likely to be clear to a listener if the person uses words that are
a. concrete.
b. abstract.
c. general.
d. technical.

___ 3. To become a better listener, it is good to
a. pay careful attention to the person who is talking.
b. avoid distracting the speaker by showing your reaction.
c. look down so that you can concentrate more easily.
d. avoid repeating what the speaker has said.

___ 4. The Johari Window includes
a. the actual self and the ideal self.
b. the open self, the hidden self, the blind self, and the unknown self.
c. the real self, the actual self, the ideal self, and the ought self.
d. the open self, the actual self, the hidden self, and the blind self.

___ 5. To increase self-disclosure, a good strategy is to proceed gradually and to begin with
a. your feelings.
b. facts about yourself.
c. "here and now" communication.
d. a confession.

___ 6. Research on how men and women communicate indicates that
a. there are no significant gender differences.
b. men and women have similar styles of communication.
c. if someone interrupts and takes over a conversation, it is more likely to be a man than a woman.
d. both men and women prefer talk that is designed to give information rather than talk designed to create a bond.

___ 7. According to Carl Rogers, if you want to communicate effectively,
a. be sure to praise the speaker.
b. avoid making judgments.
c. be direct and blunt.
d. comment on your own experiences.

___ 8. Giving advice is
a. an effective strategy for deepening relationships.
b. a first step toward self-disclosure.
c. a strategy that is sometimes constructive and sometimes destructive.
d. a strategy that establishes trust.

___ 9. When verbal and nonverbal messages seem to conflict,
a. verbal messages are more reliable because nonverbal behaviors are ambiguous.
b. both messages are likely to be important.
c. you know that the person is lying.
d. you must be misinterpreting either the verbal or the nonverbal messages.

___ 10. Compared with people who are telling the truth, liars tend to
a. give longer responses.
b. include more repetitions and slips of the tongue in their statements.
c. speak in a lower pitch.
d. speak faster and more specifically.

___ 11. The way people use touch to communicate
a. is innate and universal.
b. is learned during adolescence.
c. varies with gender and culture.
d. varies with gender but not with culture.

___ 12. Silence during a conversation
a. signifies a lack of interest.
b. indicates a breakdown in communication.
c. offers opportunities for effective listeners.
d. indicates lost opportunities for strengthening a relationship.

Answers to Chapter Questions

Guided Review
1. message
2. channel
3. encoding; decoding
4. noise
5. relationship
6. transactional
7. senders; receivers
8. context
9. relationship; sociocultural
10. ethnic (*or* cultural)
11. encoding; decoding
12. listeners
13. denotative; connotative

14. concrete
15. specific
16. examples
17. verbal; nonverbal
18. hearing
19. listening
20. monopolizing
21. reflective
22. feedback
23. self-disclosure
24. Johari Window
25. unknown
26. open
27. blind
28. risky self-disclosures
29. self-disclosure
30. gradually; facts
31. passively
32. guilty
33. assertive
34. assertive
35. rapport; report
36. rapport
37. self-disclosure; self-disclosure
38. vulnerability
39. judging
40. advice
41. one-upping
42. logical solutions
43. nonverbal communication
44. ambiguous
45. nonverbal leakage
46. negative; irrelevant; generalized
47. clusters
48. styles
49. women; men
50. gestures
51. dominance
52. public
53. power
54. traffic signals
55. paralanguage

Practice Test A
1. c
2. b
3. a
4. c
5. d
6. c
7. b
8. d
9. a
10. c
11. c
12. d

Identifying Concepts
1. THE JOHARI WINDOW
   a. hidden self
   b. open self
   c. blind self
2. TYPES OF BODILY COMMUNICATION
   a. gesture
   b. facial expression
   c. touch
   d. eye communication

Practice Test B
1. b
2. a
3. a
4. b
5. b
6. c
7. b
8. c
9. b
10. b
11. c
12. c

CHAPTER **8**   **FRIENDSHIP AND LOVE RELATIONSHIPS**

Chapter Outline

I. FORMING CLOSE RELATIONSHIPS: ATTRACTION

A. Familiarity and Similarity

- Familiarity and similarity increase the chances that we will like another person.
- In general, we are attracted to people who are similar to ourselves, with similar attitudes, behavior patterns, tastes, and personal characteristics.

B. Physical Attractiveness

- Men tend to value attractiveness in a romantic partner more than women do.
- Although people value attractiveness, they end up choosing as partners people whose level of attractiveness is similar to their own, as the matching hypothesis predicts.

C. Personality Traits

People are attracted to people with traits such as sincerity, honesty, understanding, loyalty, truthfulness, intelligence, and dependability.

II. FRIENDSHIPS

People tend not only to form friendships with people similar to themselves but also to become more similar to their friends.

A. The Benefits of Friendship

Friendship can reduce loneliness, boost self-esteem, and provide emotional support.

B. Gender and Friendship

Compared with men, women tend to have more close friends, and their friendships tend to involve more self-disclosure and mutual support, more emphasis on talking, and less emphasis on activities and competition.

III. LOVE

A. What Is Love?

Zick Rubin proposed that loving involves some degree of closeness, dependency, selflessness, absorption, and exclusivity.

1. **ROMANTIC LOVE**

   Romantic or passionate love has strong components of sexuality and infatuation, and it often is the predominant type of love early in a love relationship.

2. **AFFECTIONATE LOVE**

   Affectionate or companionate love involves deep, caring affection, and it becomes increasingly important as love matures.

3. **CONSUMMATE LOVE**

   - Sternberg proposed a model in which love relationships include varying combinations of passion, intimacy, and commitment.
   - According to Sternberg, consummate love involves all three ingredients—passion, intimacy, and commitment—and is the strongest, fullest type of love.

B. Attachment

Researchers have found that the quality of romantic relationships is linked with the quality of attachment to caregivers during infancy and childhood.

1. **ATTACHMENT STYLES**

   Mary Ainsworth identified different styles of attachment between infants and their caregivers, including secure, avoidant, and ambivalent attachment styles.

2. **LINKS BETWEEN ATTACHMENT STYLES AND ADULTHOOD**

   - Researchers have found correlations between a secure attachment with parents during childhood and secure relationships later in life, between avoidant attachment in childhood and difficulty developing intimate relationships in adulthood, and between ambivalent attachment in childhood and possessiveness during adulthood.
   - Attachment styles can change over time, and links between earlier and later styles are lessened by stressful life experiences.

C. Gender and Love

- Compared with men, women tend to give affection more importance, are more likely to think of love in terms of friendship, and are less likely to conceptualize love in terms of passion.
- Men and women tend to have different styles of communicating and interacting, with women being more expressive.

D. Falling Out of Love

Although falling out of love is painful, it can be beneficial if the relationship is harmful.

Breaking the Bonds of Love

1. Identify the feelings that make it hard to end the relationship.
2. Develop self-esteem and independence.
3. Stop self-defeating thoughts that prevent you from leaving the relationship.
4. Fall in love with someone else only when you're emotionally ready.

IV. THE DARK SIDE OF CLOSE RELATIONSHIPS

A. Anger

- Anger in close relationships can be very destructive and generate cyclic patterns in which anger leads to more anger.
- Carol Tavris suggests that a first step in breaking the destructive cycle of anger is to give up the dream of rescuing or changing your partner.

B. Jealousy

- Jealousy is the fear of the possibility of losing someone's exclusive love.
- Men tend to be especially upset about sexual infidelity, whereas women are often more upset by emotional infidelity.
- Jealousy is often stimulated by a specific event or situation, but people with certain characteristics such as low self-esteem are especially prone to jealousy.
- Strategies for overcoming jealousy include reducing insecurities and thinking more rationally.

C. Spouse and Partner Abuse

- Domestic violence is learned behavior, and it provides a means of control.
- Lenore Walker describes a three-phase cycle of domestic violence: tension building, battering, and loving contrition.
- Battering continues for several reasons, including the batterer's pattern of blaming the victim, dependence, jealousy, low self-esteem, and family scripts in which problems are solved through physical force or psychological abuse.

D. Dependence

- Excessive dependence often generates resentment and hostility.
- Excessively dependent people tend to have low self-esteem and are prone to jealousy.

Overcoming Excessive Dependence

1. Admit that the problem exists.
2. Explore the reasons for such neediness.
3. Initiate strategies that will lead to increased independence.

E. Loneliness

Chronic loneliness is linked with impaired physical and mental health.

1. LONELINESS AND LIFE'S TRANSITIONS
   - Transitions such as beginning college often bring loneliness.
   - The ability to overcome loneliness is linked with optimism and high self-esteem.
   - Loneliness is linked with a decreased ability to cope with stress.
2. LONELINESS AND TECHNOLOGY
   Watching television and using the Internet may contribute to social disengagement, although the Internet also offers opportunities for forming new ties.

ADJUSTMENT STRATEGIES *for*

Reducing Loneliness

1. Participate in activities that you can do with others.
2. Be aware of the early signs of loneliness.
3. Diagram your social network.
4. Engage in positive behaviors when you meet new people.
5. See a counselor or read a book about loneliness.

Learning Goals

After reading and studying this chapter, you should be able to

1. **Discuss the factors involved in attraction.**
   a. Describe the roles that familiarity and similarity play in attraction.
   b. Explain the link between physical attractiveness and attraction.
   c. Describe the relationship between personality traits and attraction.

2. **Describe friendship.**
   a. Describe the benefits of friendship.
   b. Outline gender differences in friendship.

3. **Characterize the types of love and factors involved in love.**
   a. Identify various forms of love.
   b. Describe the link between attachment during childhood and adult relationships.
   c. Outline gender differences related to love.
   d. Discuss the process of falling out of love.

4. **Explain the dark side of close relationships.**
   a. Describe characteristics of anger in close relationships.
   b. Outline the sources of jealousy.
   c. Outline the sources of domestic violence.
   d. Explain the sources and consequences of excessive dependence in a relationship.
   e. Describe factors involved in loneliness.

Guided Review

After you have read this chapter in the textbook, complete these statements. Topics are discussed in the same order as in the chapter. Answers are provided at the end of the study guide chapter.

Learning Goal 1: Discuss the factors involved in attraction

Goal 1a: Describe the roles that familiarity and similarity play in attraction

1. _____ increases the chances that we will like someone and is a necessary condition for a close relationship.
2. People like to associate with people who are _____ to themselves.
3. We are attracted to people with attitudes and behavior patterns similar to our own in part because of _____ _____; in other words, their attitudes and behavior validate our own.

Goal 1b. Explain the link between physical attractiveness and attraction

4. Compared with women, men tend to give more importance to the _____ of an intimate partner.
5. People usually seek out someone at their own level of attractiveness in both _____ _____ and social attributes.
6. Although people may prefer a more attractive person in the abstract, their actions follow the _____ _____, which says that people end up choosing someone who is close to their own level.
7. To make themselves attractive to others, men tend to use tactics that showcase their resources, whereas women tend to focus on their _____.

Goal 1c: Describe the relationship between personality traits and attraction

8. People tend to be attracted to people who have desirable personality traits such as sincerity, _____, _____, and _____.

Learning Goal 2: Describe friendship

9. _____ are close relationships that involve intimacy, trust, acceptance, mutual liking, and understanding.
10. People tend to form friendships with people who are _____ to themselves and to become more similar to their friends as the friendship develops.

Goal 2a: Describe the benefits of friendship

11. Friendship can reduce _____, buoy self-esteem, and provide emotional support.
12. Harry Stack Sullivan emphasized that friendship plays an important role in _____, helping people fulfill such social needs as needs for attachment and for playful companionship.
13. Some psychologists argue that during adulthood friends are more important than _____ _____ for psychological well-being.

Goal 2b: Outline gender differences in friendship

14. Compared with men, women tend to have more _____ _____, and their friendships tend to involve more self-disclosure and mutual support.

15. Male friends are more likely than female friends to engage in _____ and to be _____.

16. Problems can arise in cross-gender friendships because of differing _____.

Learning Goal 3: Characterize the types of love and factors involved in love

17. Whereas liking involves a positive evaluation of a person, loving involves feeling _____ to someone.

Goal 3a: Identify various forms of love

18. Key types of love are _____ love, _____ love, and consummate love.

19. Romantic love, also called _____ love, has strong components of sexuality and infatuation and often predominates early in a love relationship.

20. Affectionate love, also called _____ love, is characterized by a deep, caring affection.

21. According to Sternberg, the strongest, fullest type of love is what he called _____ love.

22. In Sternberg's triangular model of love, three dimensions or ingredients are involved in love relationships: _____, _____, and commitment.

23. In Sternberg's model of love, _____ is our cognitive appraisal of the relationship and our intent to maintain it even in the face of problems.

Goal 3b: Describe the link between attachment during childhood and adult relationships

24. Research indicates that the quality of romantic relationships is linked to the quality of _____ during infancy and childhood.

25. People learn an attachment style as infants, and that style seems to serve as a _____ for their adult relationships.

26. _____ described three styles of attachment between infants and their caregivers: secure, avoidant, and ambivalent.

27. A _____ attachment style is characterized by a caregiver who is responsive to an infant's needs and shows positive emotions when interacting with the infant and by an infant who trusts the caregiver and isn't afraid to explore the world.

28. An _____ attachment style is characterized by a caregiver who is distant, rejecting, and fails to respond to the infant and by an infant who appears uninterested in being close to the caregiver.

29. An _____ attachment style is characterized by a caregiver who is inconsistently available to the infant and overbearing when present and by an infant who clings to the caregiver and then pushes the caregiver away.

30. Research indicates that adults who report that they were _____ _____ to their parents as children are more likely than adults who report having had an insecure attachment to say that they have a secure attachment to their romantic partners.

31. Research also indicates that having an _____ attachment to a caregiver in childhood is linked with having problems developing an intimate relationship in adulthood and that having an _____ attachment in childhood is linked with being less trusting than securely attached adults.

32. Attachment styles can change during adulthood, and the links between early and later attachment styles are lessened by _____ life experiences.

Goal 3c: Outline gender differences related to love

33. Research indicates that men tend to conceptualize love in terms of _____, whereas women are likely to think of love more in terms of _____.

34. Both women and men include affection in their definitions of love, but women usually rate affection as _____ important than men do.

35. Overall, women are more _____ and affectionate than men in marriage.

36. Sensitivity to deficiencies in caring may help explain why wives are _____ likely than their husbands to initiate a divorce.

Goal 3d: Discuss the process of falling out of love

37. Painful as it is, falling out of love may be beneficial if you are _____ with a person who betrays your trust or if you are in love with someone who drains you emotionally or financially or does not return your feelings.

38. Detecting whether a relationship has evolved in a way that creates _____ and _____ roles is an important step toward learning whether to reconstruct or to end a relationship.

39. _____ can help us to identify the destructive aspects of a relationship and to rebuild our identity and self-esteem.

40. Strategies for breaking the bonds of love in a destructive relationship include (1) identifying the feelings that make breaking up difficult, (2) developing _____-_____ and _____, (3) recognizing the self-defeating thoughts that make breaking up difficult, and (4) falling in love with someone else when you are emotionally ready to do so.

Learning Goal 4: Explain the dark side of close relationships
Goal 4a: Describe characteristics of anger in close relationships

41. Anger in close relationships can generate a destructive, self-perpetuating _____.

42. Three cyclic patterns of anger that often occur in close relationships are (1) an anger-justifies-itself pattern, in which your belief in your justifications for anger generate more anger; (2) a _____-and-outburst pattern, in which a failure to confront problems breeds resentment that builds to a outburst of anger, followed by remorse and a renewed failure to confront problems; and (3) a pattern in which a spouse's outburst of anger leads to a counterattack, which generates another outburst in return.

43. According to Tavris, the first step in breaking a destructive cycle of anger in close relationships is to drop the dream of _____ or _____ your partner.

44. Tavris suggest that it is best to let your anger _____.

Goal 4b: Outline the sources of jealousy

45. Men tend to be especially upset about _____ infidelity, whereas women are often more upset by _____ infidelity.

46. Jealousy is often stimulated by a specific event or situation, but it also has been linked to low _____-_____ and feelings of insecurity.

47. Jealous individuals often perceive their partners as very desirable possessions and tend to _____ their partners.

48. To overcome jealousy, people should try to reduce their feelings of insecurity, to think more _____ about the relationship, and to discuss their concerns and needs with their partners in a nonaccusing way.

Goal 4c: Discuss the sources of domestic violence

49. Research indicates that battering behavior is _____ and that men batter women in order to show their power and exercise control.

50. Most women who stay in violent relationships do so, not because of masochism, but because of _____.

51. According to Lenore Walker, domestic violence is a three-phase cycle in which the phases are tension building, battering, and _____ _____.

52. Obstacles to change among batterers include a tendency to _____ the victim, dependence on the victim, low self-esteem, and a family script that calls for solving problems with _____ _____ and psychological abuse.

Goal 4d: Explain the sources and consequences of excessive dependence in a relationship

53. Excessively dependent people are likely to generate feelings of resentment and _____ in their partners.

54. Excessively dependent people tend to have low _____-_____ and feelings of insecurity.

Goal 4e: Describe factors involved in loneliness

55. Each of us feels lonely at times, but chronic loneliness is linked with impaired _____ and _____ _____.

56. Married individuals are _____ lonely than their nonmarried counterparts.

57. Men tend to blame _____ for their loneliness whereas women tend to blame _____ _____.

58. Loneliness is linked with many life _____.

59. Loneliness has been linked to using _____ and the _____, perhaps because these may encourage social disengagement.

60. People often feel _____ or _____ before loneliness becomes pervasive.

Key Terms

Briefly define each key term and provide an example or application.

1. consensual validation

2. matching hypothesis

3. friendship

4. romantic love

5. affectionate love

6. consummate love

7. secure attachment style

8. avoidant attachment style

9. ambivalent attachment style

10. jealousy

Practice Test A

Answer these multiple-choice questions to assess your understanding of the chapter. Answers are provided at the end of the study guide chapter.

____ 1. Overall, people are attracted to people who
a. offer a contrast with their own attitudes.
b. offer a contrast with their own tastes and behavior patterns.
c. are similar to themselves.
d. have attitudes similar to their own but display different behavior patterns.

____ 2. According to one study, the characteristics that women rate most highly in a romantic partner are traits such as
a. good looks, intelligence, and power.
b. good looks, strength, and resourcefulness.
c. strength, dependability, and good health.
d. considerateness, honesty, dependability, and kindness.

_____ 3. In forming relationships we usually seek out
a. the most attractive person we know.
b. the person with the most attractive social attributes.
c. a person who is moderately attractive.
d. a person close to our own level of attractiveness.

_____ 4. People are attracted to people similar to themselves
a. when they form romantic relationships but not when they form friendships.
b. only if they have low self-esteem.
c. when they form friendships as well as when they form romantic relationships.
d. only if they have high self-esteem.

_____ 5. Which of the following is NOT a true statement about romantic love?
a. Romantic love has strong components of sexuality and infatuation.
b. Romantic love is what we mean when we say we are "in love" with someone.
c. Romantic love often predominates in the early part of a love relationship.
d. Romantic love is also called companionate love.

_____ 6. According to Ellen Berscheid, sexual desire
a. is not an important component of love.
b. is the most important component of romantic love.
c. is only one of several equally important components of romantic love.
d. is the most important component of consummate love.

_____ 7. According to Robert Sternberg, affectionate love occurs when there is
a. passion and commitment but little or no intimacy.
b. passion and intimacy but little or no commitment.
c. intimacy and commitment but little or no passion.
d. passion, commitment, and intimacy.

_____ 8. According to Ainsworth, infants who have a secure attachment to their caregivers
a. will be so attached to their caregivers they will fear being abandoned by them.
b. will be so attached to their caregivers they will not want to explore on their own.
c. will cling anxiously to their caregivers.
d. will feel safe enough to explore their world.

_____ 9. Attachment styles during adulthood
a. may change.
b. are solidified by stressful experiences.
c. are established by the age of 21.
d. are established by about the age of 35.

_____ 10. Which of the following is NOT a good strategy for breaking the bonds of love if you are in a destructive relationship?
a. Identify the feelings that make it hard to break up.
b. Fall in love with someone else as soon as possible.
c. Develop your self-esteem and independence.
d. Stop self-defeating thoughts that prevent you from taking steps to break up.

_____ 11. People who are excessively dependent and people who are prone to jealousy share a tendency to
a. seek control.
b. have low-self-esteem
c. be masochistic.
d. have a history of secure attachments.

___ 12. Strategies for reducing loneliness include
a. joining an organization.
b. drawing a diagram of your social network and asking whether it is meeting your social needs.
c. engaging in positive behavior when you meet new people.
d. all of the above.

Identifying Concepts

Answers are provided at the end of the study guide chapter.

1. TYPES OF LOVE   Identify the type of love illustrated by each description.

a. Marked by passion with little or no intimacy or commitment

b. Marked by passion and commitment without intimacy

c. Being in love

d. Dominates the early part of a romantic relationship

e. Characterized by a deep, caring affection and the desire to be near someone

f. Marked by passion as well as by commitment and intimacy

2. STUDENTS OF RELATIONSHIPS   Identify the person whose contribution is described in each example.

a. Emphasized the importance of friendships to human development

b. Identified styles of attachment

c. Developed triangular theory of love

d. Described how to break the cycle of anger

Understanding Concepts

Complete these exercises to develop your understanding of important ideas in this chapter.

1. What characteristics make people attractive to other people?

2. Why are friends important to development and to psychological well-being?

3. List three ways in which friendships and relationships with family members differ.

4. How are friendships like and unlike romantic relationships?

5. Summarize Shaver's description of what happens to romantic love over time.

6. Describe Sternberg's triangular model of love.

7. Summarize the key characteristics of the secure, avoidant, and ambivalent attachment styles.

8. What is the relationship between attachment style during infancy and childhood and adult relationships?

9. What are three cyclic patterns of anger that are common in close relationships?

10. What is the relationship between use of the Internet and loneliness?

Applying Concepts and Strategies

Complete these exercises to develop your ability to apply this chapter's material to your life and the world. Your responses will differ from those of other students in the class, and it is helpful to share your ideas with other students.

1. Do your friends offer you consensual validation? Describe how they do or don't. Have you altered your attitudes or behavior as a result of your friendships? If so, how would you evaluate the change?

2. How can researchers who study the matching hypothesis show that people match on physical attractiveness? Can you think of ways that researchers could measure physical attractiveness?

3. Complete Self-Assessment 8.1: What Type of Love Do I Have? and evaluate the results. Does Sternberg's triangular theory of love give you new insight into your relationship?

4. Is it possible that a person always loves in the same way?

5. Complete Self-Assessment 8.2: What Is My Attachment Style and evaluate the results. What do you think are the sources of your style? Do you want to change it?

6. Summarize strategies for falling out of love. Under what circumstances would you find it important to end a relationship?

7. Have anger, jealousy, or excessive dependency ever significantly affected your close relationships? If so, what did you do?

8. Anger, jealousy, and dependency tend to occur together in relationships. What is the link among these emotions?

9. How do gender differences make it difficult to sustain harmonious relationships?

10. Do your attitudes and behavior follow the patterns for your gender that are described in the discussions of friendships and romantic relationships in the text? If not, describe how they differ. What do you think are the reasons for the differences?

11. What elements of modern life make it more likely that people will be lonely? What elements of modern life help to decrease loneliness?

12. Which of the strategies for reducing loneliness would you apply? How would you determine whether the people in your social network are meeting your social needs?

Practice Test B

Answer these multiple-choice test questions to help you assess your understanding of the textbook chapter. Answers are provided at the end of the study guide chapter.

___ 1. In a study in which students were shown slides of women and asked to rate how much they liked them, the women's ratings
a. were positively linked with the number of times the students had seen the women in the classroom.
b. were negatively linked with the number of times the students had seen the women in the classsroom.
c. were not affected by the number of times the students had seen the women in the classroom.
d. depended solely on how attractive they were.

___ 2. The idea that opposites attract
a. is one of the most powerful lessons generated by the study of close relationships.
b. is very frequently but not always true in the case of cross-gender relationships.
c. is true in some limited cases for some isolated characteristics.
d. has not been carefully studied.

___ 3. According to one study, the characteristics that men rate most highly in a romantic partner are traits such as
a. considerateness, honesty, dependability, and kindness.
b. understanding, good looks, and dependability.
c. good looks, frugality, and cooking skill.
d. kindness, dependability, and good health.

___ 4. The idea that we end up choosing people who are close to our own level of attractiveness is known as
a. consensual validation.
b. the matching hypothesis.
c. the triangular model of love.
d. ambivalent attachment.

___ 5. In adulthood relationships with friends may be more important to our well-being than relationships with family members because
a. friendships are more enduring.
b. friendships are optional and chosen, not ascribed, relationships.
c. friendships are ascribed relationships.
d. friends are less similar to ourselves.

___ 6. Cross-gender friendships are
a. less common among adults than among elementary school children.
b. as common as same-gender friendships.
c. more common among adults than among elementary school children.
d. as common among adults as among elementary school children.

___ 7. Romantic relationships
a. are perceived as more stable than friendships.
b. involve a less complex mixture of emotions than friendships.
c. are more likely than friendships to be the cause of depression.
d. do not resemble friendships in any significant way.

___ 8. Adults who had an avoidant attachment in childhood are more likely than adults who had a secure attachment
a. to be jealous.
b. to find it easy to get close to others.
c. to quickly end a relationship.
d. to have little concern about being abandoned.

___ 9. In the anger-justifies-itself pattern,
a. your resentment builds as a result of a failure to confront problems until you express the anger.
b. you make arguments to justify your anger and then allow your belief in those arguments and thoughts about your grievance to fuel further anger.
c. your partner's anger makes you angry, which makes your partner angry.
d. resolution comes through the quick expression of any angry feelings.

___ 10. According to Tavris, trying to reform your partner
a. is a first step in breaking the cycle of anger.
b. reinforces the intimacy of your relationship.
c. tends to push your partner into the role of incompetent helpee.
d. should motivate both of you to sustain the relationship.

___ 11. Research on domestic violence indicates that
a. battering behavior is a response to provocation by women.
b. alcohol and drug use causes domestic violence.
c. increased violence is linked with alcohol and drug use.
d. genetic differences account for different rates of domestic violence.

___ 12. A lonely man is likely to attribute his loneliness to
a. other people.
b. a past relationship.
c. himself.
d. his childhood.

Answers to Chapter Questions

Guided Review
1. familiarity
2. similar
3. consensual validation
4. attractiveness
5. physical characteristics
6. matching hypothesis
7. appearance
8. honesty; understanding; loyalty (*or* truthfulness; intelligence; dependability)
9. friendships
10. similar
11. loneliness
12. development
13. family members
14. close friends
15. activities; competitive
16. expectations
17. close
18. romantic; affectionate
19. passionate
20. companionate
21. consummate
22. passion; intimacy
23. commitment
24. attachment
25. blueprint (*or* working model)
26. Ainsworth
27. secure
28. avoidant
29. ambivalent
30. securely attached
31. avoidant; ambivalent
32. disruptive (*or* stressed)
33. passion; friendship
34. more

35. expressive
36. more
37. obsessed
38. dominant; submissive
39. friends
40. self-esteem; independence
41. cycle
42. passivity
43. rescuing; changing
44. subside
45. sexual; emotional
46. self-esteem
47. idolize
48. rationally
49. learned
50. fear
51. loving contrition
52. blame; physical violence
53. hostility
54. self-esteem
55. physical; mental health
56. less
57. themselves; external factors
58. transitions
59. television; Internet
60. bored; alienated

Practice Test A
 1. c
 2. d
 3. d
 4. c
 5. d
 6. b

 7. c
 8. d
 9. a
10. b
11. b
12. d

Identifying Concepts
1. TYPES OF LOVE
   a. infatuation
   b. fatuous love
   c. romantic love
   d. romantic love
   e. affectionate or companionate love
   f. consummate love
2. STUDENTS OF RELATIONSHIPS
   a. Sullivan
   b. Ainsworth
   c. Sternberg
   d. Tavris

Practice Test B
 1. a
 2. c
 3. c
 4. b
 5. b
 6. c
 7. c
 8. c
 9. b
10. c
11. c
12. c

CHAPTER 9

ADULT LIFE STYLES

Chapter Outline

I. THE DIVERSITY OF ADULT LIFE STYLES

A. Single Adults Living Alone

- In recent years, the percentage of single adults in the U.S. population has risen dramatically, and the percentage of single adults who live alone has multiplied.
- Along with advantages, being single and living alone brings the potential challenges of forming intimate relationships with other adults, confronting loneliness, and finding a niche in a marriage-oriented society.
- The benefits and challenges of living alone vary to some extent with age.

B. Cohabiting Adults

- Cohabitation refers to living together in a sexual relationship without being married.
- The percentage of U.S. couples who cohabit before marriage has multiplied in recent years.
- Cohabiting arrangements tend to be short-lived compared with marriages, and relationships between cohabiting men and women tend to be more equal than those between husbands and wives.
- Research comparing the quality of marriages among couples who first cohabited and those who did not has found either no differences or lower rates of marital satisfaction among couples who cohabited before marriage.

C. Married Adults

- The overwhelming majority of U.S. adults marry at some point in their lives, but currently only about 60 percents of U.S. adults are married.
- U.S. adults have been waiting longer before getting married, and about one-third of married couples divorce within ten years.
- The sociocultural context is a powerful influence on marriage and on the adjustments faced by married couples.
    1. FINDING A PARTNER
        - In many cultures, people see chastity and domestic skill as very important characteristics to look for in a martial partner.

- In the United States, young adults see emotional depth and the ability to communicate as very important characteristics to look for in a marital partner.

2. MARITAL EXPECTATIONS AND MYTHS
   - Unrealistic expectations about marriage are linked with low levels of marital satisfaction.
   - Myths about marriage include the idea that conflict must be avoided, that affairs are the main cause of divorce, that men are philanderers by nature, and that gender differences are the cause of marital problems.

3. WHAT MAKES MARRIAGES WORK

   John Gottman and his colleagues have studied hundred of couples over decades in order to assess what makes marriages work.

   ADJUSTMENT STRATEGIES *for*

   Making Marriages Work

   1. Establish love maps.
   2. Nurture fondness and admiration.
   3. Turn toward each other.
   4. Let your partner influence you.
   5. Solve solvable conflicts.
   6. Overcome gridlock.
   7. Create shared meaning.

   ---

4. DEALING WITH CONFLICT
   - Marital conflicts include perpetual conflicts and solvable conflicts.
   - The right strategy for dealing with marital conflict varies with the type of conflict, the problem, and the couple.
   - In general, Gottman concludes that conflicts are most likely to be resolved if couples avoid a harsh approach, are motivated to repair the relationship, regulate their emotions, compromise, and are tolerant of each other's faults.

5. THE BENEFITS OF A GOOD MARRIAGE

   Individuals who are happily married live longer, healthier lives than either divorced individuals or those who are unhappily married.

D. Divorced Adults
- The U.S. divorce rate, although high, has been declining since the mid-1980s.
- About 10 percent of U.S. adults are divorced.

1. THE TIMING OF DIVORCE
   - The most likely time for divorce to occur is between the fifth to tenth year of a marriage.
   - Young adults who divorce tend to have volatile, expressive relationships whereas couples who divorce in midlife tend to have cool and distant relationships with suppressed emotions.
   - The stress of divorce is influenced by whether a divorced parent has custody of children and by the economic effects of the divorce.

2. THE STRESSES OF DIVORCE

   Compared with married adults, separated and divorced adults have higher rates of psychiatric disorders, alcoholism, and psychosomatic problems such as sleep disorders.

3. COPING WITH DIVORCE

   According to E. Mavis Hetherington, factors that enable people to cope effectively with divorce include social maturity, autonomy, internal locus of control, religiosity, work, social support, and a new intimate relationship.

4. DIVERSITY OF POST-DIVORCE PATHWAYS

Hetherington examined how people deal with divorce and described six common outcomes.

ADJUSTMENT STRATEGIES *for*

Divorced Adults*

1. Look at divorce as an opportunity.
2. Think carefully about your decisions.
3. Focus on the future.
4. Capitalize on your strengths and available resources.
5. Don't expect to be successful and happy in everything you do.
6. Never consider yourself trapped by your current pathway.

* Based on E. M. Hetherington and M. Stanely-Hagan, "Parenting in Divorced and Remarried Families," in *Handbook of Parenting,* ed. M. Burnstein (Mahway, NJ: Erlbaum, 2002).

E. Remarried Adults

On average, divorced adults remarry within four years, but only one third of stepfamily couples stay remarried.

ADJUSTMENT STRATEGIES *for*

Remarried Adults

1. Have realistic expectations.
2. Develop new positive relationships within the family.
3. Allot time to be alone with each other.
4. Learn from the first marriage.
5. Don't expect instant love from stepchildren.

F. Gay and Lesbian Relationships

- Gay and lesbian relationships are similar, in their satisfactions and their conflicts, to heterosexual relationships.
- Contrary to stereotypes, one partner is masculine and other feminine in only a small percentage of homosexual couples, but about half of committed gay male couples have an open relationship (one that allows sex but not affectionate love with others).

II. THE FAMILY LIFE CYCLE

The way families change over time can be described as a process with six stages.

A. Leaving Home and Becoming a Single Adult

The first stage in the family life cycle involves launching, the process in which youth move into adulthood and exit the family of origin.

B. The New Couple

The second stage of the family life cycle begins with marriage, which unites two family systems and creates a new, third system.

C. Becoming a Family with Children

In the third stage of the family life cycle the couple become parents and face the difficult task of juggling roles as parents, spouses, and individuals.

D. The Family with Adolescents

The fourth stage of the family life cycle comes when children reach adolescence, which forces parents to adapt as the adolescent moves toward independence.

ADJUSTMENT STRATEGIES *for*

Parenting Adolescents

1. Show warmth and respect; avoid the tendency to be too controlling or permissive.
2. Demonstrate sustained interest in their lives.
3. Adapt to their cognitive and socioemotional development.
4. Communicate expectations for high standards.
5. Display constructive ways of dealing with problems and conflict.
6. Understand that adolescents don't become adults overnight.

E. Midlife Family

The family at midlife, which is the fifth stage in the family life cycle, is a time for launching children, linking generations, and adapting to midlife.

1. THE EMPTY NEST AND ITS REFILLING
   - The empty nest syndrome is a decrease in marital satisfaction and an increase in feelings of emptiness brought on by the launching of children.
   - In fact, most parents experience an increase rather than a decrease in marital satisfaction when their children leave home.
   - Today, more young adults are continuing to live with their parents, an arrangement that brings different benefits and challenges to adjustment.

2. INTERGENERATIONAL RELATIONSHIPS
   - Similarity between parents and an adult child is most likely in religion and politics.
   - As adult children become middle-aged, they often develop more positive perceptions of their parents.
   - Intergenerational relationships differ by gender.

F. The Family in Later Life

Retirement and grandparenting are often key features of the sixth and final stage of the family life cycle.

III. PARENTING

A. Timing of Parenthood

People in the United States today are having fewer children and having them later than they did decades ago.

B. Parenting Styles

- Diana Baumrind described four styles of parenting: authoritarian, authoritative, neglectful, and indulgent.

- Authoritarian parenting is a restrictive, punitive style; children may respond by becoming fearful and anxious.
- Authoritative parenting is warm and nurturant but still places limits on children; children often respond by becoming cheerful, self-controlled, self-reliant, and achievement-oriented.
- Neglectful parenting is a style in which the parent is very uninvolved in the child's life; the result often is children who are socially incompetent, with poor self-control and low self-esteem.
- Indulgent parenting is a style of parenting in which parents are very involved with their children but place few demands or controls on them; children often respond by becoming domineering and egocentric, with poor self-control.
- Research indicates that authoritative parenting is likely to be the most effective approach.

ADJUSTMENT STRATEGIES *for*

Effective Parenting

1. Use authoritative parenting.
2. Understand that parenting takes time and effort.
3. Be a good manager.
4. Don't use physical punishment.

C. Working Parents

- Because of decreases in family size and in the time needed for housework, children whose mothers work outside the home today may receive as much attention as children in the past whose mothers were not employed.
- A number of researchers have found that in general maternal employment does not have detrimental effects on children's development; however, negative effects may occur if a mother goes to work during the first nine months of a child's life.

D. Children in Divorced Families

- Research suggests that children of divorced parents show poorer adjustment than children of nondivorced parents; still, most children of divorced parents do not have significant problems.
- The child's adjustment after divorce depends in part on the relationship between the divorced parents and on their parenting skills and styles.
- Many characteristics of the child, as well as the custody arrangements, also influence how well a child will adjust to the parents' divorce.

ADJUSTMENT STRATEGIES *for*

*Communicating with Children about Divorce**

1. Explain the separation in a sensitive way.
2. Explain that the separation is not the child's fault.
3. Explain that it takes time to feel better.
4. Keep the door open to further discussion.
5. Provide as much continuity as possible.
6. Provide support for your children.

*Based on E. Galinsky & J. David, *The Preschool Years: Family Strategies That Work—from Experts and Parents* (New York: Times Books, 1988).

E. Ethnicity and Parenting

- In the United States large families and extended families are more common among minority groups than among the white majority.
- Children in minority groups are more likely than white children to face poverty, prejudice, and discrimination.
- Families play an important role in buffering the extra stressors faced by minority children.

F. Child Abuse

The main types of child maltreatment are physical abuse, child neglect, sexual abuse, and emotional abuse.

1. THE CULTURAL CONTEXT OF ABUSE
   - Child abuse is usually mild to moderate in severity, and the personality characteristics of the abuser are only part of its cause.
   - Violence in American families reflects the extensive violence in American culture.
   - About a third of parents who were abused as children in turn abuse their own children.

2. CONSEQUENCES OF ABUSE
   - The wide-ranging consequences of child maltreatment include problems during childhood in emotion regulation, in attachment, in peer relations, and in school as well as psychological problems such as anxiety and depression.
   - The scars of being maltreated as a child may be carried into adulthood.

Learning Goals

After reading and studying this chapter, you should be able to

1. **Discuss the diversity of life styles and how they influence people's lives.**
   a. Characterize the lives of single adults living alone.
   b. Discuss cohabitation.
   c. Describe key features of married life.
   d. Discuss divorce and how people cope with it.
   e. Describe the stresses faced by adults who remarry after divorce.
   f. Describe gay and lesbian relationships.

2. **Describe the family life cycle.**
   a. Identify the tasks of the first stage of the family life cycle.
   b. Describe the second stage of the family life cycle.
   c. Describe the third stage of the family life cycle.
   d. Describe the challenges of the fourth stage of the family life cycle.
   e. Discuss adjustment during the fifth stage of the family life cycle.
   f. Describe the final stage of the family life cycle.

3. **Discuss parenting and how it affects children's adjustment.**
   a. Discuss the implications of the timing of parenthood.
   b. Describe four parenting styles.
   c. Discuss how mothers' working outside the home affects children.
   d. Describe how divorce affects children.
   e. Discuss how ethnicity affects children.
   f. Discuss child abuse and its consequences.

Guided Review

After you have read this chapter in the textbook, complete these statements. Topics are discussed in the same order as in the chapter. Answers are provided at the end of the study guide chapter.

Learning Goal 1: Discuss the diversity of life styles and how they influence people's lives

Goal 1a: Characterize the lives of single adults living alone

1. The percentage of single adults in the U.S. population and the percentage of single adults who live alone have _____ dramatically.

2. Although being single and living alone brings advantages such as privacy, this life style also brings challenges such as forming intimate relations with other adults, confronting _____, and finding a niche in a marriage-oriented society.

Goal 1b: Discuss cohabitation

3. _____ refers to living together in a sexual relationship without being married.

4. The percentage of U.S. couples who cohabit before marriage has increased to almost _____ percent.

5. In the United States cohabiting arrangements tend to be _____.

6. Research indicates that compared with married couples who did not cohabit, married couples who lived together before marrying either show no differences in marital quality or have _____ rates of marital satisfaction.

Goal 1c: Describe key features of married life

7. About 95 percent of Americans have been married at least once by the time they are 55 years old, but only about _____ percent of adults are married at any particular time.

8. Americans are marrying _____ in life, and about _____ of couples divorce before their 10th wedding anniversary.

9. In one large-scale study of the traits desired in a spouse by people in 37 cultures, people varied most regarding how much they valued _____.

10. Young adults in the United States view emotional depth and the ability to _____ as very important traits in a spouse.

11. John Gottman's extensive research suggests that individuals in successful marriages have _____ _____ of each other's life and world, which Gottman calls "love maps."

12. The characteristics that Gottman's research suggests are linked to successful marriages include having insights into each other's lives, praising each other, turning toward each other as friends, sharing _____, and solving solvable conflicts.

13. According to Gottman, more than two thirds of marital problems are _____ conflicts.

14. For marital problems that are perpetual conflicts, tension will decrease only when both partners feel comfortable _____ _____ the difference.

15. For marital problems that are resolvable conflicts, Gottman suggests that conflict resolution depends not on one person making changes but on _____ and accommodating each other.

16. An unhappy marriage increases an individual's risk of _____ _____ by about one third and can even shorten a person's life.

Goal 1d: Discuss divorce and how people cope with it

17. The U.S. divorce rate, which increased dramatically from the 1960s through the mid-1980s, has been _____ since then.

18. Increases in divorce are associated with youthful marriage, premarital pregnancy, low _____ _____, and low _____.

19. If a divorce is going to occur, it is most likely to occur between the _____ and _____ year of marriage.

20. Couples who divorce within the first seven years of marriage typically have relationships marked by _____ emotions, whereas couples who divorce in midlife tend to have _____ relationships.

21. Regardless of who initiated the divorce, it places men and women at risk for _____ and _____ difficulties.

22. Compared with married adults, separated and divorced men and women may face reduced functioning of the _____ system as well as higher rates of mental disorders, including depression, _____, and psychosomatic problems such as sleep disorders.

23. After a divorce _____ show modest declines in income, whereas _____ face significant declines.

24. Hetherington identified seven factors that enabled divorced adults to cope effectively: (a) social _____, (b) autonomy, (c) internal locus of control, (d) religiosity, (e) work, (f) social _____, and (g) a new intimate relationship.

25. In Hetherington's research social _____ consisted of characteristics such as planfulness, self-regulation, adaptability, and social responsibility.

26. Hetherington identified six so-called pathways that people took after divorce, the most common of which she labeled the _____ _____.

Goal 1e: Describe the stresses faced by adults who remarry after divorce

27. On average, divorced adults remarry within 4 years after their divorce, with men remarrying _____ than women.

28. Only _____ of stepfamily couples in the United States stay remarried.

29. Possible reasons for the high rate of divorce among remarried adults include their motives for remarrying (such as for help, not for love), the _____ _____ that they bring from their first marriage, and the extra stress of rearing children in stepfamilies.

Goal 1f: Describe gay and lesbian relationships

30. Researchers have found that gay and lesbian relationships are _____—in their satisfactions, loves, joys, and conflicts—to heterosexual relationships.

31. Lesbian couples especially place a high priority on _____ in their relationships.

32. Researchers have found _____ differences between the adjustment of children living in gay and lesbian families and the adjustment of children living in heterosexual families.

Learning Goal 2: Describe the family life cycle

33. Six stages in a family life cycle have been proposed to reflect the changes that families experience through the years, but critics argue that clearly defined stages often do not develop and that the stages do not always occur in _____.

34. Entry into the stages of the family life cycle is increasingly independent of _____.

Goal 2a: Identify the tasks of the first stage of the family life cycle

35. The first stage in the family life cycle involves _____, the process in which youth move into adulthood and leave their family of origin.

36. Launching is a time to formulate _____, to develop an identity, and to become more independent before forming a new family.

Goal 2b: Describe the second stage of the family life cycle

37. In the second stage of the family life cycle the marriage of two individuals not only creates a new family but also _____ the two families of origin.

Goal 2c: Describe the third stage of the family life cycle

38. During the third stage of the family life cycle (becoming a family with children), adults move up a generation, becoming _____ to the younger generation, and face the challenge of juggling multiple roles.

Goal 2d: Describe the challenges of the fourth stage of the family life cycle

39. During the fourth stage of the family life cycle (the family with adolescents), when adolescents push for _____, a flexible, adaptive approach is best for parents.

40. According to current thinking, most parent-adolescent conflict is _____, but even the best parents may find their relationship with their adolescent strained.

Goal 2e: Discuss adjustment during the fifth stage of the family life cycle

41. The family at midlife (the fifth stage of the family life cycle) is a time of _____ children, linking generations, and adapting to midlife changes.

42. Most parents experience an _____ in marital satisfaction after their children have left home.

43. Similarities between parents and adult children are most likely in _____ and politics and least likely in attitudes toward gender roles, life style, and work.

Goal 2f: Describe the final stage of the family life cycle

44. During the sixth stage of the family life cycle (family in later life), _____ and grandparenting are often key features.

45. Retirement alters a couple's life style, but the changes are likely to be greatest in _____ families.

Learning Goal 3: Discuss parenting and how it affects children's adjustment

46. The many myths about parenting include the idea that the birth of a child will _____ a failing marriage, that parents can mold their children, and that parenting is an instinct.

Goal 3a: Discuss the implications of the timing of parenthood

47. Currently, adults in the United States are having _____ children and having children _____ in life.

48. Possible advantages of having children in one's twenties include the fact that parents are likely to have more physical energy than when they are older and the fact that the mother is likely to have fewer _____ _____.

49. Possible advantages of having children later in life are that parents will have had more time to consider their goals in life, will be more mature, will have the benefit of experiences that might improve their parenting skills, and might have more _____.

Goal 3b: Describe four parenting styles

50. Diana Baumrind identified four types of parenting styles: authoritarian, _____, neglectful, and _____.

51. Authoritarian parenting is a restrictive, punitive style in which parents place firm limits on the child and allow little _____ _____.

52. Children of authoritarian parents are often unhappy, fearful, and anxious about comparing themselves to others; they fail to take _____ and have weak communication skills.

53. Authoritative parents are warm, allow extensive verbal give-and-take, encourage children to be _____, but place limits on children's actions.

54. Neglectful parents are very uninvolved in their children's lives, and their children tend to be socially _____ and to have poor self-control.

55. Indulgent parents are very involved with their children but place few _____ on them.

56. Children of indulgent parents tend to have difficulty controlling their behavior and might be _____ and egocentric.

57. Baumrind's four styles of parenting involve combinations of acceptance and _____ on the one hand and demand and _____ on the other.

58. Research documents more positive links between _____ parenting and the well-being of children than between children's well-being and the other parenting styles.

Goal 3c: Discuss how mothers' working outside the home affects children

59. Because technology has lessened the time needed for housework and because _____ _____ has decreased, it is not certain that U.S. children receive less attention than children in the past whose mothers were not employed.

60. A number of researchers have found no detrimental effect of maternal employment on children's development, but when a child's mother works in the _____ _____ of the child's life, it can have a negative effect on the child's later development.

61. Researchers have found that any detrimental effects of maternal employment during the child's first nine months are lessened if the mother works less than _____ _____ a week and if the child receives high-quality _____ _____.

Goal 3d: Describe how divorce affects children

62. Most researchers agree that children whose parents are divorced show _____ _____ than their counterparts whose parents are not divorced.

63. A number of researchers have shown that in the year following divorce parents tend to display _____ _____ _____ .

64. Among the factors that influence children's vulnerability to adjustment problems when their parents divorce are the child's adjustment before divorce, _____, temperament, and gender, as well as the custody arrangements.

65. One recent analysis found that children in joint-custody families were _____ adjusted than children in sole-custody families.

Goal 3e: Discuss how ethnicity affects children

66. African American and Latino children interact _____ with grandparents, aunts, uncles, cousins, and more distant relatives than do white children.

67. Ethnic minority children are more likely than white children to face certain stressors, including the difficulties associated with _____, poverty, prejudice, and discrimination.

Goal 3f: Discuss child abuse and its consequences

68. In 2001 about 84 percent of the children in the United States who were victims of child abuse were abused by _____ .

69. The four main types of child maltreatment are physical abuse, child neglect, sexual abuse, and _____ _____ .

70. Experts on child abuse believe that it is important to recognize that child abuse is a diverse condition, that it is usually _____ to _____ in severity, and that it is only partially caused by the personality characteristics of the abuser.

71. About _____-_____ of parents who were abused themselves when they were young abuse their own children.

72. Physical child abuse has been linked to wide-ranging problems in the victims, including anxiety, personality problems, depression, conduct disorder, and _____ .

73. Adults who were maltreated as children show increased violence toward others and increased rates of substance abuse problems, anxiety, and _____ .

Key Terms

Briefly define each key term and provide an example or application.

1. leaving home and becoming a single adult

2. launching

3. new couple

4. becoming parents and a family with children

5. family with adolescents

6. family at midlife

7. empty nest syndrome

8. family in later life

9. authoritarian parenting

10. authoritative parenting

11. neglectful parenting

12. indulgent parenting

Practice Test A

Answer these multiple-choice questions to assess your understanding of the chapter. Answers are provided at the end of the study guide chapter.

___ 1. Which of the following is true?
a. The percentage of U.S. couples who cohabit before marriage has multiplied since 1970.
b. Many couples see cohabitation as an ongoing life style, not a precursor to marriage.
c. In Sweden, cohabitation before marriage is almost universal.
d. All of the above statements are true.

___ 2. In the United States today
a. people are marrying earlier in life than they did in decades past.
b. less than half of the adult population is married.
c. people are marrying later in life than they did in decades past.
d. about 60 percent of U.S. adults have been married at some time in their lives.

___ 3. The divorce rate in the United States has been
a. declining since the mid-1980s.
b. rising since the mid-1990s.
c. stable since the 1960s.
d. declining since the 1960s.

___ 4. If people are going to divorce, they usually do so
a. within the first couple of years.
b. only after children have left home.
c. in the fifth to tenth year of marriage.
d. when they have reached middle age.

___ 5. According to Hetherington's research, the most powerful buffer against post-divorce stress is
a. a successful career.
b. a new intimate relationship.
c. participation in a church.
d. a close friend.

___ 6. Which of the following is true?
a. In most homosexual couples one partner is masculine and one is feminine.
b. Most lesbian couples have an open relationship.
c. Few homosexuals prefer long-term, committed relationships.
d. None of the above statements is true.

___ 7. The stages of the family life cycle
a. provide a framework for understanding how families tend to change over time.
b. have been clearly defined by research.
c. are closely tied to chronological age.
d. establish a sequence that must be followed to ensure satisfactory adjustment.

___ 8. Research on relationships between parents and their adolescent children has
a. found that conflicts have become much more intense in recent years.
b. linked an active parental role with lower drug use and positive peer relations among adolescents.
c. linked an active parental role with rebellious behavior such as higher drug use among adolescents.
d. found that most parent-adolescent relationships are free of conflict.

___ 9. When children leave home most parents
a. feel empty.
b. experience the empty nest syndrome.
c. experience a decrease in marital satisfaction.
d. experience an increase in marital satisfaction.

___ 10. In the United States today
a. the number of one-child families is increasing.
b. people are having children at a younger age than in the past.
c. the number of three-child families is increasing.
d. there is a tendency to have more children.

___ 11. A rigid, punitive parenting style is known as
a. authoritarian parenting.
b. authoritative parenting.
c. neglectful parenting.
d. permissive parenting.

___ 12. Research studies suggest that the most effective parenting style is
a. authoritarian parenting.
b. authoritative parenting.
c. neglectful parenting.
d. indulgent parenting.

___ 13. A majority of children with divorced parents
a. display externalized problems.
b. display internalized problems.
c. display externalized and internalized problems.
d. do not have significant adjustment problems.

___ 14. Of parents who were abused when they were children
a. the overwhelming majority abuse their own children.
b. about 10 percent abuse their own children.
c. about a third abuse their own children.
d. none of the above is true.

Identifying Concepts

Answers are provided at the end of the study guide chapter.

1. FAMILY LIFE CYCLE   Identify the stage of the family life cycle illustrated in each example.

a. Two individuals unite to form a new family system

b. An individual moves out of his or her parent's home and becomes a single adult

c. A couple become caretakers of the younger generation

d. Retirement

2. PARENTING STYLES   Identify the parenting style illustrated in each example.

a. Sets limits but encourages children to be independent

b. Places few control but is very involved with the children

c. No involvement with the children

d. Places firm, rigid limits on children and allows little verbal exchange

Understanding Concepts

Complete these exercises to develop your understanding of important ideas in this chapter.

1. What are some advantages and disadvantages of living alone as a single adult?

2. Summarize the trends in cohabitation.

3. Why might divorce rates be higher among people who cohabit before marriage than among those who do not?

4. What do people look for in a spouse?

5. What are love maps?

6. What does Gottman mean by "perpetual conflicts" in marriage, and how does he recommend dealing with them?

7. Summarize the benefits of a happy marriage.

8. How does divorce affect physical and psychological health?

9. Based on statistics, what are the prospects for people who remarry after divorce, and what are the special problems they face?

10. Compare and contrast the problems faced by lesbian and gay couples with those faced by heterosexual couples.

11. Describe and evaluate four parenting styles.

12. Is there such a thing as intergenerational transmission of abuse?

Applying Concepts and Strategies

Complete these exercises to develop your ability to apply this chapter's material to your life and the world. Your responses will differ from those of other students in the class, and it is helpful to share your ideas with other students.

1. What are your views on the advantages and disadvantages of cohabitation? Do you approve of its growing popularity?

2. What are (were) the major factors involved in your own mate selection?

3. What are (or were) your pushes toward marriage and pulls away from being single?

4. Complete Self-Assessment 9.2: My Knowledge of Marital Myths and Realities and evaluate the results. For any myths that you believed were true, what was the source of your opinion?

5. Watch four television shows in which families are prominent. How are marriage and parenthood portrayed? Do the shows reflect actual trends? What characteristics do they say are important in good relationships? What kinds of parenting styles are illustrated?

6. List the strategies for making marriages work based on Gottman's research. Which would you find most difficult to implement? Why?

7. Would you legalize homosexual marriages? Why or why not?

8. Which parenting style did your parents use? Which style do you or would you use in rearing your own children? Do you think these parenting styles are also reflected in styles of teaching and administration?

9. The text discusses how maternal employment affects a child's development. Do you think the effect of paternal employment should receive equal attention? Why or why not?

10. Suppose you are drawing up a proposal for a project that would reach out to child abusers and their victims in your city with the aim of reducing the intergenerational transmission of abuse. List at least five goals or services that would be part of your program.

Practice Test B

Answer these multiple-choice test questions to help you assess your understanding of the textbook chapter. Answers are provided at the end of the study guide chapter.

___ 1. Research on how cohabiting before marrying affects couples
a. has produced varying results.
b. has indicated that it improves marital satisfaction.
c. has shown that it improves communication during marriage.
d. has found that it is linked to lower divorce rates.

___ 2. Researchers have found that unrealistic expectations about marriage
a. are linked to greater marital satisfaction.
b. are linked to lower divorce rates.
c. are linked to lower levels of marital satisfaction.
d. have no effect on marital satisfaction.

___ 3. Marital conflicts
a. must be resolved if a marriage is to endure.
b. often involve perpetual problems that do not have to be solved for the marriage to work.
c. should be avoided at all costs.
d. usually involve daily hassles and can be easily solved.

___ 4. Researchers have found that children growing up in gay or lesbian families
a. usually grow up to be gay or lesbian.
b. are just as popular with their peers as children growing up in heterosexual families.
c. have fewer problems than children growing up in heterosexual families.
d. have unusually high rates of mental health problems.

___ 5. To achieve a successful launching, a young adult should
a. seek complete independence from the family of origin.
b. try to comply with parental expectations.
c. find emotional refuge outside the family of origin.
d. learn to deal with his or her parents as one adult to another.

___ 6. A longitudinal investigation of couples from late pregnancy until $3^{1}/_{2}$ years after the baby was born found that
a. marital relations improved after the baby's birth.
b. the baby's birth had no effect on marital satisfaction.
c. marital relations were less positive after the baby was born.
d. men but not women were more satisfied with the marriage after the baby was born.

___ 7. As adult children become middle-aged,
a. conflicts between mothers and daughters increase.
b. most have little or no contact with their parents.
c. they often develop more positive perceptions of their parents.
d. none of the above is true.

___ 8. According to a study of intergenerational relationships,
a. mothers and their daughters have closer relationships in their adults years than mothers and sons or fathers and sons or daughters.
b. married men are more involved with their wives' relatives than with their own.
c. maternal grandmothers are much more likely than paternal grandmothers to be considered the most important relative.
d. all of the above are true.

___ 9. Having children later in life
a. is best for children.
b. is best for parents.
c. is best for parents and children.
d. has advantages and disadvantages.

___ 10. Children who are fearful, anxious about being compared with others, and lack initiative often have parents with
a. an authoritarian style.
b. an authoritative style.
c. a neglectful style.
d. an indulgent style.

___ 11. Cameron and Dan want their children to be free and independent spirits, so they try to set no rules and exact no punishments in their home. This parenting style is often linked with
a. children who are cheerful, self-controlled, and achievement-oriented.
b. children who fail to initiate activity and have weak communication skills.
c. children who have difficulty controlling their behavior and difficulty relating to their peers.
d. children who have low self-esteem and little social competence.

___ 12. Evidence that links authoritative parenting with children's competence
a. has been found only in the United States.
b. has been found only in middle class families.
c. has been found only in white families.
d. has been found for a range of ethnic groups, social strata, and cultures.

___ 13. Children with divorced parents
a. are at increased risk for academic problems, externalized problems, and internalized problems.
b. usually show significant adjustment problems.
c. are no more likely than other children to have adjustment problems.
d. are less likely than other children to have internalized problems.

___ 14. Adults who were maltreated as children
a.   usually abuse their own children
b. have increased rates of substance abuse, anxiety, and depression.
c. usually abuse their spouses.
d. show none of the above effects.

Answers to Chapter Questions

Guided Review

1. increased
2. loneliness
3. cohabitation
4. 60
5. short-lived
6. lower
7. 60
8. later; one third
9. chastity
10. communicate
11. detailed maps
12. power
13. perpetual
14. living with
15. negotiating
16. getting sick
17. declining
18. educational level; income
19. fifth; tenth
20. heated; distant
21. physical; psychological
22. immune; alcoholism
23. men; women
24. maturity; support
25. maturity
26. good enoughs
27. sooner
28. one-third
29. negative patterns
30. similar
31. equality
32. no
33. sequence
34. age
35. launching
36. goals
37. realigns
38. caregivers
39. autonomy
40. moderate
41. launching
42. increase
43. religion
44. retirement
45. traditional
46. save
47. fewer; later
48. medical problems
49. income
50. authoritative; indulgent
51. verbal exchange
52. initiative
53. independent
54. incompetent
55. demands (*or* controls)
56. domineering
57. responsiveness; control
58. authoritative
59. family size
60. first year
61. 30 hours; child care
62. poorer adjustment
63. diminished parenting skills
64. personality
65. better
66. more
67. acculturation
68. parents
69. emotional abuse
70. mild; moderate
71. one third
72. delinquency
73. depression

Practice Test A

1. d
2. c
3. a
4. c
5. b
6. d
7. a
8. b
9. d
10. a
11. a
12. b
13. d
14. c

Identifying Concepts

1. FAMILY LIFE CYCLE
   a. new couple (stage 2)
   b. leaving home (stage 1)
   c. becoming a family with children (stage 3)
   d. family in later life (stage 6)
2. PARENTING STYLES
   a. authoritative
   b. indulgent
   c. neglectful
   d. authoritarian

Practice Test B

1. a
2. c
3. b
4. b
5. d
6. c
7. c
8. d
9. d
10. a
11. c
12. d
13. a
14. b

CHAPTER **10**   **ACHIEVEMENT, CAREERS,**
AND WORK

Chapter Outline

I. ACHIEVEMENT

A. Intrinsic and Extrinsic Motivation
- Extrinsic motivation refers to the influence of external rewards and punishments; intrinsic motivation refers to the influence of internal factors such as self-determination and curiosity.
- Many psychologists argue that intrinsic motivation is more likely than extrinsic motivation to produce competent behavior and mastery.

B. Goal Setting, Planning, and Monitoring
- Goals may take the form of personal projects, personal strivings, and life tasks.
- Researchers have found that achievement improves when people set goals that are specific, short term, and challenging.
- Planning how to reach a goal and monitoring progress toward it are critical aspects of achievement; researchers have found that high-achieving individuals systematically monitor their progress toward goals.

ADJUSTMENT STRATEGIES *for*

Setting Goals

1. Set goals that are challenging, reasonable, and specific.
2. Set schedules and completion dates for meeting goals.
3. Create subgoals.
4. Make a commitment.
5. Monitor your progress.

C. Time Management
Time management will help you be more productive and less stressed.

1. **PLAN AND SET PRIORITIES**

   Create plans within time frames of a year, month, week, and day and set priorities within these plans.

2. **CREATE AND MONITOR TIME PLANS**

   Create a to-do list for each day.

D. Some Obstacles to Achievement

1. **PROCRASTINATION**

   Reasons for procrastination include poor time management, difficulty concentrating, fear and anxiety, personal problems, boredom, unrealistic expectations and perfectionism, and fear of failure.

   ADJUSTMENT STRATEGIES *for*

   Conquering Procrastination

   1. Acknowledge that procrastination is a problem.
   2. Identify your values and goals.
   3. Work on your time management.
   4. Divide the task into smaller parts.
   5. Use behavioral strategies.
   6. Use cognitive strategies.

   ---

2. **PERFECTIONISM**

   Perfectionism is sometimes the underlying cause of procrastination.

   ADJUSTMENT STRATEGIES *for*

   Coping with Perfectionism*

   1. List the advantages and disadvantages of trying to be perfect.
   2. Become more aware of the self-critical nature of all-or-none thinking.
   3. Be realistic about what you can do.
   4. Set strict time limits on each of your projects; when the time is up, move on.
   5. Learn how to accept criticism.

   *Based on University of Texas at Austin Counseling and Mental Health Center, *Coping with Perfectionism* (Austin, TX: University of Texas at Austin, 1999).

   ---

3. **PROTECTING SELF-WORTH BY AVOIDING FAILURE**

   To protect their self-worth some people engage in self-handicapping strategies such as not trying, shamming an effort, procrastinating, setting unreachable goals, or admitting to a minor personal weakness in order to avoid acknowledging incompetence.

II. CAREERS AND JOBS

A. Career Development across the Life Span

- Eli Ginzberg has proposed that people go through three stages of career development: fantasy (birth through age 11), tentative (ages 11 through 17), and realistic (ages 18 to 25).

- Donald Super has described five stages of career development: growth (birth to age 14), exploration (15 through 24), establishment (25 through 44), maintenance (45 to 64), and decline.
  1. CHILDHOOD
     - Growth stage is Super's label for the period from birth through early adolescence when children move from having no interest in vocations to having extensive fantasies about careers and then to having career interests based on likes and dislikes.
     - Parents may be an important influence on the selection of an occupation.
  2. ADOLESCENCE
     - Although Ginzberg and Super divide the years of adolescence and early adulthood differently in their descriptions of stages, both depict adolescents and young adults as beginning to explore the world of work in a more realistic way.
     - Career counselors recommend exploring many career options.
  3. EARLY ADULTHOOD

     Establishment stage is Super's label for the period when adults from 25 to 45 years old pursue a permanent career and attain a stable pattern of work in a particular career.
  4. MIDDLE ADULTHOOD
     - Maintenance stage is Super's label for the period when adults from about 45 to 64 years old maintain their career status.
     - For many adults middle adulthood brings a reassessment and readjustment of their careers.
  5. LATE ADULTHOOD
     - Decline stage is Super's label for the period when people are 65 or older and reduce their career activity and retire.
     - Some people maintain their productivity throughout their lives, and the percentage of older adults who work part-time has steadily increased since the 1960s.

B. Skills and Personality Traits

- To discover the career that is best for you, it is important to evaluate your academic and personal skills.
- John Holland argues that it is important for your career to fit your personality type.
- Holland's personality type theory outlines six career-related personality types: realistic, investigative, artistic, social, enterprising, and conventional.
- Most people reflect a combination of two or three of Holland's personality types.

C. Knowledge, Goals, and Careers

To discover the career that is best for you, it is also important to become knowledgeable about careers and to set career goals.

1. BECOMING KNOWLEDGEABLE ABOUT CAREERS

   It is critical to keep up with the occupational outlook in various fields.
2. SET CAREER GOALS

   If setting goals is difficult for you, begin with general goals and move toward more specific ones.

D. Getting a Job

To obtain a great job, take the following steps:

1. BE AWARE OF WHAT EMPLOYERS WANT
2. DO A THOROUGH JOB SEARCH
3. CREATE A RESUME
4. LEARN HOW TO HAVE A GREAT JOB INTERVIEW

ADJUSTMENT STRATEGIES *for*

Knocking 'Em Dead in a Job Interview*

1. Create an excellent resume.
2. Prepare for the interview.
3. Be prepared to give positive examples of your work experience.
4. Anticipate questions that will be asked in the interview.
5. Ask appropriate job-related questions.
6. Keep your cool.
7. As the interview closes, decide whether you want the job.
8. Immediately after the interview, send a follow-up letter.

*Based on M. Yate, *Knock 'Em Dead* (Boston: Adams Media, 2005).

III. WORK

A. The Role of Work in People's Lives

- Work is an important influence on financial standing as well as on the way people spend their time, where they live, their friendships, their health, their identity, and stress.

- Four characteristics of work settings that are linked to stress are high job demands, inadequate opportunities to participate in decision making, a high degree of supervisor control, and lack of clarity about criteria for competent performance.

- Problems in balancing work with the rest of life may be especially acute for workaholics and dual-career couples.

  1. WORKAHOLICS

     Workaholics do not necessarily experience their work as stressful; they tend to identify strongly with their careers and to be very satisfied with their jobs.

  2. DUAL-CAREER COUPLES

     As the number of U.S. women working outside the home increased in recent decades, the division of responsibility for taking care of the home and family changed somewhat.

  3. DIVERSITY IN THE WORKPLACE

     The percentage of women and ethnic minorities in the U.S. workplace increased greatly in recent decades.

  4. UNEMPLOYMENT

     - Unemployment is related to physical problems, mental problems, marital and family problems, and crime.

     - Individuals who cope best with unemployment are those who have financial resources.

B. Working during College

- Most U.S. undergraduates are also employed.

- Although work can contribute to a student's education, researchers have found that as the number of hours worked rises, grades fall and drop-out rates rise.

C. Work and Retirement

In the second half of the twentieth century federal laws and programs gave many U.S. workers both the option of retiring and protection from being forced to retire because of their age.

1. **RETIRING PART-TIME**

   Many retirees only partially retire, moving to part-time employment.

2. **ADJUSTING TO RETIREMENT**

   Adults who adjust best to retirement are healthy, have adequate income, are active, are better educated, have an extended social network including both friends and family, and usually were satisfied with their lives before retiring.

D. Leisure
- Leisure can be an especially important part of middle adulthood.
- Taking part in fulfilling leisure activities during midlife may ease the transition to retirement.

Learning Goals

After reading and studying this chapter, you should be able to

1. **Discuss achievement and related adjustment strategies.**
   a. Describe extrinsic and intrinsic motivation.
   b. Discuss the relationship between goals and achievement.
   c. Identify the keys to good time management.
   d. Discuss the major obstacles to achievement.

2. **Describe important aspects of careers and jobs.**
   a. Outline stages in career development.
   b. Discuss how skills and personality traits are related to a successful career.
   c. Describe how to obtain the knowledge and set the goals useful for career development.
   d. Identify steps to take to obtain a good job.

3. **Summarize key aspects of work.**
   a. Discuss the relationships between work and life.
   b. Identify advantages and disadvantages of working while in college.
   c. Discuss how people adjust to retirement.
   d. Describe the role of leisure in people's lives.

Guided Review

After you have read this chapter in the textbook, complete these statements. Topics are discussed in the same order as in the chapter. Answers are provided at the end of the study guide chapter.

Learning Goal 1: Discuss achievement and related adjustment strategies

Goal 1a: Describe internal and external motivation

1. Research on operant conditioning demonstrates the power of _____ motivation—that is, the power of external rewards and punishments to shape behavior.

2. _____ _____ refers to the influence of internal factors such as self-determination and curiosity.

3. Research reveals that people whose motivation is _____ tend to show more interest, excitement, and confidence in what they are doing than people whose motivation is _____.

Goal 1b: Discuss the relationship between goals and achievement

4. _____ help people increase self-discipline and maintain interest in achievement.

5. Researchers have found that achievement improves when people set goals that are _____, short term, and challenging.

6. Researchers have also found that high-achieving individuals systematically evaluate their progress toward their goals _____ than low-achieving individuals.

Goal 1c: Identify the keys to good time management

7. To manage your time efficiently, you should create _____ and set priorities.

8. Covey classifies activities into those that are important and those that are _____ and says that you should do important activities early, before they become _____.

9. To stay focused on what is important for you to do each day, you should create a _____-_____ _____ and monitor how well you are doing with your time plans.

Goal 1d: Discuss the major obstacles to achievement

10. Besides failing to set goals, major obstacles to achievement include _____, perfectionism, and self-handicapping strategies for protecting self-worth.

11. Strategies for conquering procrastination include _____ a task so that what seems an unmanageable task becomes manageable and using behavioral and cognitive strategies to overcome diversions.

12. Sometimes the underlying reason for procrastination is _____, which holds that mistakes are never acceptable.

13. Depression, anxiety, and _____ _____ are common outcomes of perfectionism.

14. Some individuals protect their self-worth by using _____-_____ strategies so that if they fail, the cause seems to be circumstances, not lack of ability.

15. Self-handicapping strategies include not trying, pretending to make an effort, procrastinating, setting _____ _____, or admitting to a minor weakness to avoid acknowledging incompetence.

Learning Goal 2: Describe important aspects of careers and jobs

Goal 2a: Outline stages in career development

16. Eli Ginzberg proposes three stages of career development: _____ (birth through age 11), tentative (ages 11 through 17), and realistic (ages 18 to 25).

17. Donald Super proposes five stages of career development: growth (birth to 14 years of age), exploration (15 through 24), _____ (25 through 44), _____ (45 through 64), and decline (beginning at 65).

18. According to Super, during the growth stage of career development children move from having no interest in vocations to having extensive _____ about careers to basing their career interests on likes and dislikes.

19. Despite differences in their analyses of the stages of career development, both Ginzberg and Super say that adolescents and young adults begin to explore the world of work in a more _____ way.

20. Most career advancement occurs _____ in adulthood.

21. By the time they are in their _____, most people have gone as far as they will go up the career ladder and will remain in the same career.

22. Although Super labels the years from 45 to 64 as the maintenance stage of career development, middle-aged adults may reassess their careers or be forced to make a career change as a result of _____ or other large-scale changes in the economy.

23. Older workers have a _____ attendance record than younger workers along with fewer accidents and higher job satisfaction.

24. A strong psychological commitment to work and a distaste for _____ are the most important characteristics linked to continued employment into one's 70s and 80s.

25. The percentage of older adults who work part-time has steadily _____ since the 1960s.

Goal 2b: Discuss how skills and personality traits are related to a successful career

26. Realistically evaluating your _____ is key to finding the career that is best for you.

27. _____ argues that it is also important to find a career that fits your personality.

28. Holland's personality-type theory outlines six career-related personality styles: realistic, investigative, _____, _____, enterprising, and conventional.

29. In Holland's classification, _____ individuals like the outdoors, enjoy manual activities, and are practical and often anti-intellectual; jobs such as farming, truck driving, and construction suit them.

30. The investigative type in Holland's classification is interested in _____ more than people and is the type with the highest educational level and most prestige.

31. The _____ type in Holland's classification has a creative orientation and a distaste for conformity and values ambiguity.

32. The _____ type enjoys helping others, is more interested in people than in intellectual pursuits, and has excellent interpersonal skills.

33. The _____ type is more oriented toward people than toward things or ideas, is good at coordinating the work of others and at persuading people to do something or to change their attitudes, and seeks to dominate others.

34. The _____ type in Holland's classification prefers working with numbers rather than with people or ideas, works best in well-structured circumstances, and is skilled at working with details.

35. Most individuals reflect a _____ of Holland's types.

36. Holland's ideas are reflected in tests used by careers counselors, including his Self-Directed Search and the _____-_____ Interest Inventory.

Goal 2c: Describe how to obtain the knowledge and set the goals useful for career development

37. Sources for keeping up with the outlook for jobs in various fields include the _____ _____ _____, social networks, college career centers, and websites.

38. People who have difficulty articulating career goals should begin by stating _____ goals and use them to determine more _____ goals.

Goal 2d: Identify steps to take to obtain a good job

39. First steps in obtaining a good job are to be aware of what _____ want, to conduct a thorough job search, and to create a high-quality resume.

40. Frequently used types of resumes are _____ resumes, resumes that focus on marketable skills, and resumes that emphasize achievements.

41. Strategies for having a successful job interview include learning about the prospective employer, being prepared to give examples of work experience, and _____.

Learning Goal 3: Summarize key aspects of work

Goal 3a: Discuss the relationships between work and life

42. Most individuals spend about _____ - _____ of their lives at work.

43. Work defines people in fundamental ways and can create _____.

44. Four characteristics of work settings are linked with stress and health problems: high job demands such as heavy workloads and time pressure, inadequate opportunities to participate in _____ _____, a high level of supervisor control, and lack of clarity about the criteria for _____ _____.

45. _____ seem to be addicted to their work, may enjoy their work as much as other people enjoy their hobbies, and are likely to identify strongly with their careers.

46. Unlike workaholics, people with the _____ _____ personality are likely to experience stress and pressure related to their work.

47. Like workaholics, _____ - _____ _____ may have particular problems finding a balance between work and the rest of their lives.

48. As more women work outside the home, U.S. husbands are taking _____ responsibility for maintaining the home and showing _____ interest in their families and parenting.

49. The increased ethnic diversity of the U.S. workplace since the 1980s includes a doubling of the percentage of Latinos and _____ _____.

50. Women and ethnic minorities face what is called the _____ _____, an invisible barrier to advancement into executive positions.

51. Unemployment produces _____ and is linked to physical and mental problems, marital and family problems, and crime.

52. A longitudinal study found that _____ _____ dropped considerably following unemployment and increased after re-employment but did not completely return to pre-unemployment levels.

Goal 3b: Identify advantages and disadvantages of working while in college

53. Recent studies found that as the number of hours students worked increased, _____ suffered and the risk of dropping out increased.

54. Many colleges offer _____ programs, which are paid apprenticeships.

Goal 3c: Discuss how people adjust to retirement

55. On average, today's workers will spend _____ to _____ percent of their lives in retirement.

56. Adults who adjust best to retirement are _____, have an adequate income and an extended social network, are active and educated, and usually were satisfied with their lives before they retired.

57. _____ is also a key factor in adjusting to retirement because retirement brings a loss of the structured environment created by employment.

Goal 3d: Describe the role of leisure in people's lives

58. _____ refers to the times when individuals are free to pursue activities and interests of their own choosing.

59. Developing fulfilling leisure activities during _____ _____ can ease the transition to retirement.

Key Terms

Briefly define each key term and provide an example or application.

1. intrinsic motivation

2. extrinsic motivation

3. self-handicapping

4. fantasy stage

5. growth stage

6. tentative stage

7. realistic stage

8. establishment stage

9. maintenance stage

10. decline stage

11. personality type theory

12. glass ceiling

13. leisure

Practice Test A

Answer these multiple-choice questions to assess your understanding of the chapter. Answers are provided at the end of the study guide chapter.

___ 1. Extrinsic motivation
a. is the source of achievement.
b. refers to the influence of external factors such as rewards and punishments.
c. refers to the influence of factors such as curiosity.
d. has little power to shape behavior.

___ 2. Researchers have found that achievement improves when people
a. set goals that are specific.
b. set short-term goals.
c. set goals that are challenging.
d. do all of the above.

___ 3. Research indicates that perfectionism is linked to
a. high self-esteem.
b. productivity.
c. realistic goal setting.
d. impaired health.

___ 4. Self-handicapping strategies are
a. ways to protect your self-worth in case of failure.
b. methods for gauging your chances of success.
c. methods for determining your goals.
d. ways of setting priorities.

___ 5. Ginzberg's fantasy stage and Super's growth stage both occur during
a. childhood.
b. puberty.
c. adolescence.
d. young adulthood.

___ 6. Both Ginzberg and Super describe adolescence as a time when individuals
a. have no interest in the world of work.
b. begin to create elaborate fantasies about careers.
c. begin to explore the world of work in a more realistic way.
d. are very pragmatic in their ideas about their careers.

___ 7. In advising college students about how to increase their chances of obtaining a job, career counselors
a. agree that undergraduates should study a wide range of subjects.
b. agree that undergraduates should specialize as soon as possible.
c. agree that undergraduates should specialize by their sophomore year.
d. disagree about whether studying a wide range of subjects or specializing is the best course.

_____ 8. Most advancement in a career occurs
a. early in our adult lives.
b. by the time a person is 30 years old.
c. in a person's early 50s.
d. just before retirement.

_____ 9. Compared with younger workers, older workers have
a. a higher rate of accidents.
b. poor attendance records at work.
c. better attendance records at work.
d. none of the above.

_____ 10. A person who is enterprising according to Holland's classification is most likely to fit which type of career?
a. Scientist
b. Clerk
c. Nurse
d. None of the above

_____ 11. A functional resume
a. emphasizes academic accomplishments.
b. organizes accomplishments by skill or career area and thus emphasizes marketable skills.
c. is useful when your accomplishments are restricted to a specific skill or experience.
d. organizes information chronologically.

_____ 12. When U.S. men become fathers today,
a. they decrease the amount of time they spend at work by about 10 percent.
b. they may increase or decrease their working hours depending on their attitude toward gender roles.
c. they double the amount of time spent helping with housework.
d. they do not alter their working patterns.

_____ 13. The glass ceiling is the term
a. for a law that requires equal opportunity for women.
b. for a law that requires equal opportunity for minorities.
c. for a quota that limits the number of men in managerial positions.
d. for the invisible barrier that keeps women and minorities out of executive positions.

_____ 14. Researchers have found that unemployment
a. is linked to physical as well as mental problems.
b. has no long-lasting effect.
c. produces stress only for full-time workers.
d. is linked to psychological but not physical problems.

_____ 15. One recent study of men 35 to 57 years of age found that men who took annual vacations
a. were less likely to die of coronary heart disease than men who never took vacations.
b. showed no benefits from the vacations.
c. were more likely to die of coronary heart disease than men who never took vacations.
d. were less likely to succeed than men who never took vacations.

Identifying Concepts

Answers are provided at the end of the study guide chapter.

1. SUPER'S STAGES OF CAREER DEVELOPMENT
Identify the stage described by each statement.

a. Children go from no interest in vocations to career fantasies

b. Retirement takes place

c. Adults pursue permanent careers

d. Adults continue in their chosen careers

2. HOLLAND'S PERSONALITY TYPE THEORY
Identify the personality type that according to Holland fits best with the following jobs.

a. Blue-collar positions

b. Bank tellers, secretaries, and file clerks

c. Sales, management, politics

d. Teaching, social work, counseling

Understanding Concepts

Complete these exercises to develop your understanding of important ideas in this chapter.

1. Identify three self-handicapping strategies and give an example of each.

2. Identify Ginzberg's three stages of career development.

3. Identify Super's five stages of career development.

4. How well does the label "maintenance stage" suit the period from ages 45 to 64?

5. How well does the label "decline stage" suit the period when people are 65 and older?

6. Describe each of Holland's six career-related personality types: realistic, investigative, artistic, social, enterprising, and conventional.

7. Give an example of at least one career that is a good match for each of Holland's personality types.

8. Compare and contrast a workaholic and a Type A personality.

9. What problems have been linked to unemployment, and what characteristics distinguish those people who cope best with unemployment?

10. Describe the characteristics of people who adjust best to retirement.

Applying Concepts and Strategies

Complete these exercises to develop your ability to apply this chapter's material to your life and the world. Your responses will differ from those of other students in the class, and it is helpful to share your ideas with other students.

1. Think about your motivation for studying and for one other activity. Do you think extrinsic motivation or intrinsic motivation is more important to your efforts? Does the existence of rewards or punishments affect your intrinsic motivation?

2. During the 1990s, some schools began to offer money to elementary school students for each book they read. How would you evaluate this attempt to motivate students?

3. What are your goals? Are they challenging but reasonable? Are they specific enough for you to set schedules for meeting them? Take one of your goals and create subgoals for meeting it.

4. Complete Self-Assessment 10.1: Am I a Procrastinator? and evaluate the results. Are you a procrastinator? Whether you are or not, describe a specific behavioral or cognitive strategy that you could use to conquer procrastination. List other strategies for overcoming procrastination.

5. Complete Self-Assessment 10.2: Am I a Perfectionist? and evaluate the results. One strategy for coping with perfectionism is to learn how to accept criticism. Whether or not you are a perfectionist, describe specific steps that you might take to implement this strategy. Can you use any of the strategies for coping discussed in Chapter 5?

6. How do parents influence the selection of an occupation according to Anne Roe? What effects if any have your parents had on your career goals?

7. Which of Super's stages of career development best describes your current situation? Do you think that current trends in the workplace will affect the stages of career development?

8. Evaluate how your characteristics fit the descriptions of Holland's career personality types: realistic, investigative, artistic, social, enterprising, and conventional. Which is most like you? Least like you? Do your college major and career goals fit with your personality type?

9. How do you balance education, work, and leisure?

10. Define the glass ceiling and discuss its possible causes.

Practice Test B

Answer these multiple-choice test questions to help you assess your understanding of the textbook chapter. Answers are provided at the end of the study guide chapter.

___ 1. Intrinsic motivation
a. is the source of achievement
b. refers to the influence of factors such as rewards and punishments.
c. refers to the influence of internal factors such as curiosity.
d. has little power to shape behavior.

___ 2. Many research studies indicate that
a. people whose motivation is intrinsic show more interest in what they are doing than people whose motivation is extrinsic.
b. intrinsic motivation is neither necessary nor sufficient to produce mastery.
c. people whose motivation is extrinsic show more interest in what they are doing than people whose motivation is intrinsic.
d. none of the above statements is true.

___ 3. According to Ginzberg, individuals move away from fantasies about careers during which stage of career development?
a. Tentative
b. Exploration
c. Realistic
d. Pragmatic

___ 4. According to Ginzberg, individuals discard their fantasies about the world of work and make pragmatic decisions when they are about
a. 11 to 17 years old.
b. 18 to 25 years old.
c. 25 to 45 years old.
d. 45 to 65 years old.

___ 5. According to Levinson, individuals need to develop a distinct occupational identity
a. during Super's exploration stage.
b. during the second part of Super's exploration stage.
c. during the first part of Super's establishment stage.
d. during Super's maintenance stage.

___ 6. The period from about 45 to 64 years of age
a. is Super's maintenance stage of career development.
b. is a time when people must adjust idealistic hopes about their careers to realistic possibilities.
c. is a time when some people redefine their identity through a career change.
d. may be characterized by all of the above statements.

___ 7. Ken is most interested in dealing with people, but he is also interested in science. According to Holland's theory, which types may characterize him?
a. Social, investigative
b. Conventional, social
c. Interpersonal, investigative
d. Conventional, interpersonal

___ 8. The Myers-Briggs Type Indicator (MBTI)
a. has been replaced by the Self-Direct Search.
b. is a test frequently used by career counselors.
c. was developed by John Holland.
d. measures motivation to achieve.

___ 9. If you have limited experience related to the job you are seeking, it might be best to
a. avoid submitting a resume.
b. submit a functional resume.
c. submit a chronological resume.
d. submit a resume that emphasizes accomplishments.

___ 10. When supervisors exercise tight control on a job,
a. stress is likely to be low for everyone else.
b. employees' intrinsic motivation is likely to be high.
c. they increase the risk that work will be stressful for employees.
d. they raise morale.

___ 11. Which is most likely true about workaholics?
a. They dislike what they do.
b. They have Type A personalities.
c. Their work is like a hobby.
d. They experience stress on the job.

___ 12. In the U.S. workplace today,
a. gender segregation is the norm.
b. some occupations continue to be sex-segregated.
c. sex segregation has been eliminated.
d. women participate much less than they do in other countries.

___ 13. Unemployment is likely to upset
a. men more than women.
b. women as much as men.
c. younger workers more than middle-aged workers.
d. full-time but not temporary workers.

___ 14. In 1986 the U.S. government
a. established the Social Security system.
b. raised the mandatory retirement age to 65.
c. lowered the mandatory retirement age to 65.
d. banned mandatory retirement in all but a few occupations.

Answers to Chapter Questions

Guided Review

1. extrinsic
2. intrinsic motivation
3. intrinsic; extrinsic
4. goals
5. specific
6. more
7. plans
8. urgent; urgent
9. to-do list
10. procrastination
11. dividing
12. perfectionism
13. eating disorders
14. self-handicapping
15. unreachable goals
16. fantasy
17. establishment; maintenance
18. fantasies
19. realistic
20. early
21. forties
22. outsourcing
23. better
24. retirement
25. increased
26. skills
27. Holland
28. artistic; social
29. realistic
30. ideas
31. artistic
32. social
33. enterprising
34. conventional
35. combination
36. Strong-Campbell
37. Occupational Outlook Handbook
38. general; specific
39. employers
40. chronological
41. practicing
42. one third
43. stress
44. decision making; competent performance
45. workaholics
46. Type A
47. dual-career couples
48. more; more
49. Asian Americans
50. glass ceiling
51. stress
52. life satisfaction
53. grades
54. cooperative
55. 10; 15
56. healthy
57. flexibility
58. leisure
59. middle age

Practice Test A

1. b
2. d
3. d
4. a
5. a
6. c
7. d
8. a
9. c
10. d
11. b
12. b
13. d
14. a
15. a

Identifying Concepts

1. SUPER'S STAGES OF CAREER DEVELOPMENT
   a. growth
   b. decline
   c. establishment
   d. maintenance
2. HOLLAND'S PERSONALITY TYPE THEORY
   a. realistic
   b. conventional
   c. enterprising
   d. social

Practice Test B

1. c
2. a
3. a
4. b
5. c
6. d
7. a
8. b
9. b
10. c
11. c
12. b
13. b
14. d

CHAPTER **11** | # EMERGING ADULTHOOD, ADULT DEVELOPMENT, AND AGING

Chapter Outline

I. BECOMING AN ADULT

A. The Nature of Development

- Development refers to the pattern of change in human capabilities that begins at conception and continues throughout the life span.
- To analyze how people develop, it helps to organize the years into distinct periods.
- Early adulthood is the developmental period that begins in the late teens or early 20s and lasts through the 30s.
- Middle adulthood is the developmental period from approximately 40 to about 60 years of age.
- Late adulthood is the developmental period from the 60s to death.
- A person's goals and priorities are likely to change over these periods, but each period has its pluses and minuses, and no particular age group is happier than the others.

B. Emerging Adulthood

Emerging adulthood is the term for the transition from adolescence to adulthood, which occurs from approximately 18 to 25 years of age.

1. WHO IS AN ADULT?

- The transition from adolescence to adulthood is determined by cultural standards and experiences.
- In the United States, individuals reach adulthood at some point in the late teens through the early twenties as they accept responsibility for themselves, become capable of making independent decisions, and gain financial independence.

2. PERSONAL AND SOCIAL ASSETS

Well-being in adolescence and emerging adulthood is tied to intellectual assets, psychological assets, and social assets.

3. CHANGE AND CONTINUITY

Although change characterizes the transition to adulthood, research has found considerable continuity in religious views and behavior, attitudes toward drugs, and level of self-esteem and achievement orientation.

4. ADAPTING TO COLLEGE

- The transition from high school to college brings many changes.
- Special challenges may face returning students—students who either did not go to college right out of high school or went to college, dropped out, and have returned.

II. PHYSICAL DEVELOPMENT IN ADULTHOOD

A. Early Adulthood

Most adults reach their peak physical development and are healthiest during their 20s.

B. Middle Adulthood

- Physical changes during middle adulthood include changes in appearance, a general decline in physical fitness, and some deterioration in health.
- Menopause—the cessation of a woman's menstrual periods—usually occurs in U.S. women in their late 40s or early 50s.

C. Late Adulthood

From 1950 to 1990 the world's population of individuals 65 and older doubled.

1. LIFE SPAN AND LIFE EXPECTANCY

- The human life span is the maximum number of years that human beings can live, and it does not seem to have increased since the beginning of recorded history.
- Life expectancy refers to the number of years that will probably be lived by the average person born in a particular year, and it has increased.
- Diet, a low-stress life style, a caring community, activity, and spirituality may contribute to longevity.

2. HORMONAL STRESS THEORY

Hormonal stress theory states that aging of the body's hormonal system can lower resilience to stress and increase the likelihood of disease.

3. PHYSICAL CHANGES AND HEALTH

- Changes in physical appearance become more pronounced in older adults.
- Normal aging brings some loss of bone tissue in late adulthood, and chronic diseases become more common.
- A substantial portion of individuals in late adulthood are still robust and active.
- A sense of control over one's life is linked with health and even survival in late adulthood.

4. DEMENTIAS

- Dementia is a global term for any neurological disorder in which the primary symptoms involve a deterioration of mental functioning.
- The most common form of dementia is Alzheimer's disease, a progressive, irreversible disorder characterized by gradual deterioration of memory, reasoning, language, and eventually physical functioning.

5. THE BRAIN

Even in late adulthood, the brain has remarkable repair capability.

III. COGNITIVE DEVELOPMENT IN ADULTHOOD

A. Early Adulthood

- According to Piaget, adults do not think differently than adolescents; Piaget believed that the highest stage of thinking is the formal operational stage, which appears between the ages of 11 and 15.
- In the formal operational stage individuals begin to think in abstract and more logical terms.
- Unlike Piaget, some theorists argue that adults move into a new stage of cognitive development, postformal thought, which is marked by thinking that is reflective, relativistic, and contextual.

B. Middle Adulthood

- Findings about whether cognitive skills decline in middle age vary depending on which skills are studied and whether cross-sectional or longitudinal research is used.
- Crystallized intelligence refers to an individual's accumulated information and verbal skills whereas fluid intelligence refers to the ability to reason abstractly.
- In a cross-sectional study differences might be due not to age but to cohort effects—that is, the effects of living during a certain historical time in a certain culture.
- Based on cross-sectional research, John Horn concluded that fluid intelligence peaks in early adulthood and that crystallized intelligence peaks in middle age.
- Based on longitudinal research, K. Warner Schaie concluded that middle adulthood is a time of peak performance for some aspects of both crystallized and fluid intelligence.

C. Late Adulthood

- A decline in speed of processing is apparent in middle-aged adults and becomes more pronounced in older adults.
- Older adults do more poorly than their younger counterparts when tasks involve speed of processing and in most areas of memory, such as remembering the where and when of life's happenings.
- Some aspects of cognition might improve with age, including wisdom, which is expert knowledge about the practical aspects of life.
- For those aspects of cognitive ability that decline with age, education and training can make a difference.

IV. SOCIOEMOTIONAL DEVELOPMENT IN ADULTHOOD

A. Early Adulthood

- Erik Erikson proposed eight stages of development, with each stage defined by a unique developmental task.

- According to Erikson, during early adulthood individuals enter the sixth stage of development, the intimacy-versus-isolation stage.

- During the intimacy-versus-isolation stage individuals either form intimate relations with others or become socially isolated.

B. Middle Adulthood

1. GENERATIVITY

- Erikson believed that middle-aged adults enter the seventh stage of development, generativity versus stagnation.

- Generativity encompasses the desire to leave a legacy of oneself to the next generation and can be achieved in many ways—for example, by nurturing children, by passing skills on to younger workers, by creating or conserving some aspect of culture.

2. MIDLIFE CRISES

- Daniel Levinson argued that by age 40 adults enter a transition period during which they experience a crisis and must come to grips with the conflict between being young versus being old, being destructive versus being constructive, being masculine versus being feminine, being attached versus being separated.

- Research indicates that few middle-aged adults experience a midlife crisis and most have less anxiety than younger adults.

- Middle-aged adults do experience midlife consciousness, becoming aware of the shrinking time left in their lives.

3. MEANING OF LIFE AND LIFE THEMES

- Because middle-aged adults are likely to experience the death of people close to them and to experience midlife consciousness, they may become more aware of the finiteness of life.

- Recognition of life's finiteness may lead many middle-aged adults to think more deeply about the meaning of life and to search for life themes, or meaningful, optimal experiences.

C. Late Adulthood

1. INTEGRITY VERSUS DESPAIR

- According to Erikson, people in late adulthood enter the integrity-versus-despair stage of development, in which the task is to reflect on one's life with the assurance that it has been meaningful.

- A prominent feature of late adulthood is life review, which involves looking back on one's experiences, evaluating and interpreting them.

- Compared with younger adults, older adults report experiencing more positive emotion and less negative emotion, having better control over their emotions, and experiencing less extreme emotions.

2. SOCIAL NETWORKS

- Connections with family, friends, and others can improve the physical and mental health of older adults in many ways.

- Older adults tend to have far smaller social networks than younger adults.

- Carstensen's socioemotional selectivity theory states that older adults emphasize goals related to emotion and become more selective about their social networks.

3. SELF-REGULATION

- Self-regulation of capacities and activities allows people to deal with the losses that are part of aging.
- According to selective optimization with compensation theory, successful self-regulation in aging involves three processes: selection (a reduction in performance in most domains), optimization (the maintenance of standards of performance in some areas), and compensation (strategies for offsetting lost abilities).

4. RELIGION

- Religion may help older people to face impending death, to find and maintain a sense of meaningfulness, and to accept the inevitable losses of old age.
- Religious beliefs or activities among older adults have been linked with higher levels of life satisfaction, self-esteem, optimism, and health.

5. SOCIOECONOMIC STATUS AND ETHNICITY

- The percentage of older people living in poverty in the United States has remained about the same since the 1980s.
- Poverty rates soar among older women who live alone and among older people who are members of ethnic minority groups.

6. MENTAL HEALTH AND AGING

Older adults do not have a higher incidence of mental disorders than younger adults, but they do lack mental health services.

7. POSITIVE PSYCHOLOGY AND AGING

- The more active and involved older adults are, the more likely they are to stay healthy.
- Positive emotions early in adulthood are linked with longevity.
- The chances of being alive and happy at 75 to 80 years of age rise if at 50 years of age a person is not a heavy smoker, does not abuse alcohol, has a stable marriage, exercises, maintains a normal weight, and has good coping skills.

ADJUSTMENT STRATEGIES *for*

Successful Aging

1. Don't abuse alcohol and don't smoke.
2. Exercise regularly and avoid being overweight.
3. Be well-educated.
4. Use your intellectual skills.
5. Develop coping skills.
6. Have good friends and/or a loving partner.

V. DEATH AND GRIEVING

A. Facing One's Own Death

- Elisabeth Kübler-Ross divided the behavior and thinking of dying persons into five stages: denial and isolation, anger, bargaining, depression, and acceptance.
- The existence of Kübler-Ross's five-stage sequence has not been demonstrated, and some psychologists prefer to describe these responses not as stages but as potential reactions to dying.
- The extent to which people have found meaning and purpose in their lives is linked with how they approach death.

B. Coping with the Death of Someone Else

1. COMMUNICATING WITH A DYING PERSON

Most psychologists believe that it is best for dying individuals and those close to them to know that they are dying.

ADJUSTMENT STRATEGIES *for*

Communicating with a Dying Person

1. Establish your presence.
2. Eliminate distractions.
3. Be sensitive to how long you should stay.
4. Don't insist that the dying person feel acceptance of death.
5. Encourage the expression of feelings.
6. Don't be afraid to ask the person what the expected outcome for their illness is.
7. Ask the dying person if there is anyone he or she would like to see.
8. Encourage the dying person to reminisce.
9. Talk with the individual when he or she wishes to talk.
10. Express your regard for the dying person.

---

2. GRIEVING

- Grief is the emotional numbness, disbelief, separation anxiety, despair, sadness, and loneliness that accompany the loss of someone we love.
- Grieving is an evolving process, not a progression of stages, and often involves rapidly changing emotions.
- For most individuals, grief becomes more manageable over time, but long-term grief can predispose individuals to become depressed and even suicidal.

C. Death in Different Cultures

- Most societies throughout history have had philosophical or religious beliefs about death and rituals to deal with death.
- In most societies death is not viewed as the end of existence.
- The United States in many ways has developed a culture of avoiding and denying death.

Learning Goals

After reading and studying this chapter, you should be able to

1. Describe the nature of development and becoming an adult.
 a. Characterize development.
 b. Outline the key features of emerging adulthood.

2. Explain physical changes in adulthood.
 a. Outline the physical changes that characterize early adulthood.
 b. Outline the physical changes that characterize middle adulthood.
 c. Outline the physical changes that characterize late adulthood.

3. **Characterize cognitive changes in adulthood.**
   a. Outline the cognitive changes that take place in early adulthood.
   b. Outline the cognitive changes that take place in middle adulthood.
   c. Outline the cognitive changes that take place in late adulthood.

4. **Summarize the socioemotional changes of adulthood.**
   a. Describe the socioemotional changes that characterize early adulthood.
   b. Describe the socioemotional changes that characterize middle adulthood.
   c. Describe the socioemotional changes that characterize late adulthood.

5. **Discuss death and grieving.**
   a. Discuss how people face their own death.
   b. Describe how people cope with the death of someone else.
   c. Describe variations in how different cultures deal with death.

Guided Review

After you have read this chapter in the textbook, complete these statements. Topics are discussed in the same order as in the chapter. Answers are provided at the end of the study guide chapter.

Learning Goal 1: Describe the nature of development and becoming an adult
Goal 1a: Characterize development

1. _____ refers to the pattern of change in human capabilities that begins at conception and continues throughout the life span.

2. The pattern of development is the product of _____, cognitive, and socioemotional processes.

3. To analyze how we develop through the life span, it helps to organize the years of life into distinct periods such as childhood, _____, early adulthood, middle adulthood, and late adulthood.

4. Early adulthood is the developmental period that begins in the late teens or early twenties and lasts through the _____.

5. Middle adulthood is the developmental period from approximately _____ years of age to about 60.

6. Late adulthood is the developmental period that begins in the 60s and lasts until _____.

7. From ages 25 to 34 people are likely to give priority to _____, friends, family, and independence.

8. From ages 35 to 54 or 55, _____ is likely to become more important than friends.

9. For those more than 85 years old, _____ is likely to become the most important personal investment.

10. No age group is more satisfied with life than another, and in every age group slightly less than _____ percent of people say that they are very happy.

Goal 1b: Outline the key features of emerging adulthood

11. Unlike adolescence, the transition from adolescence to adulthood is determined by _____ _____ and experiences.

12. _____ _____ is the term given to the transition from adolescence to adulthood, which occurs from approximately 18 to 25 years of age.

13. _____ and exploration characterize the emerging adult.

14. In developing countries _____ is often a more significant marker for entry into adulthood than it is in the United States.

15. In the United States, the most widely recognized marker for entry into adulthood is holding a _____-_____ job, but other criteria for adulthood are far from clear.

16. Reaching adulthood involves more than reaching a chronological age and in the United States usually means accepting responsibility for oneself, becoming capable of making _____ _____, and gaining financial independence from parents.

17. Well-being in adolescence and emerging adulthood is linked with intellectual assets such as academic success and good decision-making skills, with _____ assets such as optimism and self-confidence, and with social assets such as feelings of belongingness.

18. Research suggests that _____ views and behaviors tend to be stable during emerging adulthood.

19. A person's degree of _____-_____ and achievement orientation tend to be stable from adolescence through emerging adulthood.

20. Compared with less happy students, college students who are very happy are likely to be very social and more _____ and to have stronger romantic and social relationships.

Learning Goal 2: Explain physical changes in adulthood

Goal 2a: Outline the physical changes that characterize early adulthood

21. Most adults reach their peak physical development and are their healthiest during their _____.

22. Early adulthood is when strength, _____, and many physical skills begin to decline.

Goal 2b: Outline the physical changes that characterize middle adulthood

23. Individuals begin to lose height in _____ _____, and many gain weight.

24. The three greatest health concerns of middle age are _____ _____, cancer, and weight.

25. Usually in a woman's late 40s or early 50s the production of _____ by the ovaries declines dramatically.

26. The average age of _____, when menstrual periods cease, is 52.

27. For most women, menopause does not produce _____ or _____ _____.

Goal 2c: Outline the physical changes that characterize late adulthood

28. The number of years that human beings can live, the _____ _____, is about 120 to 125.

29. _____ _____ refers to the number of years that will probably be lived by the average person born in a particular year.

30. Individuals live longer on _____ than anywhere else in the world, perhaps because of their diet, low-stress life style, caring community, active life style, and spirituality.

31. According to _____ _____ _____, as we age, the hormones that flow through the neuroendocrine-immune pathway remain elevated longer than when we were younger, and these elevated levels of stress-related hormones increase risks for many diseases.

32. After age 60, weight frequently declines because of _____ _____.

33. _____ _____ often rises in older adults, and normal aging also brings some loss of bone tissue.

34. Chronic diseases are _____ in early adulthood, increase in middle adulthood, and become more common in late adulthood.

35. The most common chronic disorder is late adulthood is _____.

36. _____ slows the aging process.

37. _____ _____ over one's life is linked with the health, well-being, and even survival of older adults.

38. _____ is a global term for any neurological disorder in which the primary symptoms involve a deterioration of mental functioning.

39. An estimated _____ percent of individuals who are more than 80 years old have some form of dementia.

40. Approximately 10 to 20 percent of dementias stem from _____ _____.

41. The most common form of dementia is _____ _____, a progressive, irreversible disorder that is characterized by gradual deterioration of memory, reasoning, language, and eventually physical functioning.

42. _____-_____ Alzheimer's affects individuals younger than 65 and is rare.

43. The brains of victims of Alzheimer's deteriorate and _____.

44. The formation of tangles and _____ in the brain is a normal part of aging, but these are much more pervasive in victims of Alzheimer's disease.

45. Even in late adulthood, the brain has remarkable ability to _____ _____.

46. Research supports the idea that _____ _____ _____ helps to keep the brain healthy.

47. High levels of _____ _____ may decrease the chance of having a stroke and thus help protect the brain from decline.

Learning Goal 3: Characterize cognitive changes in adulthood

Goal 3a: Outline the cognitive changes that take place in early adulthood

48. According to Piaget, people enter the _____ _____ stage between the ages of 11 and 15 and begin to think in abstract and more logical terms.

49. Piaget believed that the formal operational stage is the highest stage of thinking and that no _____ changes in cognition take place in adulthood.

50. Some theorists believe that young adults move into a new stage of cognitive development, _____ thought, which is characterized by reflective, relativistic, and contextual thinking.

51. Whether or not there are qualitative changes in cognition in adulthood, some cognitive skills such as verbal memory tend to _____ during early adulthood.

Goal 3b: Outline the cognitive changes that take place in middle adulthood

52. _____ intelligence refers to accumulated information and verbal skills.

53. _____ intelligence refers to the ability to reason abstractly.

54. _____-_____ studies assess a number of people at one point in time, whereas longitudinal studies assess the same participants over a lengthy period.

55. The results of a cross-sectional study may reflect _____ effects, which are the effects of living through a certain historical time in a certain culture.

56. In Schaie's longitudinal studies _____ _____ and _____ _____ declined in middle age, but some other abilities improved.

57. In Schaie's longitudinal studies middle adulthood was the time of peak performance for some aspects of both _____ intelligence (vocabulary) and fluid intelligence (spatial orientation and inductive reasoning).

58. In Horn's cross-sectional studies, fluid intelligence peaked in _____ _____ and crystallized intelligence peaked in middle age.

Goal 3c: Outline the cognitive changes that take place in late adulthood

59. When tasks involve _____ of processing, older adults do more poorly than their younger counterparts.

60. For tasks involving most aspects of memory older adults tend to perform more _____ than younger adults.

61. _____, or expert knowledge about the practical aspects of life, might improve with age.

62. The memories of older adults can be improved through _____.

Learning Goal 4: Summarize the socioemotional changes of adulthood

Goal 4a: Describe the socioemotional changes that characterize early adulthood

63. In _____ theory, through the life span people go through eight stages of development, with each stage defined by a unique developmental task.

64. According to Erikson, during early adulthood people go through the sixth stage of development, _____ versus _____.

65.By intimacy Erikson meant a _____ to another person that includes a willingness to choose a joint identity.

Goal 4b: Describe the socioemotional changes that characterize middle adulthood

66. According to Erikson, middle-aged adults enter the _____-versus-_____ stage.

67. Generative adults commit themselves to the _____ and _____ of society as a whole through their connection to the next generation.

68. Daniel Levinson argued that around the age of 40 people enter a transition period and experience a _____ _____.

69. Research indicates that _____ people experience a midlife crisis and that middle-aged individuals tend to have _____ anxiety levels than younger people.

70. During midlife many people do develop _____ _____, which is the awareness of the gap between being young and being old and the shrinking time left in their lives.

71. The recognition of life's _____ leads many people to think about life's meaning and to seek _____ _____, or meaningful, optimal experiences.

Goal 4c: Describe the socioemotional changes that characterize late adulthood

72. According to Erikson, in late adulthood people enter the _____-versus-_____ stage.

73. A prominent feature of this stage is _____ _____, which involves looking back at one's experiences and evaluating, interpreting, and often reinterpreting them.

74. Research indicates that during adulthood _____ emotion increases with age at an accelerating rate.

75. In diverse populations researchers have found that older adults _____ emotion better than younger adults and that their emotions are more _____.

76. According to Carstensen's _____ _____ theory, older adults emphasize goals related to emotion and become more selective about their social networks, spending more time with individuals with whom they have had rewarding relationships.

77. Baltes and his colleagues proposed _____ _____ _____ _____ theory, which holds that successful self-regulation in aging involves selection, optimization, and compensation.

78. Individuals over 65 years old are more likely than younger people to say that _____ _____ is the most significant influence in their lives, that they try to put it into practice, and that they attend religious services.

79. Research has linked religious beliefs and religious practices among older adults with higher levels of _____ _____, self-esteem, optimism, and health.

80. Although the overall number of older people living in poverty in the United States has declined since the 1960s, the percentage of older persons living in poverty has remained in the _____ to _____ percent range since the early 1980s.

81. Poverty rates soar among elderly women who _____ _____ and among older people who are members of ethnic minority groups.

82. Older adults who are members of an ethnic minority are _____ likely than others to become ill and _____ likely to receive treatment.

83. Older adults do not have a higher incidence of mental disorders than younger adults but do lack _____ _____ _____.

84. The more _____ and _____ older people are, the more satisfied they are, and the more likely they are to stay healthy.

85. A longitudinal study found that poor social connections, infrequent participation in social activities, and social disengagement predicted _____ _____ in older adults.

86. Successful aging has been linked with having _____ emotions early in adulthood and with having healthy habits, education, a stable marriage, and good coping skills at 50.

Learning Goal 5: Discuss death and grieving

87. Of all life's stressors death of a _____ is ranked as requiring the most difficult adjustment.

Goal 5a: Discuss how people face their own death

88. Kübler-Ross proposed that dying people go through five stages: _____ and isolation, anger, bargaining, depression, and _____.

89. Critics argue that there is no evidence that dying people go through Kübler-Ross's stages but instead that many emotions _____ and _____.

Goal 5b: Describe how people cope with the death of someone else

90. Most psychologists believe that it is _____ for dying individuals and those close to them to know that they are dying.
91. Grief often involves _____ _____ emotions, not a progression of stages.
92. Long-term grief can predispose individuals to become _____ and even suicidal.

Goal 5c: Describe variations in how different cultures deal with death

93. Most societies have _____ or _____ beliefs about death, such as a belief that death brings redemption or reincarnation, as well as rituals related to death.
94. Many aspects of U.S. culture seem to reflect an attempt to _____ and _____ death.

Key Terms

Briefly define each key term and provide an example or application.

1. development

2. early adulthood

3. middle adulthood

4. late adulthood

5. emerging adulthood

6. life span

7. life expectancy

8. hormonal stress theory

9. dementia

10. Alzheimer's disease

11. formal operational stage

12. post-formal thought

13. crystallized intelligence

14. fluid intelligence

15. wisdom

16. Erikson's theory

17. intimacy versus isolation

18. generativity versus stagnation

19. integrity versus despair

20. socioemotional selectivity theory

21. selective optimization with compensation theory

22. major depression

23. dementia

24. Kubler-Ross's stages of dying

Practice Test A

Answer these multiple-choice questions to assess your understanding of the chapter. Answers are provided at the end of the study guide chapter.

___ 1. The process of development
a. is a story of growth.
b. is a story of decline.
c. is a story of both growth and decline.
d. is the story of physical processes.

___ 2. Early adulthood is the developmental period
a. that begins in the late teens or early 20s and lasts through the 30s.
b. that begins in the twenties and ends at 45.
c. that occurs during the 20s.
d. that occurs from approximately 18 to 25 years of age.

___ 3. An individual becomes an adult
a. at puberty.
b. at a time determined by the culture.
c. at 18.
d. at 21.

___ 4. Most people reach their peak of physical fitness and health
a. during childhood.
b. during adolescence.
c. during early adulthood.
d. during middle adulthood.

___ 5. The life span
a. has been increasing since 1900.
b. has been increasing since 1950.
c. is about 73 to 80 years.
d. is about 120 to 125 years.

___ 6. A classic experiment by Rodin and Langer found that encouraging nursing home residents to make day-to-day choices
a. created stress.
b. increased anxiety and fear.
c. increased alertness and satisfaction.
d. had no effect.

___ 7. The most common type of dementia is
a. schizophrenia.
b. depression.
c. Alzheimer's disease.
d. obsessive compulsive disorder.

___ 8. Research suggests that intellectually challenging activity
a. helps keep the brain healthy.
b. creates plaques.
c. can overstress the aging brain.
d. has no physical effects.

___ 9. According to Piaget, our way of thinking
a. changes radically after adolescence.
b. does not change qualitatively after we reach the formal operational stage.
c. become provisional and realistic during adolescence.
d. is qualitatively the same once we learn to speak.

___ 10. One consistent finding in studies of cognitive skills is that
a. crystallized intelligence declines in middle adulthood.
b. all abilities decline in late adulthood.
c. when tasks involve speed of processing, older adults do more poorly than their younger counterparts.
d. all of the above statements are true.

___ 11. According to Erikson, the central task of early adulthood is to
a. learn to form intimate relationships and thus avoid isolation.
b. begin the quest for personal fulfillment.
c. find a career that suits your identity.
d. form a family.

___ 12. According to Erikson, middle-aged adults enter
a. the intimacy-versus-isolation stage.
b. the generativity-versus-stagnation stage.
c. the integrity-versus-despair stage.
d. none of the above.

___ 13. Research on middle adulthood suggests that
a. most people do not experience a midlife crisis.
b. compared with people under 40, middle-aged adults report more negative life events.
c. compared with people under 40, middle-aged adults worry less.
d. all of the above statements are true.

___ 14. Grieving is a process that
a. typically follows a five-stage sequence.
b. often involves rapidly changing emotions.
c. should not last more than a week.
d. should not last more than a month.

Identifying Concepts

Answers are provided at the end of the study guide chapter.

1. ERIKSON'S STAGES OF DEVELOPMENT   Name the developmental stage associated with each task.

a. Assist the younger generation

b. Develop a close, committed relationship

c. Conduct a life review

2. PEOPLE IN ADULT DEVELOPMENT AND AGING Identify the person whose contribution is summarized in each statement.

a. Proposed eight stages of development through the life span

b. Described the midlife crisis

c. Proposed socioemotional selectivity theory

d. Described eight stages of dying

Understanding Concepts

Complete these exercises to develop your understanding of important ideas in this chapter.

1. Define development and explain why it is complex.

2. Summarize the changes that occur from early to late adulthood in the domains that are likely to attract a person's greatest personal investment.

3. When do people reach their peak performance?

4. Differentiate between life span and life expectancy. What is the upper limit of the human life span? What is life expectancy in the United States today?

5. Summarize how cognition and memory typically change during middle and late adulthood.

6. Describe the study by Rodin and Langer that examined how opportunities to have control and responsibility affect nursing home residents.

7. Describe Alzheimer's disease.

8. Does "use it or lose it" apply to the brain? Why or why not?

9. Summarize what researchers have discovered about emotional life during late adulthood.

10. Explain Carstensen's socioemotional selectivity theory.

11. Describe the three processes in Baltes's theory of successful self-regulation among older adults.

12. What influence does religious belief or religious activity have on the lives of older adults?

13. Which characteristics of your life at 25 and 50 might predict whether you will age successfully?

Applying Concepts and Strategies

Complete these exercises to develop your ability to apply this chapter's material to your life and the world. Your responses will differ from those of other students in the class, and it is helpful to share your ideas with other students.

1. List your intellectual, psychological, and social assets. Describe how one of these assets is linked to your well-being. What asset could you develop further to improve your well-being, and how could you develop it?

2. Have you changed since you were 18? If so, how?

3. Describe the physical changes in appearance that are typical of middle age. Would you try to mask these changes? If so, describe what steps you would be willing to take to do so. How does our culture's emphasis on a youthful appearance affect you?

4. Summarize how the age of the world's population and the U.S. population has changed since 1950. What effects do you think this change is having?

5. Complete Self-Assessment 11.3: Can You Live to Be 100? How did you score? What are your greatest unchangeable liabilities? Which liabilities could you modify?

6. What are the characteristics of postformal thought? Do these characteristics describe how you think? Has your way of thinking changed since you were an adolescent?

7. Define cohort effects and explain their importance. What differences between you and your mother or father might be the result of cohort effects? Between you and your grandmother or grandfather?

8. How can a slowdown in the speed of cognitive processing affect the everyday lives of older Americans? Give two or three specific examples. For one example, describe how the processes in Baltes's selective optimization with compensation theory could be applied to help an older adult adapt to this change.

9. What are some examples of ageism in our culture?

10. If you were a nursing home administrator, what information in this chapter would you apply to your nursing home, and how would you do so?

Practice Test B

Answer these multiple-choice test questions to help you assess your understanding of the textbook chapter. Answers are provided at the end of the study guide chapter.

___ 1. In human development
a. physical processes determine cognition and socioemotional development.
b. physical, cognitive, and socioemotional processes interact.
c. socioemotional processes determine the course of physical and cognitive processes.
d. cognitive processes determine the course of physical and socioemotional processes.

___ 2. Middle adulthood is the developmental period
a. from the 30s through the 50s.
b. that occurs during the 40s.
c. from approximately 40 years of age to about 60.
d. from approximately 35 years of age to about 55.

___ 3. In the United States individuals are generally considered adults
a. when they obtain a driver's license and a job.
b. when they are married and have a job.
c. when they accept responsibility for themselves, make independent decisions, and are financially independent.
d. when they consider themselves adults.

___ 4. For most women, menopause occurs
a. when they are in their early 40s.
b. when they are in their early 50s.
c. when they are in their early 60s.
d. when they are in late adulthood.

___ 5. In Alzheimer's disease
a. the brain deteriorates and shrinks.
b. there is a deficiency of acetylcholine.
c. more tangles and plaques form than in the normally aging brain.
d. all of the above occur.

___ 6. In Schaie's longitudinal studies of cognitive skills,
a. many people reached their peak for many cognitive skills in middle adulthood.
b. most cognitive skills peaked in early adulthood.
c. no skills improved during middle age.
d. most cognitive skills continued improving until people reached their 70s.

___ 7. In Schaie's longitudinal studies of cognitive skills,
a. all skills declined in middle age.
b. numerical ability and perceptual speed declined in middle age.
c. vocabulary and verbal memory declined after early adulthood.
d. none of the above is true.

___ 8. The ability to remember and use information to solve problems and make decisions
a. remains stable throughout late adulthood.
b. declines in late adulthood.
c. declines in early adulthood.
d. improves until individuals reach their 80s.

____ 9. In Erikson's theory of development, each stage has a crisis, which is
a. a point of danger.
b. a state of increased vulnerability and enhanced potential.
c. a defining event.
d. a point at which an irreversible decision must be made.

____ 10. By generativity, Erikson meant
a. having children.
b. nurturing and guiding children.
c. developing a positive legacy of the self and offering it to the next generation.
d. reviewing one's life and finding that it had meaning.

____ 11. Older adults tend to have
a. small social networks dominated by peripheral contacts.
b. wider and older social networks than younger adults.
c. fewer peripheral contacts than younger people but about the same number of emotional relationships.
d. very few emotional relationships.

____ 12. According to Carstensen's socioemotional selectivity theory,
a. older adults choose to become more selective about their social networks.
b. older adults focus on nonemotional goals.
c. people select people their own age to be part of their social networks.
d. old age forces people to be more selective about their social interactions.

____ 13. Which of the following statements about Kübler-Ross's stages of dying is true?
a. Her work encouraged people to pay greater attention to the quality of life of dying patients.
b. The stages are denial and isolation, anger, bargaining, depression, and acceptance.
c. Research has not demonstrated the existence of this five-stage sequence.
d. All of the above statements are true.

____ 14. Communication about death with a person in the process of dying may
a. improve coping for the dying but not survivors.
b. improve coping for survivors but not the dying.
c. increase death anxiety of survivors.
d. improve coping for all involved.

Answers to Chapter Questions

Guided Review

1. development
2. physical
3. adolescence
4. 30s
5. 40
6. death
7. work
8. family
9. health
10. 20
11. cultural standards
12. emerging adulthood
13. experimentation
14. marriage

15. full-time
16. independent decisions
17. psychological
18. religious
19. self-esteem
20. extraverted
21. 20s
22. speed
23. middle adulthood
24. heart disease
25. estrogen
26. menopause
27. physical; psychological problems
28. life span

29. life expectancy
30. Okinawa
31. hormonal stress theory
32. muscle loss
33. blood pressure
34. rare
35. arthritis
36. exercise
37. perceived control
38. dementia
39. 20
40. vascular disease
41. Alzheimer's disease
42. early-onset
43. shrink
44. plaques
45. repair itself
46. stimulating intellectual activity
47. folic acid
48. formal operational
49. qualitative
50. postformal
51. improve
52. crystallized
53. fluid
54. cross-sectional
55. cohort
56. numerical ability; perceptual speed
57. crystallized
58. early adulthood
59. speed
60. poorly
61. wisdom
62. training
63. Erikson's
64. intimacy; isolation
65. commitment
66. generativity; stagnation
67. continuation; improvement
68. midlife crisis
69. few; lower
70. midlife consciousness
71. finiteness; life themes
72. integrity; despair
73. life review
74. positive
75. regulate; mellow
76. socioemotional selectivity
77. selective optimization with compensation
78. religious faith
79. life satisfaction
80. 10; 12
81. live alone
82. more; less
83. mental health services
84. active; involved
85. cognitive decline
86. positive
87. spouse
88. denial; acceptance
89. come; go
90. best
91. rapidly changing
92. depressed
93. philosophical; religious
94. avoid; deny

Practice Test A

1. c
2. a
3. b
4. c
5. d
6. c
7. c
8. a
9. b
10. c
11. a
12. b
13. d
14. b

Identifying Concepts

1. ERIKSON'S STAGES OF DEVELOPMENT
   a. generativity versus stagnation
   b. intimacy versus isolation
   c. integrity versus despair
2. PEOPLE IN ADULT DEVELOPMENT AND AGING
   a. Erikson
   b. Levinson
   c. Carstensen
   d. Kübler-Ross

Practice Test B

1. b
2. c
3. c
4. b
5. d
6. a
7. b
8. b
9. b
10. c
11. c
12. a
13. d
14. d

CHAPTER **12**   # GENDER

Chapter Outline

I. PERSPECTIVES ON GENDER

A. Defining Gender
- Gender is the psychological and social dimension of being female or male.
- Recent decades have seen dramatic revisions in gender roles, which are sets of expectations that prescribe how females and males should think, act, and feel.

B. Evolutionary Psychology Theory
- Evolutionary psychology theory argues that adaptation during the human evolution produced psychological differences between males and females.
- Critics of evolutionary psychology theory argue that its hypotheses are backed by speculations about prehistory, not evidence, and that it pays too little attention to cultural and individual variations in gender differences.

C. Social Theories
- Alice Eagly's social role theory states that gender differences result from the contrasting roles of women and men which give women less power and status than men.
- The social cognitive theory of gender holds that gender development occurs as a result of observation and imitation as well as rewards and punishments for gender-appropriate and gender-inappropriate behaviors.

D. Cognitive Theories
- According to Kohlberg's cognitive developmental theory of gender children come to think of themselves as boys or girls, see that they will always be male or female, and then select models of their own sex to imitate.
- Kohlberg's theory predicts that gender constancy will precede gender typing, but research indicates that gender typing occurs before children develop gender constancy.
- According to gender schema theory, children gradually develop schemas of what is gender-appropriate and gender-inappropriate and are motivated to conform with these gender schemas.

II. GENDER COMPARISONS

A. Gender Stereotypes

Gender stereotypes are general beliefs about females and males.

1. TRADITIONAL MASCULINITY AND FEMININITY
   - Gender stereotypes traditionally associate instrumental traits such as independence and aggression with males and expressive traits such as warmth and sensitivity with females.
   - The traits assigned by stereotypes to men and women suit them for different roles, roles that are unequal in status and power.

2. STEREOTYPING AND CULTURE
   - Researchers find pervasive gender stereotyping in cultures around the world.
   - Males are widely believed to be dominant, independent, aggressive, achievement-oriented; females are widely believed to be nurturant, affiliative, and more helpful in times of stress.

3. GENDER STEREOTYPES AND ETHNICITY

   People form subtypes or subcategories of stereotypes and thus may have stereotypes not only of men and women in general but also of men and women of specific ethnic groups.

4. SEXISM

   Sexism is prejudice or discrimination against an individual because of his or her sex.

B. Gender Similarities and Differences

- Gender differences are averages and do not apply to all females or all males.
- Even when gender differences occur, there often is considerable overlap between males and females.
- Gender differences may have many sources, including both biological and sociocultural factors.

1. PHYSICAL SIMILARITIES AND DIFFERENCES
   - Among the host of physical differences between the average man and the average woman are the following: Women have about twice the body fat of men. The primary sex hormones in males are androgens; in females, estrogens. Women have a longer life expectancy than men and are less likely to develop physical or mental disorders. The sizes of specific parts of the brain in men and women also seem to differ on average.
   - Physical differences might be due not only to evolution and heredity but also to experience since even the brain changes as a result of experience.

2. COGNITIVE SIMILARITIES AND DIFFERENCES
   - In the classroom and on standardized tests, boys do slightly better than girls at math and science.
   - Overall, girls are superior students and do better at reading than boys do.
   - These measures of differences in achievement may reflect many factors besides cognitive ability.

3. SOCIOEMOTIONAL SIMILARITIES AND DIFFERENCES
   - Earlier chapters have discussed some of the many socioemotional differences between men and women; for example, compared with men, women have more close friends, engage in more self-disclosure, and provide more social support in friendships.
   - In all cultures boys are more physically aggressive than girls.
   - When verbal aggression is examined, females are often as aggressive or more aggressive than males.
   - Girls are more likely than boys to engage in relational aggression, which involves behavior such as spreading malicious rumors or ignoring someone.
   - Males usually show less self-regulation of emotions and behavior than females.

4. INTERPRETING GENDER DIFFERENCES

   Controversy continues over whether gender differences are rare and small or common and large.

5. GENDER IN CONTEXT
- The context influences gender differences in behavior.
- Whether males or females are more likely to engage in helping behavior depends in part on the context. When there is a perceived danger and they feel competent to help, males are more likely than females to help.
- In many cultures traditional gender roles still guide the behavior of males and females; in other cultures gender roles have become more flexible.

C. Masculinity, Femininity, and Androgeny

- Androgeny is the presence of a high degree of masculine and feminine characteristics in the same individual.
- The Bem Sex-Role Inventory is a test designed to measure androgeny.
- Some people argue that we should stop thinking of ourselves and others as masculine, feminine, or androgynous; in other words, we should aim for gender-role transcendence.

III. WOMEN'S AND MEN'S LIVES

A. Women's Lives

1. WOMEN'S STATUS AROUND THE WORLD

In many cultures people are still governed by traditional gender roles that assign a subordinate status to women, a subordination evident in politics, work, and education.

2. ETHNIC MINORITY WOMEN IN THE UNITED STATES

Women from ethnic minority groups in the United States may face the double jeopardy of racism and sexism, and they may find themselves caught in a clash between the attitudes toward gender roles in the mainstream culture and attitudes in their ethnic culture.

3. PSYCHOLOGICAL HEALTH

- Some women face special stressors such as domestic violence and sexism.
- The continuation of gender differences in work roles may be stressful for women as working wives often still bear the largest share of the burden of taking care of house, children, and family relationships.
- Beginning in elementary school, girls are more dissatisfied with their bodies than boys are, a gender difference that increases with age, and dissatisfaction with their bodies may contribute to eating disorders and depression.
- In general, women are more likely than men to be diagnosed with mood and anxiety disorders.

4. COPING WITH STRESS

- When faced with stressful situations, women tend to seek alliances with others.
- Women are more likely than men to ruminate about stressful events.

5. CONCLUSIONS

Jean Baker Miller proposes that a large part of women's lives consists of active participation in the development of other people, a tendency that leaves them dependent on others to maintain their self-esteem.

ADJUSTMENT STRATEGIES *for*

Women

1. Recognize your competencies.
2. Pay attention to developing your self as well as your relationships.
3. Don't put up with sexism.

B. Men's Lives

   1. ETHNIC MINORITY MALES

     • Poverty and racism are special burdens placed most heavily on African-American males.

     • Ethnic minority men, like women, may find themselves caught in a clash between the attitudes toward gender roles in the mainstream culture and attitudes in their ethnic culture.

   2. ROLE STRAIN

     • Because of gender stereotypes, men are far less likely than women to be granted custody of their children.

     • William Pollack argues that despite changes in gender roles, little has been done to change "boy code."

     • Joseph Pleck argues that men face role strain because their roles today are contradictory and inconsistent.

     • Men today are penalized both for violating traditional male roles and for conforming to them.

     • Compared with women, men have lower life expectancy and higher rates of stress-related disorders, alcoholism, car accidents, homicide, and suicide.

ADJUSTMENT STRATEGIES *for*

Men

1. Understand your self and your emotions.
2. Improve your social relationships.
3. Lower your health risks.

Learning Goals

After reading and studying this chapter, you should be able to

1. Define gender and explain evolutionary, social, and cognitive theories of gender.

   a. Define gender and gender roles.

   b. Discuss the evolutionary psychology theory of gender differences.

   c. Identify social theories of gender.

   d. Describe two cognitive views of gender.

2. Discuss gender comparisons and classifications.

   a. Describe gender stereotypes.

   b. Outline physical, cognitive, and socioemotional differences between males and females.

   c. Identify alternatives to masculine and feminine classifications.

3. Characterize women's and men's lives.

   a. Describe some key characteristics of women's lives.

   b. Describe some key characteristics of men's lives.

Guided Review

After you have read this chapter in the textbook, complete these statements. Topics are discussed in the same order as in the chapter. Answers are provided at the end of the study guide chapter.

Learning Goal 1: Define gender and explain evolutionary, social, and cognitive theories of gender

Goal 1a: Define gender and gender roles

1. Sex refers to biological characteristics; _____ refers to the psychological and social dimension of being female or male.

2. _____ _____ are sets of expectations that prescribe how females and males should think, act, and feel.

Goal 1b: Discuss the evolutionary psychology theory of gender differences

3. _____ _____ argues that adaptation during human evolution produced psychological differences between males and females.

4. According to evolutionary psychology theorists, because having _____ _____ _____ improves the chances that a male will pass on his genes, natural selection favored males who were able to win the competition for access to the greatest number of females.

5. According to evolutionary psychology theorists, the pressures of natural selection favored the evolution of males who were disposed to _____, _____, and risk taking.

6. Evolutionary psychology theorists say that a female's chances of passing on her genes are improved by finding a mate who can provide offspring with _____ and _____.

7. David Buss argues that men and women differ psychologically only in those domains in which they faced different _____ _____ during evolutionary history.

8. Critics argue that evolutionary psychology is based on speculation about _____ and pays insufficient attention to cultural and individual variations.

Goal 1c: Identify social theories of gender

9. Alice Eagly proposed _____ _____ theory, which holds that gender differences result from the social hierarchy and division of labor that assign different roles to men and women.

10. In Eagly's view, as women adapted to roles with little power and little status, they developed more _____, less _____ behaviors.

11. According to _____ _____ theory, gender development occurs through observation and imitation and through rewards and punishments for gender-appropriate and gender-inappropriate behavior.

12. Children learn gender-typed behavior by _____ adults and the media and by being rewarded and punished by their parents for masculine or feminine behavior.

13. As children grow up, _____ become increasingly important as sources of rewards and punishments for gender-appropriate or gender-inappropriate behavior.

14. Researchers who observed preschoolers found that the more time boys spent interacting with other boys, the more their activity level, _____-_____-_____ _____, and gender-typed choice of toys and games increased.

15. The more time preschool girls spent interacting with other girls, the more their _____ level and _____ decreased.

Goal 1d: Describe two cognitive views of gender

16. Some critics of social cognitive theory argue that it pays too little attention to the child's own

_____.

17. Cognitive theories stress that individuals _____ _____ their gender world.

18. According to Lawrence Kohlberg's cognitive developmental theory, gender development depends on

_____.

19. According to cognitive developmental theory of gender, children first think of themselves as boys or

girls, see that they will always be male or female, and then select _____ of their own sex to

_____.

20. Research findings that children select gender-typed toys and games and clothes before they develop

gender constancy _____ Kohlberg's cognitive developmental theory of gender.

21. According to gender schema theory, children gradually develop _____ of what is gender-

appropriate and inappropriate in their cultures and then conform to these _____.

22. A _____ _____ is a cognitive structure that organizes the world in terms of

female and male and guides a person's perceptions, thinking, and behavior.

Learning Goal 2: Discuss gender comparisons and classifications

Goal 2a: Describe gender stereotypes

23. Gender _____ are general beliefs about males and females.

24. Traits generally associated with males such as being independent and aggressive are _____

traits.

25. Traits generally associated with females such as being warm and sensitive are _____ traits.

26. The instrumental traits associated with males suit them for roles out in the world whereas the expressive

traits associated with females are suited for _____.

27. The traits and roles associated with males and females are not only different but also

_____.

28. Cross-cultural studies indicate that gender stereotypes are _____.

29. Males are widely believed to be _____, independent, aggressive, and achievement-oriented.

30. People not only have stereotypes for men and women in general but also may assign certain

characteristics to men and women from particular _____ _____.

31. _____ is prejudice and discrimination against an individual because of his or her sex.

Goal 2b: Outline physical, cognitive, and socioemotional differences between males and females

32. Interpretations of reported gender differences should take into account the fact that the differences are

_____ and do not apply to all males and females and that there is often considerable

_____ between males and females.

33. Females have a longer _____ _____ than males and are _____

likely than males to develop physical or mental disorders.

34. Males have _____ levels of stress hormones than females.

35. Research to date suggests that the sizes of parts of the _____, _____

_____, and parietal lobe differ in males and females.

36. Even if the brains of most men differ from the brains of most women, those differences might be

_____.

37. In U.S. classrooms and on standardized tests, boys do slightly better than girls on _____ and _____.

38. Overall, compared with U.S. boys, girls are better students and do significantly better in

_____.

39. Grades and scores on standardized tests reflect _____ and may have causes other than cognitive ability.

40. Gender differences in the classroom and on standardized tests may reflect attempts to conform to _____ _____ as well as differences in motivation, self-regulation, or other socioemotional characteristics.

41. Compared with men, women have more _____ _____, engage in more self-disclosure, and provide more social support in their friendships.

42. In all cultures boys are more _____ _____ than girls.

43. When _____ aggression and _____ aggression are considered, girls are as aggressive or more aggressive than boys.

44. Relational aggression includes behaviors such as spreading _____ _____ or ignoring someone.

45. Compared with females, males show less _____-_____ of emotions and behavior, which can translate into behavioral problems.

46. When a perceived _____ exists, males are more likely than females to help if they feel competent to help.

47. _____ are more likely than _____ to show anger toward strangers and to turn their anger into aggressive actions.

48. Women are displaying more _____ traits as gender roles become more flexible in many Western cultures.

Goal 2c: Identify alternatives to masculine and feminine classifications

49. _____ is the presence of a high degree of masculine and feminine characteristics in the same individual.

50. A male who is both _____ and _____ to others' feelings might be described as androgynous.

51. Sandra Bem constructed the _____ _____-_____ _____ to assess androgeny.

52. In Bem's classification an _____ individual is low on both feminine and masculine traits.

53. One recent study found that androgynous individuals were more _____ _____ than masculine or feminine individuals.

54. To some degree, _____ influences which gender role is most adaptive.

55. Some critics argue that the concept of androgyny encourages continued gender stereotyping and that a better ideal is _____-_____ _____.

Learning Goal 3: Characterize women's and men's lives
Goal 3a: Describe some key characteristics of women's lives

56. In much of the world traditional gender roles continue to assign a _____ role to women.

57. In the United States the conditions of women vary significantly with _____.

58. Asian-American and Mexican-American women are among those who might find themselves caught in a conflict between the attitudes of the mainstream culture and the _____ gender roles that are part of their cultural heritage.

59. Compared with non-Latino white women, _____ _____ women are more likely to ponder their options before taking action, pray, or bide their time waiting for alternatives to develop.

60. Compared with men or with other women, women who experience frequent sexism have more symptoms of _____, _____, and physical complaints.

61. Beginning with elementary schools, girls are more _____ with their bodies than boys are, and this gender difference continues through adulthood.

62. Dissatisfaction with their bodies may be linked with weight-control practices, _____ _____, and depression.

63. Faced with stressful situations, women are more likely than men to seek alliances with others and to _____.

64. Jean Baker Miller concludes that women spend a large part of their lives participating in the development of other people and may become dependent on others to maintain their _____- _____.

65. Harriet Lerner has argued that it is important for women to bring a strong _____ self to their relationships.

Goal 3b: Describe some key characteristics of men's lives

66. African-American males are more likely than non-Latino white males to face _____ and _____.

67. Among Chinese-, Japanese-, and Mexican-American men, the influence of rigid traditional gender roles is _____.

68. Among the _____ _____, men take responsibility for children when not working away from the family.

69. William Pollack argues that little has been done to change the _____ _____ that tells boys to act tough.

70. According to Joseph Pleck, men face role strain because male roles are _____.

71. The strains created by the way the male role is currently defined in the United States may be reflected in statistics regarding men's _____.

72. Compared with women, men have _____ rates of stress-related disorders, alcoholism, car accidents, and suicide, and their life expectancy is lower.

73. The current view of men's role encourages expectations that men should _____ women and has been blamed for encouraging _____ toward women and inadequate emotional connections with other males.

Key Terms

Briefly define each key term and provide an example or application.

1. gender

2. gender roles

3. evolutionary psychology theory

4. psychoanalytic theory of gender

5. social cognitive theory of gender

6. cognitive developmental theory of gender

7. gender schema theory

8. gender stereotypes

9. androgyny

10. gender-role transcendence

Practice Test A

Answer these multiple-choice questions to assess your understanding of the chapter. Answers are provided at the end of the study guide chapter.

_____ 1. Sets of expectations that prescribe how females and males should think, feel, and act are
a. gender roles.
b. gender stereotypes.
c. gender schemas.
d. gender constancies.

_____ 2. Evolutionary psychology theory explains gender differences
a. by examining the genome.
b. as a reflection of differences in power.
c. as a result of the varying pressures placed on males and females in prehistorical times.
d. as a result of the evolution of technology.

_____ 3. In most cultures around the world
a. women have less power and status than men.
b. women perform more domestic work than men.
c. women receive lower pay than men.
d. all of the above conditions exist.

_____ 4. According to Eagly's social role theory,
a. biology assigns a subordinate role to women.
b. the social hierarchy and division of labor are important causes of gender differences.
c. gender differences create social hierarchies.
d. none of the above is true.

_____ 5. In the social cognitive theory of gender,
a. conditioning creates all gender differences.
b. cognitive structures account for all gender differences.
c. observation, imitation, rewards, and punishments are the mechanisms by which gender develops.
d. social hierarchies create gender differences.

_____ 6. Kohlberg's cognitive developmental theory of gender holds that
a. children first think of themselves as boys or girls before adopting gender-typed behaviors.
b. children adopt gender-typed behavior and then learn to think of themselves as boys and girls.
c. children adopt gender-typed behavior after they are rewarded for imitating it.
d. none of the above is true.

_____ 7. According to gender schema theory,
a. children are internally motivated to perceive the world and act in accordance with their developing gender schemas.
b. children develop gender schemas as a result of being rewarded for gender-typed behavior.
c. gender schemas are biologically encoded and determine gender-typed behavior.
d. none of the above statements is true.

_____ 8. According to gender stereotypes, the traits characteristic of males are
a. instrumental traits.
b. expressive traits.
c. androgynous traits.
d. affiliative traits.

_____ 9. The brains of males and females
a. are identical.
b. are markedly different.
c. show slight but unchangeable differences.
d. change as a result of experience.

_____ 10. Studies of aggression indicate that
a. boys are more aggressive than girls.
b. boys are more aggressive physically and verbally than girls.
c. boys are more physically aggressive than girls, but girls are as aggressive or more aggressive than boys when verbal and relational aggression are examined.
d. girls are more aggressive than boys when all types of aggression are taken into account.

_____ 11. Phil's friends all say that he is androgynous. If they are correct, this means that Phil is characterized by
a. low masculinity and high femininity.
b. high masculinity and low femininity.
c. low masculinity and low femininity.
d. high masculinity and high femininity.

_____ 12. The boy code described by William Pollack
a. is a historical description of norms of the past.
b. socializes boys to hide their feelings and act tough.
c. allows boys to adapt to changing gender roles.
d. teaches boys to develop positive emotional connections with other males.

Identifying Concepts

Answers are provided at the end of the study guide chapter.

1. ANDROGENY   Identify the gender-role classification of each description.

a. Assertive, dominant

b. Not high on any traits

c. Dominant, sensitive

d. Sensitive, nurturant

2. IMPORTANT PEOPLE IN THE STUDY OF GENDER   Identify the person whose contribution is described in each statement.

a. Developed an explanation of gender differences based on evolutionary psychology

b. Proposed social role theory as an explanation for gender differences

c. Developed the first cognitive developmental theory of gender

d. Developed sex-role inventory

e. Analyzed male role-strain

Understanding Concepts

Complete these exercises to develop your understanding of important ideas in this chapter.

1. How would you describe the gender roles in your hometown?

2. Describe how evolutionary psychology explains gender differences.

3. Summarize the social role theory of gender differences.

4. What are some of the main criticisms of the explanations of gender differences offered by evolutionary psychology and by psychoanalytic theory?

5. Describe the cognitive developmental theory of gender and the evidence against it.

6. What are schemas, and how does gender schema theory explain the development of gender?

7. Describe the traits traditionally thought to be characteristic of females and discuss the implications of this stereotype.

8. What cautions do you need to keep in mind when interpreting findings about gender differences?

9. Discuss gender differences in self-regulation and their significance.

10. Discuss how gender differences in helping and nurturing behavior are influenced by context.

Applying Concepts and Strategies

Complete these exercises to develop your ability to apply this chapter's material to your life and the world. Your responses will differ from those of other students in the class, and it is helpful to share your ideas with other students.

1. What are the advantages and disadvantages of living in a culture in which gender roles are rigidly defined?

2. If the explanation of gender differences offered by evolutionary psychology is accurate, does that tell you anything about what your attitudes toward gender differences should be today?

3. Consider the explanations of gender offered by evolutionary psychology, social role theory, social cognition theory, and gender schema theory. Are any of these theories mutually exclusive? Which elements of these theories are compatible with each other?

4. What are the implications of social role theory?

5. Recall the findings on gender differences in cognitive skills. What are the possible explanations for these findings? Describe two strategies to help boys and girls perform better.

6. Complete Self-Assessment 12.3: My Gender-Role Classification and interpret the results. How does your gender-role orientation influence your daily and life choices (e.g., favorite activities, friendships, career and family goals)?

7. Why is it important to understand gender roles in other cultures?

8. Suppose that you are a foreign policy advisor for the U.S. government. Do you think that the government should treat discrimination against women in other countries as a violation of human rights or as a cultural difference?

9. Have you ever been the victim or perpetrator of sexism? What do you think are valid measures of sexism in the United States?

10. Consider Pollack's comments on the boy code. Describe an example of coaches or other adults teaching the boy code. Do you think attempts should be made to change the boy code? If so, describe one strategy for doing so.

Practice Test B

Answer these multiple-choice test questions to help you assess your understanding of the textbook chapter. Answers are provided at the end of the study guide chapter.

____ 1. Gender roles are
a. set by our biology.
b. the legacy of evolution and essentially unchanged for eons.
c. universal and stable.
d. social constructions that may change.

____ 2. According to Freud's psychoanalytic theory of gender, gender differences arise
a. because the child identifies with the same-sex parent.
b. after the child renounces a sexual attraction to the opposite-sex parent at about 5 or 6 years of age.
c. as the child unconsciously adopts the characteristics of the same-sex parent.
d. as a result of all of the above.

____ 3. When children are about 4 to 12 years of age,
a. peers have little influence over their behavior.
b. they spend most of their free time playing with children of their own sex.
c. mixed-sex play groups play the critical role in their development.
d. the influence of peers gradually decreases.

____ 4. During childhood peers tend to
a. show little interest in whether behavior is gender appropriate or not.
b. reward gender-inappropriate behavior.
c. become increasingly less important as models or reinforcers of behavior.
d. extensively reward and punish behavior depending on whether it is considered masculine or feminine.

____ 5. The understanding that sex remains the same even though clothing and activities might change is called
a. gender identity.
b. gender constancy.
c. gender schema.
d. gender stereotype.

____ 6. Research indicates that children
a. develop gender-typed behavior after they develop gender constancy.
b. develop gender-typed behavior before they develop gender constancy.
c. do not develop gender constancy until adolescence.
d. do not develop gender-typed behavior until they enter school.

____ 7. According to gender stereotypes, the traits characteristic of females are
a. instrumental traits.
b. expressive traits.
c. androgynous traits.
d. dominant traits.

____ 8. Compared with men, women generally
a. are more susceptible to infections.
b. react to stress with higher levels of stress hormones.
c. have blood vessels that are more elastic.
d. are more vulnerable to illness.

____ 9. Research by Eleanor Maccoby in the 1970s and 1980s found that gender differences in cognitive skills
a. had increased.
b. had decreased.
c. were unchanged.
d. had disappeared.

____ 10. An androgynous individual is a
a. male with a high degree of expressive traits.
b. male with a high degree of instrumental traits.
c. male or female with a high degree of expressive traits.
d. male or female with a high degree of both expressive and instrumental traits.

____ 11. The proportion of seats held by women in national governments around the world
a. has tripled since 1990.
b. has increased 2 percent since 1990.
c. reached 25 percent in 2003.
d. reached 50 percent in 2003.

____ 12. Among Native Americans
a. males are the head of the family.
b. males share child care responsibilities.
c. females function as the core of the family.
d. some tribes are matriarchal and some patriarchal.

Answers to Chapter Questions

Guided Review
1. gender
2. gnder roles
3. evolutionary psychology
4. multiple sexual liaisons
5. violence; competition
6. resources; protection
7. adaptive problems
8. prehistory
9. social role
10. cooperative; dominant
11. social cognitive
12. observing
13. peers
14. rough-and-tumble play
15. activity; aggression
16. mind (or understanding)
17. actively construct
18. cognition
19. models; imitate
20. refute
21. schemas; schemas
22. gender schema
23. stereotypes
24. instrumental
25. expressive
26. caregivers
27. unequal
28. pervasive
29. dominant
30. ethnic groups
31. sexism
32. averages; overlap
33. life expectancy; less
34. higher
35. hypothalamus; corpus callosum
36. changeable
37. mathematics; science
38. reading
39. achievement
40. gender roles
41. close friends
42. physically aggressive
43. verbal; relational
44. malicious rumors
45. self-regulation
46. danger
47. males; females
48. instrumental
49. androgeny
50. assertive; sensitive
51. Bem Sex-Role Inventory
52. undifferentiated
53. emotionally intelligent
54. context
55. gender-role transcendence
56. subordinate
57. ethnicity
58. traditional
59. African-American
60. depression; anxiety
61. dissatisfied

62. eating disorders
63. ruminate
64. self-esteem
65. assertive (*or* independent, authentic)
66. poverty; discrimination
67. eroding
68. Mescalero Apache
69. boy code
70. contradictory (*or* inconsistent)
71. health
72. higher
73. dominate; violence

Identifying Concepts

1. ANDROGENY
   a. masculine
   b. undifferentiated
   c. androgynous
   d. feminine
2. IMPORTANT PEOPLE IN THE STUDY OF GENDER
   a. David Buss
   b. Alice Eagly
   c. Lawrence Kohlberg
   d. Sandra Bem
   e. Joseph Pleck

Practice Test A

1. a
2. c
3. d
4. b
5. c
6. a
7. a
8. a
9. d
10. c
11. d
12. b

Practice Test B

1. d
2. d
3. b
4. d
5. b
6. b
7. b
8. c
9. b
10. d
11. b
12. d

CHAPTER 13

SEXUALITY

Chapter Outline

I. SEXUAL MOTIVATION AND BEHAVIOR

Biology, cognitions, and culture all influence sexual behavior.

A. The Biology of Sex

1. THE HUMAN SEXUAL RESPONSE CYCLE

- William Masters and Virginia Johnson observed and measured the physiological responses of female and male volunteers as they masturbated or had sexual intercourse.
- According to Masters and Johnson, the human sexual response cycle consists of four phases: excitement, plateau, orgasm, and resolution.
- The excitement phase begins erotic responsiveness and can last from several minutes to several hours; the most obvious signs of responses in this phase are lubrication of the vagina and partial erection of the penis.
- The plateau phase is a continuation and heightening of the arousal begun in the excitement phase.
- The third phase of the human sexual response cycle is orgasm, which lasts 3 to 15 seconds.
- Following orgasm, the individual enters the resolution phase, in which blood vessels return to their normal state.

2. HORMONES

- The role of hormones in motivating human sexual behavior is not clear, but it is clear that estrogens and androgens can influence sexual behavior.
- Estrogens are the class of sex hormones that predominate in females; androgens (of which testosterone is the most important) are the class that prodominates in males.
- At puberty, males experience a dramatic increase in testosterone levels along with an increase in sexual thoughts and fantasies, masturbation, and nocturnal emissions.
- At puberty, females' ovaries begin to produce estrogen.

B. Sensations, Perceptions, and Cognitions

- Touch, visual cues, certain words, and smells can all be sexually arousing.
- Men are more aroused by what they see; women are more aroused by touch.

- Men are likely to become sexually aroused quickly, whereas women's sexual arousal tends to build gradually.
- Cognitions about sexual activity, about potential and actual sexual partners, and about ourselves influence decisions about having sex, our experience of sex, and our interpretations of our experiences.

C. Culture and Sexual Motivation

- Some cultures consider sexual pleasures normal; other cultures view sexual pleasures as weird or abnormal.
- Variations in sexual behavior reflect the influence of different sexual scripts, which are stereotyped patterns of expectations about how people should behave sexually.
- Two influential sexual scripts in U.S. culture are the traditional religious script, which holds that sex is acceptable only within marriage, and the romantic script, in which sex is synonymous with love and it is acceptable to have sex with a person you are in love with.

D. Gender and Sexual Motivation

- Men and women often follow different sexual scripts, with women linking sexual intercourse with love more than male do.
- Many people hold a double standard, a belief that many sexual activities are acceptable for males but not females.
- Men think about sex far more than women do, report more frequent feelings of sexual arousal, have more frequent sexual fantasies, and rate the strength of their sex drive higher than women do.
- Many gender differences found in heterosexual relationships have also been documented in homosexual relationships.

E. Sexual Orientation

- Sexual orientation refers to an enduring attraction for members of one's own sex (homosexual orientation) or members of the other sex (heterosexual orientation) or members of either sex (bisexual orientation).
- It is accepted today that sexual orientation is, not an either-or proposition, but a continuum from exclusive heterosexuality to exclusive homosexuality.
    1. WHAT CAUSES SEXUAL ORIENTATION?
        - Homosexuals and heterosexuals have similar physiological responses during sexual arousal and seem to be aroused by the same types of tactile stimulation.
        - An individual's sexual orientation is most likely determined by a combination of genetic, hormonal, cognitive, and environmental factors.
    2. DEVELOPMENTAL PATHWAYS

       Gay and lesbian youth have diverse patterns of initial attraction, often have bisexual attractions, and may have physical or emotional attraction to same-sex individuals.

ADJUSTMENT STRATEGIES *Involving*

Gays and Lesbians

1. Develop a bicultural identity.
2. Join an organization for gay, lesbian, or bisexual individuals.
3. Be tolerant of the sexual orientation of others.

F. Sexual Patterns in the United States

- A comprehensive survey of Americans' sexual lives suggests that for most Americans sexual behavior is ruled by marriage and monogamy.

- U.S. males report that their first sexual intercourse occurs at 17.4 years of age and U.S. females at 16.9 years of age.

II. SEXUALITY AND ADJUSTMENT

A. Sexual Communication

- Sex is best conceptualized as a form of communication within a relationship.
- The best way for people to improve the likelihood that their sexual needs will be met is to talk about them with a partner.

ADJUSTMENT STRATEGIES *for*

Effective Communication in Sexual Relationships*

1. Understand that it is normal to feel uncomfortable talking about sex with a partner.
2. Take responsibility for your sexual needs.
3. Learn about your partner's sexual needs.
4. Criticize constructively.
5. Handle criticisms effectively.
6. If you mean no, say, No.
7. Pay attention to nonverbal cues.

*Based on Robert Crooks and Carla Bauer, *Our Sexuality, 9th ed.* (Belmont, CA: Wadsworth, 2005).

B. Sexual Myths and Sex Education

1. SEXUAL MYTHS

   Adolescents in the United States believe a distressing number of myths about sex.

2. SEX EDUCATION

   - U.S. adolescents receive very little sex education from their parents.
   - According to a 1999 survey, the overwhelming majority of Americans support having sex education in the schools.
   - In contrast to sex education in other Western nations, U.S. sex education typically has focused on the hazards of sex.

C. Contraception

- As a result of inadequate knowledge about contraception and inconsistent use of effective contraceptive methods, the United States has one of the highest rates of adolescent pregnancy in the industrialized world.
- No single method of contraception is best for everyone.
- Major methods of contraception include oral contraceptives, condoms, diaphragms, spermacides, IUDs, Norplant, Depo-Provera, Ortho Evra, Preven and Plan B, tubal ligation, and vasectomy.

D. Psychosexual Dysfunctions and Disorders

1. PSYCHOSEXUAL DYSFUNCTIONS

   Psychosexual dysfunctions are disorders that involve impairments in the sexual response cycle, either in the desire for gratification or in the ability to achieve it.

2. TREATMENT FOR PSYCHOSEXUAL DYSFUNCTIONS

Most cases of psychosexual dysfunction now yield to techniques tailored to treat each dysfunction.

3. PARAPHILIAS

- Paraphilias are psychosexual disorders in which the source of an individual's sexual satisfaction is an unusual object, ritual, or situation.
- Paraphilias include fetishism, transvestism, exhibitionism, voyeurism, sadism, masochism, and pedophilia.

4. GENDER IDENTITY DISORDER

Transsexualism is a disorder of gender identity in which an individual has an overwhelming desire to become a member of the opposite sex.

III. SEXUALITY AND HARM

A. Sexually Transmitted Infections

Sexually transmitted infections are diseases that are contracted primarily through sexual contact.

1. GONORRHEA

Gonorrhea is a sexually transmitted disease caused by a bacterium; it can be successfully treated with antibiotics in its early stages.

2. SYPHILIS

Syphillis is a sexually transmitted infection caused by a bacterium; in its early stages it can be treated with penicillin.

3. CHLAMYDIA

Chlamydia is the most common sexually transmitted infection in the Untied States and is caused by a bacterium; in females tt can cause pelvic inflammatory disease, which can lead to infertility.

4. GENITAL HERPES

Genital herpes is a sexually transmitted infection caused by a virus; in women it brings an increased risk of cervical cancer.

5. HPV

HPV is a virus that causes genital warts; the warts can be removed by a physician.

6. AIDS

- AIDS is a sexually transmitted infection caused by HIV (human immunodeficiency virus), which destroys the immune system.
- A person who is infected with HIV is vulnerable to infections that a normal immune system could defeat.
- AIDS can be transmitted only by contact with an infected person's blood, semen, or vaginal fluids such as through sexual contact, the sharing of needles, or contaminated blood transfusions.

ADJUSTMENT STRATEGIES *for*

Protecting against STIs

1. Know your and your partner's risk status.
2. Obtain medical examinations.
3. Have protected, not unprotected, sex.
4. Don't have sex with multiple partners.

B. Rape

- Rape is forcible sexual intercourse with a person who does not give consent.
- Rape is a traumatic experience for victims and those close to them.
- Recovery after rape depends on the victim's coping abilities, psychological adjustment prior to the assault, and social support.
- Date or acquaintance rape is coercive sex forced by someone with whom the victim is at least casually acquainted.

ADJUSTMENT STRATEGIES *Involving*
Acquaintance Rape

For men and women:

1. Communicate your expectations clearly.
2. Know that women and men have the right to set limits that will be respected.
3. Consider the consequences.
4. If you use alcohol, use it in moderation.
5. Report the rape.

For women:

1. You have the right to set and reset sexual limits.
2. Think about where you go with a man.
3. Get to know the person well first.
4. Be careful about sending conflicting messages.
5. Educate yourself about men and sex.

For men:

1. Understand that "No" always means no.
2. Understand that your partner can change her mind at any time.
3. Be aware of cultural expectations.
4. Know that a woman who wears provocative clothing is not asking to have sex with you.
5. Spending money on a date does not entitle you to have sex.
6. Be aware of the consequences of your sexual conduct.

C. Sexual Harassment

Sexual harassment comes in many forms—from sexist remarks and covert physical contact to blatant propositions and sexual assaults.

D. Incest

- Incest is sex between people who are close relatives.
- Taboos against incest are virtually universal.

E. Pornography and Violence against Women

- *Pornography* means sexually explicit material.
- The nature of the pornographic material, the characteristics of those viewing it, and the surrounding culture are among the factors that influence the effects of pornography.

- Pornography showing sexual violence toward women is more likely to increase violence toward women than pornography that displays consensual sex without violence.
- For men with certain characteristics, viewing pornography may be linked with increased violence toward women.

Learning Goals

After reading and studying this chapter, you should be able to

1. **Describe the key factors that influence sexual motivation and behavior.**
   a. Identity some biological factors involved in sexual motivation and behavior.
   b. Discuss nonbiological factors that influence sexual arousal and activity.
   c. Discuss the relationship between culture and sexual behavior.
   d. Outline gender differences in sexual motivation.
   e. Discuss sexual orientation and its possible causes.
   f. Identify characteristics of the sexual activity of typical Americans.

2. **Discuss the relation between sexuality and adjustment.**
   a. Describe effective sexual communication.
   b. Discuss what Americans know about sex and how they learn it.
   c. Outline the range of available contraceptives.
   d. Describe psychosexual dysfunctions, paraphilias, and gender identity disorder.

3. **Explain aspects of sexuality that can be harmful.**
   a. Identify the main sexually transmitted infections.
   b. Discuss rape and its consequences.
   c. Describe sexual harassment.
   d. Describe incest.
   e. Discuss the relationship between pornography and violence against women.

Guided Review

After you have read this chapter in the textbook, complete these statements. Topics are discussed in the same order as in the chapter. Answers are provided at the end of the study guide chapter.

Learning Goal 1: Describe the key factors that influence sexual motivation and behavior

Goal 1a: Identity some biological factors involved in sexual motivation and behavior

1. _____ and _____ observed and measured the physiological responses of adult volunteers as they masturbated or had sexual intercourse.

2. Masters and Johnson identified the _____ _____ _____ _____ consisting of four phases—excitement, plateau, orgasm, and resolution.

3. The _____ phase can last several minutes to several hours and is characterized by engorgement of blood vessels, increased blood flow in genital areas, and muscle tension.

4. The most obvious signs of the excitement phase are partial _____ of the penis and vaginal _____.

5. The second phase, the _____ phase, is a continuation and heightening of arousal with increases in breathing, pulse rate, and blood pressure and complete penile erection and vaginal lubrication.

6. The _____ phase only lasts from three to fifteen seconds and involves an explosive discharge of neuromuscular tension and an intense pleasurable feeling.

7. For males but not females, part of the _____ phase is the refractory period during which they cannot achieve another orgasm; this period increases in length as men age.

8. Although the role of hormones in motivating human sexual behavior is not clear, it is clear that _____ and _____ have some influence.

9. _____ are the class of sex hormones that predominate in females; androgens are the class of sex hormones that predominate in males.

10. At puberty, boys experience a dramatic increase in levels of the androgen _____ along with an increase in sexual thoughts and fantasies.

11. At puberty, a girl's _____ begin to produce estrogen.

12. Estrogen levels vary over an approximately month-long cycle, but human females may be interested in _____ _____ at any time during this cycle.

13. Although _____ women have a significant drop in estrogen, they are still sexually active.

Goal 1b: Discuss nonbiological factors that influence sexual arousal and activity

14. For people, the sensory system of _____ usually predominates during sexual intimacy, but _____ also plays a prominent role for some people.

15. _____ are scented substances that are powerful sexual attractants in some animals, but it's not clear whether there are pheromones that trigger sexual attraction between humans.

16. _____ are substances that supposedly arouse sexual desire and increase the capacity for sexual activity.

17. _____ may stimulate sexual arousal or deter us from sexual activity, and they influence our decisions about having sex, our experience of sex, and our interpretations of that experience.

Goal 1c: Discuss the relationship between culture and sexual behavior

18. Among the _____ of Ireland, premarital sex is out of the question, and men avoid most sexual experiences.

19. In the _____ culture of the South Pacific, when boys turn 13, they are instructed about sexual strategies including how to aid their female partner in having orgasms.

20. _____ _____ are stereotyped patterns of expectancies about how people should behave sexually.

21. In the _____ _____ _____, extramarital sex is taboo, whereas in the romantic script it is acceptable to have sex with a person you are in love with whether you are married or not.

Goal 1d: Outline gender differences in sexual motivation

22. Females, more than males, cite _____ _____ _____ as the main reason for being sexually active.

23. Despite the movement toward equality between men and women, many people still hold a
_____ _____, a belief that many sexual activities are acceptable for males but
not for females.

24. Recent studies indicate that men think about sex far more than women do and report more frequent
feelings of _____ _____, have more frequent sexual fantasies, and rate the
strength of their sex drive higher than women.

Goal 1e: Discuss sexual orientation and its possible causes

25. _____ _____ refers to an enduring attraction toward members of one's own
sex or toward members of the other sex.

26. _____ and heterosexuals have similar physiological responses during sexual arousal, and
they seem to be aroused by the same types of tactile stimulation.

27. To date, no specific _____ _____ of homosexuality has been found.

28. Most likely, an individual's sexual orientation is determined by a combination of _____,
_____, cognitive, and environmental factors.

29. Many gay and lesbian individuals struggled with _____-_____
_____ in childhood, but others did not and instead experienced an abrupt sense of their
same-sex attraction in late adolescence.

Goal 1f: Identify characteristics of the sexual activity of typical Americans

30. A comprehensive study of Americans' sexual patterns that was published in 1994 found that
_____ rules sexual behavior for most Americans.

31. In the 1994 survey nearly _____ percent of married men and 85 percent of married women
indicated that they had never been unfaithful.

32. By their late teenage years, _____ _____ of U.S. youth say they have had
sexual intercourse.

Learning Goal 2: Discuss the relation between sexuality and adjustment

Goal 2a: Describe effective sexual communication

33. The best way for people to improve the chances that their sexual needs will be met is to
_____ _____ _____ with a partner.

34. One strategy for communicating effectively about sex is to _____ _____ with
praise and be selective about the time and place of the discussion.

Goal 2b: Discuss what Americans know about sex and how they learn it

35. One of many common myths about sex is that good sex must be _____.

36. According to one 1999 survey, _____ percent of Americans support offering sex education
in middle/junior high schools.

37. U.S. sex education typically has focused on the _____ of sex.

Goal 2c: Outline the range of available contraceptives

38. Calculations of the effectiveness of a contraceptive method often are based on the failure rates during
the _____ _____ of use.

39. Oral contraceptives offer a _____ rate of effectiveness and _____ interference with sexual activity.

40. A main advantage of condoms as a method of contraception is that they also offer protection against

_____ _____ _____ .

Goal 2d: Describe psychosexual dysfunctions, paraphilias, and gender identity disorder

41. Psychosexual _____ involve impairments in the sexual response cycle.

42. In psychosexual dysfunctions associated with the _____ phase, individuals show little sexual drive.

43. Inability to maintain an _____ is a disorder associated with the excitement phase.

44. During the orgasmic phase men may experience _____ _____ .

45. _____ cases of psychosexual dysfunction yield to techniques tailored to improve sexual functioning.

46. Viagra and other drugs that treat erectile dysfunction work by allowing _____

_____ _____ into the penis.

47. _____ are psychosexual disorders in which the source of an individual's sexual

_____ is an unusual object, ritual, or situation.

48. _____ is a disorder in which an individual relies on inanimate objects or a specific body part for sexual gratification.

49. _____ is a disorder in which individuals obtain sexual gratification by dressing up as a member of the opposite sex.

50. _____ expose their sexual anatomy to others to obtain sexual gratification whereas

_____ derive sexual gratification by observing the sex organs or sex acts of others, usually secretly.

51. _____ involves deriving sexual gratification from inflicting pain on others;

_____ involves deriving sexual gratification from being subjected to physical pain.

52. _____ is a disorder in which the sex object is a child and the intimacy usually involves manipulation of the child's genitals.

53. _____ is a disorder of gender identity in which an individual has an overwhelming desire to become a member of the opposite sex.

Learning Goal 3: Explain aspects of sexuality that can be harmful

Goal 3a: Identify the main sexually transmitted infections

54. The main sexually transmitted infections include three caused by bacterial infections—gonorrhea, syphilis, and _____ — and three caused by viruses—_____ _____ , HPV, and AIDS.

55. _____ can be successfully treated in its early stages with antibiotics but untreated can lead to infections that can move to various organs and can cause infertility.

56. _____ can be effectively treated in its early stages with penicillin but in its advanced stages can cause paralysis or even death.

57. _____ , which is the most common sexually transmitted infection in the United States, is highly infectious and in women can lead to ectopic pregnancies and infertility.

58. _____ _____ is caused by a virus and produces sores and blisters than may recur.

59. _____ is a virus that increases a woman's risk for cervical cancer.

60. _____ is caused by HIV, which destroys the immune system.

61. AIDS is transmitted by contact with _____ or sexual fluids of an infected person.

Goal 3b: Discuss rape and its consequences

62. _____ is forcible sexual intercourse with a person who does not give consent; legal definitions differ from state to state.

63. Initial reactions to rape include _____, numbness, and disorganization, reactions that may be followed by depression, fear, and anxiety.

64. About half of rape victims experience _____ _____, such as reduced sexual desire or inhibited orgasm.

65. Recovery after rape depends on _____ abilities, psychological adjustment prior to the assault, and social support.

66. Date or _____ _____ is coercive sexual activity directed at someone with whom the individual is at least casually acquainted.

Goal 3c: Describe sexual harassment

67. Sexual _____ take varied forms, from sexist remarks to sexual assaults, and can have serious psychological consequences for the victim.

Goal 3d: Describe incest

68. The most common form of incest occurs between a _____ and _____; the second most common form is a father-daughter relationship.

Goal 3e: Discuss the relationship between pornography and violence against women

69. Feminists suggest that pornography _____ women and glorifies violence against women.

70. No one factor such as pornography is likely to cause violence against women, but pornography is more likely to increase violence toward women if it displays _____ _____ toward women.

Key Terms

Briefly define each key term and provide an example or application.

1. estrogens

2. androgens

3. pheromones

4. sexual scripts

5. traditional religious script

6. romantic script

7. double standard

8. sexual orientation

9. bisexual

10. psychosexual dysfunctions

11. paraphilias

12. fetishism

13. transvestism

14. exhibitionism

15. voyeurism

16. sadism

17. masochism

18. pedophilia

19. transsexualism

20. sexually transmitted infections (STIs)

21. gonorrhea

22. syphilis

23. chlamydia

24. genital herpes

25. HPV

26. AIDS

27. rape

28. date or acquaintance rape

29. incest

Practice Test A

Answer these multiple-choice questions to assess your understanding of the chapter. Answers are provided at the end of the study guide chapter.

___ 1. The body returns to its prearousal state during which phase of the sexual response cycle?
a. Excitement
b. Plateau
c. Orgasm
d. Resolution

___ 2. For human males, sexual motivation is associated with
a. higher levels of estrogen.
b. higher levels of androgens.
c. lower levels of androgens.
d. higher levels of cortisol.

___ 3. Research suggests that U.S. women think about sex
a. much more than men do.
b. mostly as a type of conquest.
c. less than men do.
d. at least once a day.

___ 4. Research on homosexual relationships indicates that
a. lesbians have fewer sex partners than gay men.
b. the sexual motivation of lesbians has little in common with than of heterosexual women.
c. lesbians have little interest in committed relationships.
d. all of the above statements are true.

_____ 5. The sexual relationships and sexual response patterns of homosexuals are
a. symptoms of psychosis.
b. totally dissimilar from those of heterosexuals.
c. more similar than different from those of heterosexuals.
d. reflections of a dysfunctional family life.

_____ 6. The majority of U.S. teenagers
a. have had sexual intercourse before their sixteenth birthday.
b. do not have sexual intercourse until after their twenty-first birthday.
c. have had sexual intercourse before their eighteenth birthday.
d. remain abstinent until marriage.

_____ 7. Which of the following is true?
a. Male and female orgasms are necessary for sexual satisfaction.
b. Most women are not interested in sexual pleasure.
c. Good sex must be spontaneous.
d. None of the above statements is true.

_____ 8. It is estimated that if no contraception is used, then during the first year of being sexually active
a. few women would become pregnant.
b. about half of women would become pregnant.
c. about 85 percent of women would become pregnant.
d. about 95 percent of women would become pregnant.

_____ 9. For people with psychosexual dysfunctions, traditional forms of psychotherapy
a. have a high rate of success.
b. have a moderate rate of success.
c. have varying rate of success, with cognitive therapy being very successful.
d. have not been very successful.

_____ 10. Lew cannot satisfy himself sexually without first placing clothespins on his genitals in a sexual ritual. Lew probably has which paraphilia?
a. Sadism
b. Fetishism
c. Masochism
d. Inhibited male orgasm

_____ 11. Which of the following would be most likely say, "I have always thought I was a man even though I was born a girl. Now I just want my body to match my feelings."
a. A homosexual woman
b. A bisexual woman
c. A person with gender roles at odds with his anatomical features
d. A person with a gender identity disorder

_____ 12. Which of the following is true of incest?
a. It is universally taboo.
b. It only causes problems for females.
c. It is taboo only in Western cultures.
d. It has become less taboo as double standards have diminished.

Identifying Concepts

Answers are provided at the end of the study guide chapter.

1. **HUMAN SEXUAL RESPONSE CYCLE** Identify the sexual phase described in each item.

a. Engorgement of blood vessels and increased muscle tension

b. Explosive discharge of neuromuscular tension

c. More complete penile erection and vaginal lubrication

d. Blood vessels return to normal state

2. **SEXUALLY TRANSMITTED DISEASES** Identify the STD described in each item.

a. Caused by bacterium *Treponema pallidum*

b. Caused by HIV

c. Symptoms include small blisters on genitals

d. Most common STD

Understanding Concepts

Complete these exercises to develop your understanding of important ideas in this chapter.

1. Identify each of the four phases of the human sexual response cycle.

2. Discuss the roles of hormones in sexual arousal and describe how hormonal levels change during puberty.

3. Compare and contrast the advantages of oral contraceptives, condoms, diaphragm, vasectomy.

4. Identify the major psychosexual dysfunctions.

5. Identify the source of sexual gratification for fetishism, transvestism, exhibitionism, voyeurism, sadism, masochism, and pedophilia.

6. Desecribe transsexualism.

7. Describe six sexually transmitted diseases.

8. What are the transmission routes of AIDS?

9. What are the repercussions of rape?

10. Summarize what researchers know about pornography's effects.

Applying Concepts and Strategies

Complete these exercises to develop your ability to apply this chapter's material to your life and the world. Your responses will differ from those of other students in the class, and it is helpful to share your ideas with other students.

1. Because Masters and Johnson's research was based on observations of volunteers, do the results reflect the sexual functioning of the average person? Could the volunteers who were willing to be observed be different in their sexual functioning from most people?

2. What is the cultural impact of males being more sexually aroused by visual stimuli than are females?

3. After reading the descriptions of the Ines Beag and Mangaian cultures, describe the sexual values and behaviors at your college.

4. What do you think influences people's attitudes toward homosexuality?

5. Develop an educational program to help end the increase in sexually transmitted diseases.

6. Discuss the social effects of the AIDS epidemic. Has AIDS changed your life and your sexual choices?

7. What could be done to reduce the incidence of acquaintance rape at your college?

8. What could be done to reduce the incidence of sexual harassment at your college?

9. What characteristics of American culture might account for its very high rate of sexual violence against women and children?

10. How can erotic art and pornography be distinguished? How can researchers define pornographic material to distinguish it from art that involves nudity?

Practice Test B

Answer these multiple-choice test questions to help you assess your understanding of the textbook chapter. Answers are provided at the end of the study guide chapter.

___ 1. The excitement phase of the sexual response cycle is characterized by
a. engorgement of blood vessels and tightening of the skin.
b. surges of hormones and muscle tension.
c. surges of hormones and tightening of the skin.
d. engorgement of blood vessels and muscle tension.

___ 2. Sexual energy begins to mount and then becomes increasingly more intense during which phase of the sexual response cycle?
a. Excitement
b. Plateau
c. Orgasm
d. Resolution

___ 3. The influence of hormones on sexual behavior
a. is almost nonexistent among nonprimates.
b. becomes more important as we move from lower to higher animals.
c. becomes less important as we move from lower to higher animals.
d. is the dominant factor in humans.

___ 4. In human sexual behavior cognitions
a. play only a small role.
b. are overwhelmed by the power of sensations.
c. serve only an inhibitory function.
d. may be the most powerful aphrodisiac.

___ 5. The double standard toward sexual behavior
a. encourages men to treat women's feelings with respect.
b. encourages women to value their sexual relationships.
c. has virtually disappeared as women have moved toward social equality with men.
d. is still subscribed to by many people.

___ 6. Research on how people develop a sexual orientation shows that
a. differences in the size of the hypothalamus determine sexual orientation.
b. parenting style determines a child's sexual orientation.
c. individuals develop a homosexual orientation by varied pathways.
d. homosexual parents raise homosexual children.

___ 7. Oral contraceptives offer the advantage of
a. providing protection from sexually transmitted diseases.
b. having no harmful side effects.
c. having a high rate of effectiveness.
d. all of the above.

___ 8. An overwhelming desire to become a member of the opposite sex is characteristic of
a. homosexuals.
b. transsexuals.
c. bisexuals.
d. sexual dimorphism.

___ 9. Which of the following sexually transmitted diseases is not caused by a virus?
a. AIDS
b. Chlamydia
c. Genital herpes
d. None of the above

___ 10. Which of the following characterizes male rapists?
a. Aggression enhances their sense of power.
b. They are angry at women in general.
c. They want to hurt and humiliate the victim.
d. All of the above

___ 11. Which of following is the most common form of incest?
a. Father-daughter
b. Mother-son
c. Brother-sister
d. Same-sex

___ 12. Studies suggest that watching pornographic films in which there is no violence against women leads to
a. aggressive behavior toward women.
b. aggressive behavior toward men as well as women
c. no changes in aggressive behavior.
d. an increase in tendencies to rape.

Answers to Chapter Questions

Guided Review

1. Masters; Johnson	24. sexual arousal
2. human sexual response cycle	25. sexual orientation
3. excitement	26. homosexuals
4. erection; lubrication	27. biological cause
5. plateau	28. genetic; hormonal
6. orgasm	29. same-sex attractions
7. resolution	30. monogamy
8. androgens; estrogens	31. 75
9. estrogens	32. three-fourths
10. testosterone	33. talk about them
11. ovaries	34. temper criticism
12. sexual activity	35. spontaneous
13. postmenopausal	36. 84
14. touch; vision	37. hazards
15. pheromones	38. first year
16. aphrodisiacs	39. high; low
17. cognitions	40. sexually transmitted infections
18. Ines Beag	41. dysfunctions
19. Mangaian	42. arousal
20. sexual scripts	43. erection
21. traditional religious script	44. premature ejaculation
22. being in love	45. most
23. double standard	46. increased blood flow

47. paraphilias; satisfaction
48. fetishism
49. transvestism
50. exhibitionists; voyeurs
51. sadism; masochism
52. pedophilia
53. transsexualism
54. chlamydia; genital herpes
55. gonorrhea
56. syphilis
57. chlamydia
58. genital herpes
59. HPV
60. AIDS
61. blood
62. rape
63. shock
64. sexual dysfunctions
65. coping
66. acquaintance rape
67. harassment
68. brother; sister
69. demeans
70. sexual violence

Practice Test A
1. d
2. b
3. c
4. a
5. c
6. c
7. d

8. c
9. d
10. b
11. d
12. a

Identifying Concepts
1. HUMAN SEXUAL RESPONSE CYCLE
   a. excitement
   b. orgasm
   c. plateau
   d. resolution
2. SEXUALLY TRANSMITTED DISEASES
   a. syphilis
   b. AIDS
   c. genital herpes
   d. chlamydia

Practice Test B
1. d
2. a
3. c
4. d
5. d
6. c
7. c
8. b
9. b
10. d
11. c
12. c

CHAPTER **14**   # PSYCHOLOGICAL DISORDERS

Chapter Outline

I. UNDERSTANDING ABNORMAL BEHAVIOR

A. Defining Abnormal Behavior
Abnormal behavior is behavior that is deviant, maladaptive, or personally distressing.

B. Theoretical Approaches to Psychological Disorders
Possible causes of psychological disorders include biological, psychological, and sociocultural factors.

1. THE BIOLOGICAL APPROACH
- The biological approach examines organic, internal causes of psychological disorders.
- The medical model describes psychological disorders as medical diseases with a biological origin.

2. THE PSYCHOLOGICAL APPROACH
- Most psychologists do not believe that biological factors by themselves explain most psychological disorders.
- Psychological factors can be examined from psychodynamic, behavioral and social cognitive, and humanistic perspectives.

3. THE SOCIOCULTURAL APPROACH
- The sociocultural approach to psychological disorders emphasizes the influence of the social contexts in which a person lives.
- Many psychological disorders are universal, but their frequency and intensity vary across cultures.
- Socioeconomic status has a much stronger influence on psychological disorders than ethnicity.
- Women tend to be diagnosed with internalized disorders and men with externalized disorders.

4. AN INTERACTIONIST APPROACH: BIOPSYCHOSOCIAL
Biological, psychological, and sociocultural factors often interact to produce abnormal behavior.

C. Classifying Abnormal Behavior
The classification of mental disorders follows a medical model.

1. THE DSM-IV-TR CLASSIFICATION SYSTEM
   - DSM-IV-TR is the latest edition of the *Diagnostic and Statistical Manual of Mental Disorders (DSM)* first published in 1952 by the American Psychiatric Association.
   - DSM-IV-TR categorizes individuals on the basis of their symptoms and evaluates them in terms of five dimensions, or axes.
2. THE ISSUE OF LABELING
   - The DSM classification is criticized because it labels as psychological disorders what are often thought of as everyday problems, because it focuses on pathology, and because diagnostic labels can become self-fulfilling prophecies.
   - DSM is the most comprehensive classification system available and provides mental health professionals with a way of communicating with one another and making predictions about disorders.

II. ANXIETY DISORDERS

Anxiety disorders are psychological disorders that feature motor tension (jumpiness, trembling, inability to relax), hyperactivity (dizziness, racing heart, perspiration), and apprehensive expectations and thoughts.

A. Generalized Anxiety Disorder

Generalized anxiety disorder is an anxiety disorder characterized by persistent anxiety for at least one month; an individual with a generalized anxiety disorder is unable to specify the reasons for the anxiety.

B. Panic Disorder

- Panic disorder is a recurrent anxiety disorder marked by the sudden onset of intense apprehension or terror.
- Panic attacks often strike without warning and produce severe palpitations, extreme shortness of breath, chest pains, trembling, sweating, dizziness, and a feeling of helplessness.
- Panic attacks may be diagnosed with or without agoraphobia, a cluster of fears centered on the inability to escape or find help should one become incapacitated in a public place.

ADJUSTMENT STRATEGIES *for*

Coping with Panic*

1. Retreat.
2. Divert your attention.
3. Engage in deep-breathing relaxation and positive self-talk.

* Based on E. J. Bourne, *The Anxiety and Phobia Workbook, 3rd ed.* (Oakland, CA: New Harbinger, 2001).

C. Phobic Disorders

- A phobic disorder is an anxiety disorder in which an individual has an irrational, overwhelming, persistent fear of a particular object or situation; for example, social phobia is an intense fear of being humiliated or embarrassed in social situations.
- Possible factors in the etiology of phobic disorders include biological and psychological factors.

D. Obsessive-Compulsive Disorder

- Obsessive-compulsive disorder (OCD) is an anxiety disorder in which an individual has anxiety-provoking thoughts that will not go away (obsession) or urges to perform repetitive, ritualistic behaviors to prevent or produce a future situation (compulsion).

- Research has identified possible biological and psychological factors in the etiology of OCD.

ADJUSTMENT STRATEGIES *for*
Coping with an Anxiety Disorder
1. Understand that effective treatments are available.
2. Ask the therapist or physician about training or experience in treating anxiety disorders.
3. Expect a thorough diagnostic evaluation.
4. Recognize that the length of treatment required varies.
5. Know that if one treatment doesn't work, chances are that another will.

III. DISSOCIATIVE DISORDERS

Dissociative disorders are psychological disorders that involve a sudden loss of memory or change in identity; under extreme stress or shock, the individual's conscious awareness becomes dissociated (separated or split) from previous memories and thoughts.

A. Dissociative Amnesia and Fugue

- Dissociative amnesia is a dissociative disorder characterized by extreme memory loss caused by extensive psychological stress.
- Dissociative fugue is a dissociative disorder in which an individual not only develops amnesia but also unexpectedly travels away from home and assumes a new identity.

B. Dissociative Identity Disorder

- Dissociative identity disorder (DID), formerly called multiple personality, is a dramatic but very rare disorder in which individuals have two or more distinct personalities.
- The vast majority of individuals diagnosed with DID are adult females.
- Controversy exists about whether DID is a real condition.

IV. MOOD DISORDERS

The mood disorders are characterized by a disturbance of mood, which is a prolonged emotion that colors the individual's entire emotional state, and may involve cognitive, behavioral, and physical systems. Two main types of mood disorders are the depressive disorders and bipolar disorder.

A. Depressive Disorders

- Major depressive disorder (MDD) is a disorder in which the individual experiences significant distress or impairment of daily functioning as a result of a major depressive episode.
- According to DSM, a major depressive episode occurs when for at least two weeks an individual experiences at least five of a collection of specified symptoms (such as depressed mood most of the day, significant weight loss or gain, trouble sleeping or sleeping too much, fatigue or loss of energy, feelings of worthlessness or guilt, problems concentrating or making decisions, recurrent thoughts of death and suicide).
- Dysthymic disorder is a disorder in which the individual does not experience a major depressive episode but is in a depressed mood for most days for a prolonged period; symptoms are generally fewer but more chronic than in major depressive disorder.

B. Bipolar Disorder

- Bipolar disorder is a mood disorder characterized by extreme mood swings that include one or more episodes of mania, which is an overexcited, unrealistically optimistic state.
- Bipolar disorder is much less common than depressive disorders and is equally common among females and males.

C. Causes of Mood Disorders

1. BIOLOGICAL FACTORS
   - Links between mood disorders and biological factors are well established.
   - Bipolar disorders and, to a lesser extent, depressive disorders run in families.
   - Abnormalities found in individuals with mood disorders include abnormalities in brain activity, neuron death or disability, abnormalities in the monoamine neurotransmitters (norepinephrine, serotonin, and dopamine), and chronic hyperactivity in the neuroendocrine glandular system.

2. PSYCHOLOGICAL FACTORS
   - Modern psychodynamic theories see depressed individual as overly dependent on the approval of others as a result of childhood experiences.
   - Behavioral explanations of depressive disorders include Lewinsohn's focus on the reduction in positive reinforcers, Seligman's analysis of learned helplessness, and Nolen-Hoeksema's focus on a ruminative coping style.
   - Cognitive explanations of depressive disorders point to habitual negative thoughts and catastrophic thinking, self-blaming attributions, pessimistic cognitive styles, and depressive realism.

3. SOCIOCULTURAL FACTORS
   - Depressive disorders are found around the world, but their incidence is greater in industrialized, modernized cultures.
   - Rate of depressive disorders are elevated among those living in poverty and among certain minority groups.

- Bipolar disorders occur about equally among women and men, but women are about twice as likely as men to develop depression.

D. Suicide

- Although attempting suicide is abnormal, it is not uncommon for individuals to contemplate suicide at some point in their lives.
- Females are more likely than males to attempt suicide, but males are more likely to commit suicide.

   1. BIOLOGICAL FACTORS
      - Suicide tends to run in families
      - Suicide has been associated with low levels of serotonin and poor physical health.

   2. PSYCHOLOGICAL FACTORS

      Psychological disorders, very stressful circumstances, and substance abuse have been linked with suicide.

   3. SOCIOCULTURAL FACTORS

      The risk that someone will commit suicide rises with the loss of a loved one, a history of family instability and unhappiness, chronic economic hardship, and membership in certain ethnic groups.

ADJUSTMENT STRATEGIES *for*

Communicating with Someone Threatening Suicide

What to do:

1. Ask direct, straightforward questions in a calm manner.
2. Be a good listener and be supportive.
3. Take the suicide threat very seriously.
4. Encourage the person to get professional help and assist him or her in getting help.

What not to do:

1. Don't ignore the warning signs.
2. Don't refuse to talk about suicide if the person wants to talk about it.
3. Don't react with horror, disapproval, or repulsion.
4. Don't offer false reassurances or make judgments.
5. Don't abandon the person after this crisis seems to have passed.

III. SCHIZOPHRENIA

Schizophrenia is a severe psychological disorder characterized by highly distorted thought processes that indicate a split from reality. Individuals with schizophrenia may show odd communication, inappropriate emotion, abnormal motor behavior, and social withdrawal. Bizarre symptoms such as delusions, hallucinations, and word salad are characteristic of schizophrenia.

A. Types of Schizophrenia

Outward behavior patterns provide the basis for distinguishing four types of schizophrenia.

   1. DISORGANIZED SCHIZOPHRENIA

      Disorganized schizophrenia is a schizophrenic disorder in which an individual has delusions and hallucinations that have little or no recognizable meaning.

   2. CATATONIC SCHIZOPHRENIA

      Catatonic schizophrenia is a schizophrenic disorder characterized by bizarre motor behavior, which sometimes takes the form of a completely immobile stupor.

3. **PARANOID SCHIZOPHRENIA**

   Paranoid schizophrenia is a schizophrenic disorder characterized by delusions of reference, grandeur, and persecution.

4. **UNDIFFERENTIATED SCHIZOPHRENIA**

   Undifferentiated schizophrenia is the diagnosis given for a schizophrenic disorder that either does not meet the criteria for one of the other types or meets the criteria for more than one of the other types.

B. Causes of Schizophrenia

   1. **BIOLOGICAL FACTORS**
      - There is strong research support for biological explanations of schizophrenia.
      - Evidence that genetic factors are involved in schizophrenia is strong.
      - There is good evidence that the neurotransmitter dopamine plays a role in schizophrenia.
      - Enlarged ventricles and a small frontal cortex are associated with schizophrenia.

   2. **PSYCHOLOGICAL FACTORS**

      According to the diathesis-stress model, schizophrenia develops as a result of a biological predisposition plus stress.

   3. **SOCIOCULTURAL FACTORS**
      - The incidence of schizophrenic disorders and the types displayed may vary with culture.
      - Poor people are more likely than other people to be diagnosed with schizophrenia.

IV. PERSONALITY DISORDERS

Personality disorders are chronic, maladaptive cognitive-behavioral patterns that are thoroughly integrated into the individual's personality and are troublesome to others.

A. Odd or Eccentric Cluster

   This cluster includes paranoid, schizoid, and schizotypal personalities.

B. Dramatic or Emotionally Problematic Cluster

   This cluster includes histrionic, narcissistic, borderline, and antisocial personalities.

C. Anxious or Fearfulness Cluster

   This cluster includes avoidant, dependent, and obsessive-compulsive personalities.

Learning Goals

After reading and studying this chapter, you should be able to

1. **Discuss the characteristics and classification of abnormal behavior.**
   a. Define abnormal behavior.
   b. Outline the factors that might account for psychological disorders.
   c. Describe the *Diagnostic and Statistical Manual of Mental Disorders.*

2. **Distinguish among the various anxiety disorders.**
   a. Describe generalized anxiety disorder.
   b. Describe panic disorder.
   c. Discuss phobic disorders.
   d. Describe obsessive-compulsive disorder.

3. **Describe the dissociative disorders.**
   a. Identify the characteristics of dissociative amnesia and fugue.
   b. Discuss the characteristics of dissociative identity disorder.

4. **Compare the mood disorders and specific risk factors for depression and suicide.**
   a. Describe the depressive disorders.
   b. Describe bipolar disorder.
   c. Outline the possible causes of mood disorders.
   d. Identify factors linked to an increased risk of suicide.

5. **Identify characteristics and possible causes of schizophrenia.**
   a. Describe the main types of schizophrenia.
   b. Discuss the possible causes of schizophrenia.

6. **Identify the behavior patterns typical of personality disorders.**
   a. Describe the odd or eccentric cluster of personality disorders.
   b. Describe the dramatic or emotionally problematic cluster of personality disorders.
   c. Describe the anxious or fearful cluster of personality disorders.

Guided Review

After you have read this chapter in the textbook, complete these statements. Topics are discussed in the same order as in the chapter. Answers are provided at the end of the study guide chapter.

Learning Goal 1: Discuss the characteristics and classification of abnormal behavior

Goal 1a: Define abnormal behavior

1. Abnormal behavior is behavior that is _____, harmful, maladaptive, personally distressful.

Goal 1b: Outline the factors that might account for psychological disorders

2. The causes of abnormal behavior include biological, _____, and sociocultural factors.
3. The _____ model holds that abnormality is a disease or illness precipitated by internal physical causes.
4. Biological factors that may contribute to psychological disorders include abnormalities in the structure of the _____, imbalances in neurotransmitters or hormones, and disordered genes.
5. Psychological factors that may be involved in psychological disorders include unconscious conflicts, the _____ and _____ experienced by a person, observational learning, expectancies, self-efficacy, beliefs about oneself, and other cognitive factors.
6. The _____ approach emphasizes how culture, ethnicity, gender, age, and other sociocultural elements influence abnormal behavior.
7. Many psychological disturbances are _____, but their frequency and intensity may vary with sociocultural characteristics such as culture, socioeconomic status, and gender.
8. The _____ or biopsychosocial approach examines how biological, psychological, and sociocultural factors may interact to produce abnormal behavior.

Goal 1c: Describe the Diagnostic and Statistical Manual of Mental Disorders

9. DSM-IV-TR, published by the American Psychiatric Association, provides a classification of _____ _____ based on research and clinical experience, including more than 200 specific disorders.

10. DSM provides a system for evaluating individuals on the basis of five dimensions, or _____.

11. DSM classifies individuals based on their _____ and reflects the medical model.

12. DSM is controversial in part because it treats as disorders what are often thought of as _____ _____.

13. DSM is also criticized because it provides labels that may become _____-_____ _____.

14. Despite its problems, DSM offers the most _____ classification system available for psychological disorders.

15. Classification systems like DSM allow professionals to _____ with each other and make it possible for them to study and make _____ about a disorder.

Learning Goal 2: Distinguish among the various anxiety disorders

16. _____ _____ are psychological disorders that feature motor tension, hyperactivity, and apprehensive expectations and thoughts.

Goal 2a: Describe generalized anxiety disorder

17. _____ _____ disorder is an anxiety disorder in which a person experiences persistent anxiety for at least one month and is unable to specify the reasons for the anxiety.

Goal 2b: Describe panic disorder.

18. _____ disorder is an anxiety disorder marked by the recurrent sudden onset of intense apprehension or terror.

19. There may be a genetic predisposition to panic attacks, and individuals who experience panic disorder may have an autonomic nervous system that is predisposed to be _____ _____.

20. Panic disorder has also been linked with the occurrence of stressful life events and with _____ factors.

Goal 2c: Discuss phobic disorders

21. A _____ is an irrational, overwhelming fear of a specific object or situation.

22. _____ _____ is an intense fear of being humiliated or embarrassed in social situations.

23. Researchers have proposed a neural circuit that may operate in phobias while learning theorists argue that phobias are _____ _____.

Goal 2d.: Describe obsessive-compulsive disorder

24. _____-_____ disorder is an anxiety disorder in which the individual has anxiety-provoking thoughts that will not go away (obsessions) or urges to perform ritualistic, repetitive behaviors (compulsions).

25. The most common compulsions are excessive _____, cleaning, and counting.

26. OCD runs in families, and people who suffer from OCD tend to have distinct neurological patterns, which may be linked to depleted levels of the neurotransmitter_____.

27. The onset of OCD is often a time of _____.

Learning Goal 3: Describe the dissociative disorders

28. _____ disorders involve a sudden loss of memory or change in identity and include dissociative amnesia, dissociative fugue,and dissociative identity disorder.

Goal 3a: Identify the characteristics of dissociative amnesia and fugue

29. _____ amnesia is a dissociative disorder involving memory loss caused by extensive psychological stress.

30. People diagnosed with _____ _____ have suffered amnesia and suddenly traveled away from home and assumed a new identity.

Goal 3b: Discuss the characteristics of dissociative identity disorder

31. _____ _____ _____ is popularly known as multiple personality disorder and is the most dramatic and least common dissociative disorder.

32. People diagnosed with dissociative identity disorder exhibit two or more distinct _____, but some psychologists argue that the disorder is not a real condition but is instead created by therapists.

Learning Goal 4: Compare the mood disorders and specific risk factors for depression and suicide

Goal 4a: Describe the depressive disorders

33. People diagnosed with _____ _____ _____ have experienced a major depressive episode and experienced significant distress or impairment of daily functioning as a result.

34. In a major depressive episode people experience symptoms such as a depressed mood, _____ _____, trouble sleeping or sleeping too much, and problems thinking, concentrating, or making decisions for at least two weeks.

35. A second type of depressive disorder, _____ _____, is more chronic and has fewer symptoms than major depressive disorder.

Goal 4b: Describe bipolar disorder

36. Bipolar disorder is characterized by extreme mood swings that include one or more episodes of _____.

37. Bipolar disorder is much _____ common than depressive disorders and unlike those disorders is about equally common among females and males.

Goal 4c: Outline the possible causes of mood disorders

38. The mood disorders tend to run in families, but the family link is stronger for _____ _____ than for _____ _____.

39. The mood disorders are associated with unusual brain-wave activity during sleep, underactive areas of the brain, neuron death or disability, abnormalities in the class of neurotransmitters known as _____ _____, and hyperactivity in the neuroendocrine glandular system.

40. Freud suggested that depression is a turning inward of _____ instincts.

41. Nolen-Hoeksema suggests that depressed individuals are overly dependent on the approval of others for their self-esteem, mainly because of _____ _____.

42. Behavioral explanations of depression suggest that it is caused by inadequate positive reinforcers, _____ _____, or a ruminative coping style.

43. Cognitive explanations of depression point to the possible role of habitual negative thoughts, internal attributions, pessimistic cognitive styles, and _____ _____.

44. Sociocultural characteristics linked with an increased risk for depression include living in a _____ country, being poor, and being female.

Goal 4d: Identify factors linked to an increased risk of suicide.

45. Since the 1950s, the number of suicides in the United States has _____ threefold.

46. Suicide has been linked to low levels of the neurotransmitter _____.

47. Psychological factors linked to suicide include _____, very stressful circumstances, and substance abuse.

Learning Goal 5: Identify characteristics and possible causes of schizophrenia

48. _____ is a severe psychological disorders characterized by distorted thoughts and perceptions, odd communication, inappropriate emotion, abnormal motor behavior, and social withdrawal.

49. Bizarre symptoms associated with schizophrenia include _____, which are utterly implausible false beliefs, hallucinations, and _____ _____.

Goal 5a: Describe the main types of schizophrenia

50. _____ schizophrenia is characterized by delusions and hallucinations that have little or no recognizable meaning.

51. Catatonic schizophrenia is characterized by bizarre _____ behavior.

52. Paranoid schizophrenia is characterized by delusions of _____, grandeur, and persecution.

53. _____ schizophrenia is the classification used for schizophrenia that does not match the criteria for any of the other types or that meets the criteria for more than one of the other types.

Goal 5b: Discuss the possible causes of schizophrenia

54. There is good evidence that _____ and _____ play a role in schizophrenia.

55. _____ _____ found in the brains of some individuals with schizophrenia may be a cause or a symptom of the disorder.

56. According to the _____-_____ model, a combination of a biological predisposition and stress causes schizophrenia.

Learning 6: Identify the behavior patterns typical of personality disorders

57. Personality disorders are _____ _____ cognitive-behavioral patterns that are thoroughly integrated into an individual's personality.

Goal 6a: Describe the odd or eccentric cluster of personality disorders

58. People with a _____ personality disorder display odd thinking patterns.

59. Suspicion is a dominant characteristic of _____ personality disorder.

Goal 6b: Describe the dramatic or emotionally problematic cluster of personality disorders

60. Histrionic, narcissistic, borderline, and _____ personality disorders are classified in the dramatic or emotionally problematic cluster.

61. People with _____ personality disorder regularly violate other people's rights; they used to be called sociopaths or psychopaths.

Goal 6c: Describe the anxious or fearful cluster of personality disorders

62. The anxious or fearful cluster includes avoidant, _____, and obsessive-compulsive personality disorders.

63. _____ personality disorder resembles an anxiety disorder but is not marked by as much distress.

Key Terms

Briefly define each key term and provide an example or application.

1. abnormal behavior

2. medical model

3. DSM-IV

4. anxiety disorders

5. generalized anxiety disorder

6. panic disorder

7. agoraphobia

8. phobic disorder

9. obsessive-compulsive disorder (OCD)

10. post-traumatic stress disorder

11. dissociative disorders

12. dissociative amnesia

13. dissociative fugue

14. dissociative identity disorder (DID)

15. mood disorders

16. depressive disorders

17. major depressive disorder

18. dysthymic disorder

19. bipolar disorder

20. learned helplessness

21. schizophrenia

22. disorganized schizophrenia

23. catatonic schizophrenia

24. paranoid schizophrenia

25. undifferentiated schizophrenia

26. diathesis-stress model

27. personality disorders

Practice Test A

Answer these multiple-choice questions to assess your understanding of the chapter. Answers are provided at the end of the study guide chapter.

___ 1. Which of the following is true?
a. Abnormal behavior and normal behavior are qualitatively different.
b. Abnormal behavior is always bizarre.
c. Abnormal behavior is deviant, maladaptive, or personally distressful.
d. None of the above is true.

___ 2. Which of the following is true of psychological disorders?
a. They occur at the same rate across various cultures.
b. They occur at different rates across different cultures.
c. Their frequency is not related to gender.
d. They occur at the same rate in every socioeconomic group.

___ 3. DSM-IV-TR is a classification system based on
a. research and clinical evidence.
b. brain scans and genetic studies.
c. forensic and case studies.
d. psychoanalytic and behavioral theory.

___ 4. The five axes of DSM-IV-TR include
a. diagnostic categories of psychological disorders.
b. general medical conditions.
c. psychosocial problems
d. all of the above.

___ 5. Moira has all of her towels arranged by color and reorganizes them on a daily basis. She has also created lists of the sizes and colors of her towels and her clothes. Moira probably suffers from
a. panic disorder.
b. schizophrenia.
c. obsessive-compulsive disorder.
d. phobia disorder.

___ 6. Panic disorder may be caused by problems involving the neurotransmitters
a. norepinephrine and serotonin.
b. norepinephrine and GABA.
c. GABA and dopamine.
d. dopamine and serotonin.

___ 7. Panic attacks occur
a. more often among women than men in cultures all around the world.
b. more often among men than women in India.
c. more often among men than women in cultures all around the world.
d. at the same rate among women as among men.

___ 8. People who suffer from dissociative identity disorder are very likely to
a. have experienced sexual trauma.
b. suffer anxiety.
c. hallucinate.
d. imagine they are someone else.

___ 9. People diagnosed with bipolar disorder
a. experience less depression than those diagnosed with dysthymic disorder.
b. are usually female.
c. account for about 80 percent of the people in U.S. mental hospitals.
d. experience extreme mood swings.

___ 10. Enlarged ventricles in the brains of some individuals with schizophrenia
a. indicate that parts of the brain have atrophied.
b. cause hallucinations.
c. cause excess dopamine.
d. cause delusions of grandeur.

___ 11. The diathesis-stress model of schizophrenia is an example of what type of theory of abnormal behavior?
a. Biological
b. Sociocultural
c. Psychoanalytic
d. Interactionist

___ 12. Personality disorders are characterized by
a. hysterical reactions.
b. phobic anxiety.
c. maladaptive and inflexible traits.
d. aggressive behavior.

Identifying Concepts

Answers are provided at the end of the study guide chapter.

1. ANXIETY DISORDERS   Identify the type of anxiety disorder illustrated by each symptom.

a. Intense apprehension

b. Persistent anxiety

c. Thoughts and urges to perform rituals

d. Irrational fear of specific object

2. DISSOCIATIVE AND MOOD DISORDERS
Identify the psychological disorder illustrated by each symptom.

a. Deeply unhappy, demoralized

b. Memory loss caused by extensive psychological stress

c. Extreme mood swings

d. Two or more distinct selves

Understanding Concepts

Complete these exercises to develop your understanding of important ideas in this chapter.

1. What are the potential causes of abnormal behavior?

2. Discuss the advantages and disadvantages of having a system for classifying psychological disorders.

3. Describe DSM-IV-TR.

4. Compare and contrast generalized anxiety disorder, panic disorder, and phobic disorder.

5. What are the main features of the dissociative disorders?

6. Describe major depressive disorder and bipolar disorder.

7. State three explanations of depression.

8. Describe each of the four types of schizophrenia: disorganized, paranoid, catatonic, and undifferentiated.

9. Provide two explanations of schizophrenia.

10. What are personality disorders?

Applying Concepts and Strategies

Complete these exercises to develop your ability to apply this chapter's material to your life and the world. Your responses will differ from those of other students in the class, and it is helpful to share your ideas with other students.

1. Diagnosing someone is usually necessary for proper treatment of a disorder. Diagnosing can also lead to expectations for abnormal behavior that can worsen a person's emotional state. Do the benefits of diagnosing and labeling outweigh the potential costs?

2. Evaluate your current level of anxiety. What factors are contributing to your current anxiety? How are you handling your anxiety? Are you typically low, average, or high in anxiety?

3. Do you have fears or phobias? Do they interfere with your life? Are there any that you would like to reduce?

4. What aspects of being a college student increase your anxiety and depression? What aspects help to alleviate your anxiety and depression?

5. Suppose scientists identified a gene that predisposed people to develop schizophrenia and created a blood test to detect if people and their children were at risk. What are the advantages, disadvantages, and ethical implications of such a test?

Practice Test B

Answer these multiple-choice test questions to help you assess your understanding of the textbook chapter. Answers are provided at the end of the study guide chapter.

____ 1. Medical models of abnormal behavior emphasize
a. biological influences.
b. child-rearing practices.
c. unconscious mental processes.
d. life crises.

____ 2. Classification systems for psychological disorders have been criticized for
a. providing labels that become self-fulfilling prophecies.
b. focusing on pathology.
c. stigmatizing people.
d. all of the above.

____ 3. Charles feels his heart beating and breaks out in perspiration a few times each day for no apparent reason. Charles may suffer from
a. delusions.
b. generalized anxiety disorder.
c. schizophrenia.
d. a phobic disorder.

____ 4. Which of the following seems related to the onset of dissociative disorders?
a. Extreme stress
b. Amnesia
c. Sexual abuse
d. None of the above

____ 5. A diagnosis of major depressive disorder should be made only if a person
a. suffers significant distress.
b. has delusions.
c. has episodes of mania.
d. has suicidal thoughts.

____ 6. Dysthymic disorder differs from major depressive disorder in that the person
a. experiences manic episodes.
b. suffers a deeper depression.
c. has not experienced a major depressive episode.
d. has suffered depression for less than one year.

____ 7. During a manic episode a person
a. hears voices.
b. feels euphoric.
c. experiences hallucinations.
d. feels fatigued.

____ 8. The depressive disorders
a. tend to run in families.
b. have been linked to a specific genetic mutation.
c. appear to have no genetic component.
d. appear to have no biological component.

____ 9. Which theory states that depression is aggression turned inward?
a. Sociocultural
b. Learning
c. Cognitive
d. Psychoanalytic

____ 10. Bob exhibits bizarre motor behavior, sometimes showing a completely immobile stupor. He likely will be diagnosed as having
a. dissociative fugue.
b. disorganized schizophrenia.
c. bipolar disorder.
d. catatonic schizophrenia.

____ 11. The view that schizophrenia is caused by a combination of biological predispositions and environmental stress is expressed by
a. the medical model.
b. the diathesis-stress model.
c. the biogenic-stress model.
d. psychoanalysis.

___ 12. People with personality disorders
a. often display the disorder by the time they are adolescents or earlier.
b. usually also display bizarre behaviors associated with schizophrenia.
c. usually also display the intense fear and apprehension associated with anxiety disorders.
d. usually are not troublesome to other people.

Answers to Chapter Questions

Guided Review

1. deviant
2. psychological
3. medical
4. brain
5. rewards; punishments
6. sociocultural
7. universal
8. interactionist
9. psychological disorders
10. axes
11. symptoms
12. everyday problems
13. self-fulfilling prophecies
14. comprehensive
15. communicate; predictions
16. anxiety disorders
17. generalized anxiety
18. panic
19. overly active
20. sociocultural
21. phobia
22. social phobia
23. learned fears
24. obsessive-compulsive
25. checking
26. serotonin
27. stress
28. dissociative
29. dissociative
30. dissociative fugue
31. dissociative identity disorder
32. personalities
33. major depressive disorder
34. weight loss (*or* weight gain *or* appetite loss)
35. dysthymic disorder
36. mania
37. less
38. bipolar disorder; depressive disorders
39. monoamine neurotransmitters
40. aggressive
41. inadequate nurturing
42. learned helplessness
43. depressive realism
44. modernized
45. increased
46. serotonin
47. depression
48. schizophrenia
49. delusions; word salad
50. disorganized
51. motor
52. reference
53. undifferentiated
54. genetics; dopamine
55. structural abnormalities
56. diathesis-stress
57. chronic maladaptive
58. schizotypal
59. paranoid
60. antisocial
61. antisocial
62. dependent
63. avoidant

Practice Test A

1. c
2. b
3. a
4. d
5. c
6. b
7. b
8. a
9. d
10. a
11. d
12. c

Identifying Concepts

1. ANXIETY DISORDERS
   a. panic disorder
   b. generalized anxiety disorder
   c. obsessive-compulsive disorder
   d. phobic disorder

2. DISSOCIATIVE AND MOOD DISORDERS
   a. Depression
   b. Dissociative amnesia
   c. Bipolar disorder
   d. Dissociative identity disorder

Practice Test B
   1. a
   2. d
   3. b
   4. a
   5. a
   6. c
   7. b
   8. a
   9. d
   10. d
   11. b
   12. a

CHAPTER **15** **THERAPIES**

Chapter Outline

I. BIOLOGICAL THERAPIES

Biological therapies are treatments to reduce or eliminate the symptoms of psychological disorders by altering the way an individual's body functions. Psychologists and other mental health professional may provide psychotherapy in conjunction with the biological therapy administered by psychiatrists and other medical doctors.

A. Drug Therapy

Drugs are used mainly to treat three types of disorders: anxiety disorders, mood disorders, and schizophrenia.

1. ANTIANXIETY DRUGS

   - Commonly known as tranquilizers, antianxiety drugs reduce anxiety by making individuals calmer and less excitable.

   - Benzodiazepines are the antianxiety drugs that most often offer the greatest relief for symptoms of anxiety, but they can be addictive and have other harmful side effects.

   - BuSpar, a nonbenzodiazepine, is commonly used to treat generalized anxiety disorder.

2. ANTIDEPRESSANT DRUGS

   - Antidepressant drugs regulate mood, and there are three main classes: tricyclics, MAO inhibitors, and SSRIs.

   - The tricyclics, such as Elavil, are believed to work by increasing the level of certain neurotransmitters, especially norepinephrine and serotonin.

   - The MAO (monoamine oxidase) inhibitors, such as Nardil, are not as widely used as other antidepressants because they are more toxic.

   - The SSRIs (selective serotonin reuptake inhibitors) include Prozac, Paxil, and Zoloft and work mainly by interfering with the reabsorption of serotonin.

   - The popularity of the SSRIs is based on their effectiveness with relatively few side effects, but severe withdrawal symptoms can occur if their use is ended too abruptly.

   - At least 25 percent of individuals with major depressive disorder do not respond to any antidepressant drug.

   - Antidepressant drugs are often effective for a number of anxiety disorders.

3. LITHIUM
   - Lithium helps to reduce mood swings and is the most widely prescribed drug for bipolar disorder.
   - The amount of lithium that circulates in the bloodstream must be carefully monitored.
4. ANTIPSYCHOTIC DRUGS
   - Antipsychotic drugs diminish agitated behavior, reduce tension, decrease hallucinations, and improve social behavior and sleep patterns in individuals with a severe psychological disorder.
   - Neuroleptics, the most widely used antipsychotic drugs, are thought to block the action of the dopamine system.
   - Neuroleptics can produce the neurological disorder tardive dyskinesia as a side effect.
   - The atypical antipsychotic medications, such as Clozaril and Risperdal, block the reuptake of serotonin.
   - Drug therapy does not cure schizophrenia; symptoms reappear if medication is discontinued.

B. Electroconvulsive Therapy

- Commonly called shock therapy, electroconvulsive therapy (ECT) is used mainly to treat severely depressed individuals who have not responded to drug therapy or psychotherapy.
- ECT causes a seizure in the brain.
- ECT appears to be as effective as cognitive therapy or drug therapy but has more severe side effects than do antidepressants.

C. Psychosurgery

Psychosurgery removes or destroys brain tissue and is irreversible.

II. PSYCHOTHERAPIES

Psychotherapy is the process by which mental health professionals help individuals recognize, define, and overcome psychological and interpersonal difficulties.

A. Psychodynamic Therapies

Psychodynamic therapies stress unconscious conflicts, the role of early childhood experiences in the development of problems, and interpretation by the psychoanalyst.

1. FREUD'S PSYCHOANALYSIS
   - Psychoanalysis is Freud's method for analyzing an individual's unconscious.
   - Psychoanalysis includes techniques such as dream analysis and interpreting the free flow of words (or free associations), resistance, and transference.
   - In dream analysis psychoanalysts interpret the remembered aspects of a dream (the manifest content) to discover its unconscious symbolic aspects (latent content).
   - Resistance is any unconscious strategy to deter understanding of unconscious conflicts.
   - Transference is the process by which clients reproduce important earlier relationships in their relationship with the analyst.
2. CONTEMPORARY PSYCHODYNAMIC THERAPIES

Contemporary psychodynamic approaches still probe the client's early childhood and seek insight into repressed conflicts, but they emphasize the conscious mind, current relationships, and development of the self in social contexts.

B. Humanistic Therapies

Humanistic psychotherapies emphasize conscious thoughts, accurate perceptions of feelings, the present, and the client's self-healing capacities and potential for growth.

1. CLIENT-CENTERED THERAPY

- Client-centered therapy is a form of humanistic therapy developed by Carl Rogers in which the therapist provides a warm, supportive atmosphere to improve the client's self-concept and encourage the client to gain insight about problems.

- According to Rogers the therapist must enter into an intensely personal relationship with the client and should engage in unconditional positive regard for the client, genuineness, and active listening.

2. GESTALT THERAPY

Gestalt therapy is a humanistic therapy developed by Fritz Perls in which the therapist questions and challenges clients in order to help them become more aware of their feelings and face their problems.

C. Behavior Therapies

Behavior therapies use principles of learning to reduce or eliminate maladaptive behavior.

1. APPLICATIONS OF CLASSICAL CONDITIONING

- Systematic desensitization treats anxiety by associating deep relaxation with successive visualizations of increasingly intense anxiety-producing situations.

- Aversive conditioning repeatedly pairs an undesirable behavior with aversive stimuli.

2. APPLICATIONS OF OPERANT CONDITIONING

- In behavior modification therapists adjust reinforcements in order to replace maladaptive behaviors with adaptive ones.

- A token economy is a behavior modification system in which behaviors are reinforced with tokens that can be exchanged for rewards.

D. Cognitive Therapies

Cognitive therapies attempt to change the individual's feelings and behaviors by changing cognitions.

1. RATIONAL-EMOTIVE BEHAVIOR THERAPY

- Rational-emotive behavior therapy (REBT) is based on Albert Ellis's view that individuals become psychologically disordered because of their beliefs.

- REBT uses a direct, confrontational approach to show clients how to dispute dysfunctional beliefs and change them to realistic and logical thoughts.

2. BECK'S COGNITIVE THERAPY

Aaron Beck's cognitive therapy uses dialogue to help individuals (especially people with depression) to connect their patterns of thinking with their emotional responses and to identify their misconceptions and illogical automatic thoughts.

ADJUSTMENT STRATEGIES *Based on*

Beck's Cognitive Therapy*

1. Keep records of your thought content and emotional reactions.
2. Engage in thought stopping.
3. Examine options.
4. Question the evidence.
5. Become positively distracted.
6. Decatastrophize.
7. Fantasize consequences.
8. Turn adversity into advantage.

* Based on A. Freeman and . A. Reinecke, "Cognitive Therapy," in *Essential Psychotherapies,* ed. A. S. Gurman (New York: Guilford Press, 1995).

---

3. COGNITIVE-BEHAVIOR THERAPY

- Cognitive-behavior therapy combines techniques from cognitive therapy and behavior therapy.
- Cognitive-behavior therapy often uses self-instructional methods, which are techniques aimed at teaching individuals to modify their own behavior.

E. Therapy Integrations

Integrative therapy combines techniques from different therapies based on the therapist's judgment of which will provide the greatest benefit for the client.

III. SOCIOCULTURAL APPROACHES AND ISSUES IN TREATMENT

Sociocultural approaches to treatment view the individual as part of a social system of relationships, influenced by various social and cultural factors, and believe that these sociocultural aspects must be deal with in treatment.

A. Group Therapy

- Psychodynamic, humanistic, behavior, and cognitive therapies, as well as unique group approaches, are used in group therapy.
- Group therapy makes treatment more affordable and sees the client in the context of relationships.

B. Family and Couples Therapy

- Family therapy is group therapy with family members.
- Couple therapy is group therapy with married or unmarried couples whose major problem is their relationship.

ADJUSTMENT STRATEGIES *Based on*

Family Therapy

1. Validate each family member's feelings and beliefs.
2. Reframe problems.
3. Restructure coalitions in the family.
4. Reduce scapegoating.

C. Self-Help Support Groups

Self-help groups are voluntary organizations of individuals who meet regularly to discuss topics of common interest; meetings are led by members or by paraprofessionals, not by professional therapists.

ADJUSTMENT STRATEGIES *for*

Benefiting from Self-Help Support Groups

1. Do not rely on claims about the quality of national support groups.
2. Learn more about how self-help support groups work.
3. Find groups in your community.
4. If no group is available, consider starting one.

D. Community Mental Health

- Deinstitutionalization refers to the release of people with psychological disorders from institutions to community-based facilities.
- Primary prevention involves efforts to reduce the number of new cases of psychological disorders; secondary prevention refers to screening for early detection of problems, as well as early intervention; tertiary prevention involves efforts to treat psychological disorders.

E. Cultural Perspectives

1. ETHNICITY

An ethnic match between the therapist and the client as well as the use of ethnic-specific services may facilitate treatment.

2. GENDER

Feminist therapists believe that traditional psychotherapy is marked by gender bias and that women cannot realize their full potential unless they become aware of society's sexism.

IV. EVALUATING PSYCHOTHERAPY

A. Is Psychotherapy Effective?

- Many studies have examined the outcomes of psychotherapy; meta-analysis statistically combines the results of many studies.
- Researchers have found that the cognitive and behavior therapies can successfully treat anxiety and depressive disorders and that relaxation therapy can successfully treat anxiety disorders.
- Psychotherapy benefits most individuals with psychological problem, although benefits often diminish after the first six months of treatment.

B. Common Themes in Psychotherapy

- Effective psychotherapies inspire positive expectations, increase the client's sense of mastery and competence, and arouse the individual's emotions.
- Effective psychotherapy requires a relationship with the therapist in which the client has confidence and trust.

C. Funding Therapy

Managed care has been criticized for eliminating long-term therapy for all but the wealthy and for saving money by using less well-trained therapists.

D. Selecting a Therapist

- Psychotherapy is practiced by a variety of mental health professionals, including clinical psychologists, psychiatrists, social workers, and counselors.
- Licensing and certification of mental health professionals are handled by state governments.

ADJUSTMENT STRATEGIES *for*

Seeking Professional Help

1. Become informed about the services offered by therapists.
2. Consider which characteristics of a therapist are important to you.
3. Identify the professional's credentials.
4. Give therapy some time.
5. If your goals are not being met, consider finding a new therapist.
6. Evaluate your progress throughout therapy.

Learning Goals

After reading and studying this chapter, you should be able to

1. Describe the biological therapies.
   a. Identify the drugs most often used to treat anxiety disorders, mood disorders, and schizophrenia and discuss their effects.
   b. Discuss electroconvulsive therapy and its effects.
   c. Discuss psychosurgery.

2. Characterize four types of psychotherapies.
   a. Describe psychodynamic therapies.
   b. Discuss the humanistic therapies of Rogers and Perls.
   c. Outline behavior therapies based on classical and operant conditioning.
   d. Identify the key characteristics of REBT, Beck's cognitive therapy, and cognitive-behavior therapy.
   e. Describe integrative therapy.

3. Explain sociocultural approaches and issues in treatment.
   a. Describe group therapy.
   b. Discuss the characteristics of family and couples therapy.
   c. Outline features of self-help support groups.
   d. Describe the community mental health approach.
   e. Discuss how ethnicity and gender influence psychotherapy.

4. **Evaluate the effectiveness of therapy.**
   a. Summarize findings on the effectiveness of psychotherapy.
   b. Identify common features of effective therapy.
   c. Describe the funding of therapy and the role of managed care.
   d. Outline factors to consider in selecting a therapist.

Guided Review

After you have read this chapter in the textbook, complete these statements. Topics are discussed in the same order as in the chapter. Answers are provided at the end of the study guide chapter.

Learning Goal 1: Describe the biological therapies

1. Drug therapy is the most common form of biological therapy; much less widely used biological therapies are _____ _____ and psychosurgery.

Goal 1a: Identify the drugs most often used to treat anxiety disorders, mood disorders, and schizophrenia and discuss their effects

2. _____ are the antianxiety drugs that most often offer the greatest relief for symptoms of anxiety.
3. Frequently prescribed benzodiazepines include _____, Valium, and Librium.
4. Benzodiazepines can be _____ and can cause drowsiness, loss of coordination, fatigue, and mental slowing.
5. A nonbenzodiazepine—_____—is commonly used to treat generalized anxiety disorder.
6. _____ drugs regulate mood.
7. The three main classes of antidepressant drugs are tricyclics (such as Elavil), MAO inhibitors (such as Nardil), and _____ (such as Prozac, Paxil, and Zoloft).
8. The tricyclics are believed to work by increasing the level of certain neurotransmitters, especially _____ and _____.
9. The tricyclics reduce symptoms of depression in about 60 to 70 percent of cases and usually take _____ to _____ _____ to improve mood.
10. The MAO (monoamine oxidase) inhibitors are more _____ than the tricyclics and may interact with certain foods and drugs.
11. The SSRIs (selective serotonin reuptake inhibitors) interfere with the reabsorption of _____.
12. SSRIs can lead to insomnia, anxiety, headache, and diarrhea and can produce _____ _____ _____ if their use is ended abruptly.
13. At least _____ percent of individuals with major depressive disorder do not respond to any antidepressant drug.
14. Antidepressant drugs are often effective in treating a number of _____ _____ and are also used to treat eating disorders.
15. _____ is the most widely prescribed drug for treating bipolar disorder.
16. The effective dosage of lithium is precariously close to _____ _____.
17. _____ _____ diminish agitated behavior, reduce tension, decrease hallucinations, and improve social behavior and sleep patterns in individuals with schizophrenia.

18. The most widely used antipsychotic drugs are the _____, which are thought to block the action of the _____ system.

19. The major side effect of the neuroleptics is _____ _____.

20. As many as _____ percent of individuals with schizophrenia who take neuroleptics develop tardive dyskinesia, which produces grotesque, involuntary movements and twitching.

21. The _____ _____ medications such as Clozaril and Risperdal block the reuptake of serotonin and may reduce some of the symptoms of schizophrenia.

22. Although drug therapy allows individuals with schizophrenia to leave hospitals and return to the community, most have difficulty coping and are _____ _____.

Goal 1b: Discuss electroconvulsive therapy and its effects

23. Electroconvulsive therapy (ECT) is used mainly to treat _____ _____ individuals who have not responded to other treatments.

24. The goal of ECT is to cause a seizure in the brain much like what happens spontaneously in some forms of _____.

25. Research indicates that ECT is _____ _____ _____ cognitive or drug therapy, with a _____ to _____ relapse rate.

26. Adverse side effects of ECT include _____ _____ and other _____ _____.

27. An advantage of ECT is that its beneficial effects appear in _____.

Goal 1c: Discuss psychosurgery.

28. Psychosurgery is a biological therapy that involves the _____ or _____ of brain tissue.

29. A landmark in psychosurgery occurred in the 1930s when Egas Moniz developed a procedure known as _____ _____.

Learning Goal 2: Characterize four types of psychotherapies

Goal 2a: Describe psychodynamic therapies

30. Psychodynamic therapies emphasize the influence of the _____, the role of early childhood experiences, and extensive interpretation by the therapist.

31. Freud's technique for analyzing an individual's unconscious is called _____.

32. _____ _____ occurs when individuals say aloud whatever comes to mind.

33. The remembered aspects of a dream are its _____ content; its symbolic, unconscious aspects are its _____ content.

34. _____ refers to the client's unconscious strategies that prevent the analyst from understanding the client's problems.

35. As a result of _____, the client relates to the analyst in ways that reproduce an important earlier relationship.

36. Contemporary psychodynamic approaches emphasize the development of the _____ in social contexts.

37. According to Heinz Kohut therapy should aim to help clients to identify and seek out appropriate _____.

Goal 2b: Discuss the humanistic therapies of Rogers and Perls

38. _____ therapies emphasize conscious thoughts, the present rather than the past, and growth and fulfillment rather than curing an illness.

39. In Carl Rogers's _____-_____ therapy the therapist aims to provide a supportive atmosphere in which clients can improve their self-concept and gain insight about their problems.

40. Rogers believed that therapists should offer _____ _____ _____ for the client and take a _____ role, not leading the client to any particular revelation.

41. Fully attending to what a person says and means is called _____ _____.

42. Fritz Perls developed a humanistic therapy called _____ therapy in which the therapist questions and challenges clients to help them become more aware of their feelings and face their problems.

43. The Gestalt therapist often confronts the client and uses _____ _____ as a major technique.

Goal 2c: Outline behavior therapies based on classical and operant conditioning

44. _____ therapies use principles of learning to reduce or eliminate maladaptive behavior.

45. In the classical conditioning technique known as _____ _____, anxiety is treated by associating deep relaxation with successive visualizations of increasingly intense anxiety-producing situations.

46. _____ conditioning repeatedly pairs undesirable behavior with aversive stimuli to decrease the behavior's rewards.

47. Behavior modification is the application of _____ _____ techniques to change behavior.

48. In a _____ _____ behaviors are reinforced with tokens that can be exchanged for rewards.

Goal 2d: Identify the key characteristics of REBT, Beck's cognitive therapy, and cognitive-behavior therapy

49. _____ therapies are based on the idea that an individual's cognitions are the main source of abnormal behavior.

50. _____-_____ _____ therapy is based on the idea that irrational and self-defeating beliefs cause psychological disturbance.

51. In REBT clients are shown how to _____ their self-defeating beliefs and replace them with realistic and logical thoughts.

52. Beck's cognitive therapy is especially effective in treating _____.

53. The illogical thinking that cognitive therapy aims to correct includes the tendencies to perceive the world as harmful while ignoring evidence to the contrary, to overgeneralize, to magnify the importance of undesirable events, and to engage in _____ thinking.

54. In cognitive therapy, clients are taught to make connections between their patterns of thinking and their emotions, to identify their own _____ _____, and to challenge the accuracy of these thoughts.

55. _____-_____ therapy combines techniques from cognitive therapy and from behavior therapy to help individuals modify their thoughts and behaviors.

56. _____-_____ methods are techniques aimed at teaching individuals to modify their own behavior.

57. Cognitive-behavior therapy emphasizes the importance of _____-_____, which is the belief that one can master a situation and produce positive outcomes.

Goal 2e: Describe integrative therapy.

58. _____ _____ combines techniques from different therapies based on the therapist's judgment of which techniques will provide the greatest benefit for the client.

59. Future therapy integration is likely to include more attention to _____ and _____ factors in treating clients.

Learning Goal 3: Explain sociocultural approaches and issues in treatment

Goal 3a: Describe group therapy

60. Attractive features of group therapy include the _____ and support received from other members of the group as well as the opportunity it offers to see that other people have similar impulses and problems and to receive help in the development of _____ _____.

Goal 3b: Discuss the characteristics of family and couples therapy

61. _____ therapy is group therapy with family members, and _____ therapy is group therapy with married or unmarried couples whose major problem is their relationship.

62. Widely used techniques in family therapy include _____, _____, structural change, and triangulation.

63. In some families, one member is the _____ for other members who are in conflict but pretend not to be, and the therapist tries to disentangle, or detriangulate, this situation by shifting attention away from the scapegoat to the conflict itself.

Goal 3c: Outline features of self-help support groups

64. _____-_____ _____ groups are voluntary organizations of individuals who meet regularly to discuss topics of common interest.

65. Self-help groups are led by a _____ or member of the group, not by a professional therapist.

66. Self-help groups provide members with social support, _____ _____, and concrete strategies for problem solving.

Goal 3d: Describe the community mental health approach

67. _____ transferred people from inpatient mental institutions to community-based facilities.

68. _____ prevention involves efforts to reduce the number of new cases of psychological disorders.

69. _____ prevention involves screening for early detection of problems.

70. _____ prevention involves efforts to reduce the long-term consequences of psychological disorders.

Goal 3e: Discuss how ethnicity and gender influence psychotherapy

71. Researchers have found that clients are less likely to drop out of therapy and often have better outcomes when there is an _____ _____ between the therapist and the client and when ethnic-specific services are provided.

72. Feminist therapists believe that clients cannot realize their full potential unless they are aware of society's _____.

Learning Goal 4: Evaluate the effectiveness of therapy

Goal 4a: Summarize findings on the effectiveness of psychotherapy

73. Unlike later studies, a 1952 study by _____ found that psychotherapy was ineffective.

74. Using _____-_____, a researcher statistically combines the results of many studies.

75. The control group in studies of the effectiveness of psychotherapy often consists of a _____-_____ control group, which is made up of individuals who are waiting to see a psychotherapist.

76. Studies of the effectiveness of psychotherapy indicate that _____ and _____ therapies have been successful in treating anxiety disorders and depressive disorders; _____ _____ has also been successful in treating anxiety disorders.

Goal 4b: Identify common features of effective therapy

77. Jerome Frank concluded that effective psychotherapies inspire _____ _____, increase the client's sense of _____ and competence, and arouse the individual's emotions.

78. The therapeutic _____ is an essential ingredient in successful psychotherapy.

Goal 4c: Describe the funding of therapy and the role of managed care

79. _____ _____ organizations have been criticized for being reluctant to provide for more than a few therapy sessions per patient and for eliminating long-term therapy for all but the wealthy.

Goal 4d: Outline factors to consider in selecting a therapist

80. _____ _____, psychiatrists, social workers, and counselors all offer treatment for psychological disorders.

81. The various types of mental health professionals differ in their _____ and their approach to therapy.

82. Laws at the state level are used to _____ or certify mental health professionals.

83. Ethical codes for mental health professionals typically focus on the importance of doing no harm to clients, protecting their _____, and avoiding inappropriate relationships with them.

Key Terms

Briefly define each key term and provide an example or application.

1. biological therapies

2. psychotherapy

3. antianxiety drugs

4. antidepressant drugs

5. lithium

6. antipsychotic drugs

7. electroconvulsive therapy (ECT)

8. psychosurgery

9. psychodynamic therapies

10. psychoanalysis

11. free association

12. catharsis

13. dream analysis

14. transference

15. resistance

16. insight therapy

17. humanistic therapies

18. client-centered therapy

19. gestalt therapy

20. behavior therapy

21. systematic desensitization

22. aversive conditioning

23. behavior modification

24. cognitive therapies

25. rational-emotive behavior therapy

26. cognitive-behavior therapy

27. integrative therapy

28. family therapy

29. couples therapy

30. meta-analysis

Practice Test A

Answer these multiple-choice questions to assess your understanding of the chapter. Answers are provided at the end of the study guide chapter.

____ 1. Xanax, Valium, and Librium are
a. antidepressant drugs.
b. tricyclics.
c. benzodiazepines.
d. neuroleptics.

___ 2. Antidepressant drugs usually
a. improve mood immediately.
b. improve mood in a matter of days.
c. improve mood within a few weeks.
d. improve mood within a few months.

___ 3. Medications that diminish agitated behavior, reduce psychotic thinking, and improve social functioning are
a. neuroleptics.
b. MAO inhibitors.
c. tricyclics.
d. lithium.

___ 4. Contemporary ECT
a. is given without anesthesia.
b. is effective but has adverse side effects.
c. is less effective than antidepressants.
d. is less effective than cognitive therapy.

___ 5. The importance of unconscious conflicts
a. is at the core of all psychotherapy.
b. is emphasized by behavior therapists.
c. is emphasized by psychoanalysts.
d. is at the core of Rogers's therapy.

___ 6. Insight therapies
a. include psychoanalysis and humanistic therapies.
b. include behavior therapy and cognitive therapy.
c. highlight the importance of behavior modification.
d. are ideal tools for people working in community mental health.

___ 7. In Rogers's view the role of the therapist is
a. to correct absolutist thinking.
b. to offer reinforcement only for adaptive behavior.
c. to force the client to face conflicts.
d. to listen sympathetically and encourage positive self-regard.

___ 8. Systematic desensitization
a. applies the principles of classical conditioning to treat anxiety.
b. applies the principles of operant conditioning.
c. applies Bandura's idea about self-efficacy.
d. uses tokens to modify behavior.

___ 9. Homework assignments in which people engage in new self-talk and experience the effects of not viewing life in a catastrophic way are part of
a. token economies.
b. contemporary psychodynamic therapy.
c. REBT.
d. ECT.

____ 10. Cognitive-behavior therapists
a. give clients examples of reinforcing self-statements.
b. emphasize the importance of interpreting transference.
c. emphasize dream analysis.
d. do none of the above.

____ 11. Adjustment strategies for benefiting from self-help groups include
a. evaluating a group by checking the quality of the national group.
b. being sure that a group is led by a mental health professional.
c. going to a self-help group only after consulting a therapist.
d. none of the above.

____ 12. In studies of the effectiveness of psychotherapy, individuals in control and placebo groups who have not received treatment
a. never improve.
b. do as well as those receiving treatment.
c. show improvement but at lower rates than those who receive treatment.
d. usually show significant deterioration in their condition.

Identifying Concepts

Answers are provided at the end of the study guide chapter.

1. DRUG THERAPIES   Identify the drug described by each statement.

a. Antidepressants that work mainly by interfering with the reabsorption of serotonin

b. Fast-acting tranquilizers that bind to the receptor sites of certain neurotransmitters

c. Reduces mood swings

d. Most widely used class of antipsychotic drugs

2. PSYCHOTHERAPIES   Identify the therapy or technique described by each statement.

a. The therapist provides a warm, supportive atmosphere.

b. The therapist believes client's current problems can be traced to childhood experiences.

c. The therapist uses successive visualizations of increasingly intense anxiety-producing situations.

d. The therapist reinforces desired behaviors with tokens that can be exchanged for rewards.

e. The therapist helps the client to understand the connection between automatic thoughts and emotional reactions.

Understanding Concepts

Complete these exercises to develop your understanding of important ideas in this chapter.

1. Compare and contrast the main types of antidepressant drugs.

2. What are the advantages and disadvantages of neuroleptics?

3. Describe the roles that electroconvulsive therapy and psychosurgery have played in the treatment of psychological disorders.

4. Describe free association, dream analysis, transference, and resistance and their role in psychoanalysis.

5. Compare and contrast conditional positive regard and unconditional positive regard. How does each affect our self-esteem and happiness?

6. Describe two techniques that are based on conditioning.

7. What are the major features of Beck's cognitive therapy?

8. Describe the advantages of group therapy.

9. Differentiate among primary, secondary, and tertiary prevention in community mental health.

10. Summarize research findings about the effectiveness of psychotherapy.

Applying Concepts and Strategies

Complete these exercises to develop your ability to apply this chapter's material to your life and the world. Your responses will differ from those of other students in the class, and it is helpful to share your ideas with other students.

1. How would you evaluate the use of drug therapy to treat depression, anxiety disorders, and schizophrenia?

2. How can a psychoanalyst know more about clients than the clients themselves? Is it possible for psychoanalysts to confirm that their interpretations are correct?

3. Choose a specific situation (for example, taking a test, giving a speech) that increases your anxiety. Develop a 10- to 15-item hierarchy of things associated with your anxiety that could be used as a basis for systematic desensitization.

4. What ethical concerns are raised by use of aversive conditioning?

5. Design a behavior modification program to change one of your behaviors (e.g., improve your study skills, watch less television).

6. Do behavior therapists address problems or just scratch the surface, never really getting to the root of the problem?

7. Complete and interpret Self-Assessment 15.1: Do I Have Irrational Beliefs? What are some of your basic irrational beliefs? How do they affect your life as a college student? How would you dispute one of these beliefs?

8. If you were to enter psychotherapy, would you prefer an insight therapy, a behavior therapy, or a cognitive therapy? Why?

9. Suppose you were designing a health insurance plan or a national health program. Would you include psychological counseling? Would you provide coverage for individual and group therapy? Why or why not?

10. Do you think that both autonomy and relatedness are major goals of therapy? Why or why not?

Practice Test B

Answer these multiple-choice test questions to help you assess your understanding of the textbook chapter. Answers are provided at the end of the study guide chapter.

____ 1. Benzodiazepines are antianxiety drugs that can
a. be linked to birth defects.
b. be addicting.
c. lead to depression when combined with antihistamines.
d. do all of the above.

____ 2. Prozac and other SSRIs are
a. extremely toxic though effective.
b. effective and have relatively few side effects.
c. effective and have no significant side effects.
d. all of the above.

____ 3. The neuroleptics are thought to
a. block the reabsorption of serotonin.
b. increase the levels of serotonin.
c. block the action of the dopamine system.
d. block the effect of norepinephrine.

____ 4. The procedure known as prefrontal lobotomy
a. was less precise than today's psychosurgery.
b. is offered today with muscle relaxants.
c. is typically used as a last resort for depressed clients.
d. was rarely used until the 1960s.

____ 5. Psychoanalysts who follow Freud's techniques
a. emphasize the importance of a supportive atmosphere.
b. take a nondirective role with clients.
c. use thought stopping.
d. analyze resistance and transference.

____ 6. Heinz Kohut's view of therapy
a. represents a complete rejection of Freud.
b. shares with humanistic therapists an emphasis on empathy and understanding.
c. emphasizes personal autonomy above all.
d. emphasizes role playing.

____ 7. Action-oriented strategies are at the heart of
a. the therapy offered by Kohut.
b. behavior therapies.
c. contemporary psychoanalysis
d. none of the above.

____ 8. Peter Lewinsohn's approach to depression
a. teaches people how to use thought stopping.
b. teaches individuals to increase the ratio of positive life events to negative life events.
c. challenges a client's self-defeating beliefs.
d. teaches individuals to dispute their irrational thoughts.

____ 9. Adjustment strategies based on Beck's cognitive therapy include
a. keeping records of your thoughts and emotional reactions.
b. engaging in thought stopping.
c. finding positive distractions from negative thoughts or feelings.
d. all of the above.

____ 10. Treating individuals with both psychotherapy and drug therapy
a. represents a waste of scarce medical resources.
b. has been shown to be ineffective.
c. is an example of therapy integrations.
d. conflicts with the biopsychosocial model of abnormal behavior.

____ 11. Self-help support groups
a. do more harm than good.
b. include more than 10 million American participants.
c. are usually led by mental health professionals.
d. are characterized by all of the above.

___ 12. Jerome Frank found that effective psychotherapies
a. share only one element: a talented therapist.
b. develop positive expectations, a sense of mastery, and emotional arousal in their clients.
c. develop realism and fatalism in their clients.
d. share only one element: young and educated clients.

Answers to Chapter Questions

Guided Review

1. electroconvulsive therapy
2. benzodiazepines
3. Xanax
4. addicting
5. BuSpar
6. antidepressant
7. SSRIs
8. norepinephrine; serotonin
9. 2; 4 weeks
10. toxic
11. serotonin
12. severe withdrawal symptoms
13. 25
14. anxiety disorders
15. lithium
16. toxic levels
17. antipsychotic drugs
18. neuroleptics; dopamine
19. tardive dyskinesia
20. 20
21. atypical antipsychotic
22. chronically unemployed
23. severely depressed
24. epilepsy
25. as effective as; moderate; high
26. memory loss; cognitive impairments
27. days
28. removal; destruction
29. prefrontal lobotomy
30. unconscious
31. psychoanalysis
32. free association
33. manifest; latent
34. resistance
35. transference
36. self
37. relationships
38. humanistic
39. client-centered
40. unconditional positive regard; nondirective
41. active listening
42. Gestalt
43. role playing
44. behavior
45. systematic desensitization
46. aversive
47. operant conditioning
48. token economy
49. cognitive
50. rational-emotive behavior
51. dispute
52. depression
53. absolutist
54. automatic thoughts
55. cognitive-behavior
56. self-instructional
57. self-efficacy
58. integrative therapy
59. ethnic; cultural
60. information; social skills
61. family; couples
62. validation; framing
63. scapegoat
64. self-help support
65. paraprofessional
66. role modeling
67. deinstitutionalization
68. primary
69. secondary
70. tertiary
71. ethnic match
72. sexism
73. Eysenck
74. meta-analysis
75. wait-list
76. cognitive; behavior; relaxation therapy
77. positive expectations; mastery
78. relationship
79. managed care
80. clinical psychologists
81. training
82. license
83. privacy

Practice Test A

1. c
2. c
3. a
4. b
5. c
6. a
7. d
8. a
9. c
10. a
11. d
12. c

Identifying Concepts

1. DRUG THERAPIES
   a. SSRIs
   b. benzodiazepines
   c. lithium
   d. neuroleptics

2. PSYCHOTHERAPIES
   a. client-centered therapy
   b. psychoanalysis
   c. systematic desensitization
   d. token economy
   e. cognitive therapy

Practice Test B

1. d
2. b
3. c
4. a
5. d
6. b
7. b
8. b
9. d
10. c
11. b
12. b

CHAPTER **16**   # HEALTH

Chapter Outline

I. EXPLORING HEALTH AND ILLNESS

A. The Biopsychosocial Model of Health
- Seven of the ten leading causes of death in the United States today are related to personal habits and life styles.
- The biopsychosocial health model states that health is best understood in terms of a combination of biological, psychological, and social factors.

B. Psychological Factors in Health and Illness
- Among the psychological factors proposed as causes of health problems are lack of self-control, emotional turmoil, and negative thinking.
- Positive emotional states are linked with healthy physiological functioning.

C. Social Factors in Health and Illness
- Most health problems are found in most cultures, but the frequency and intensity of problems vary across cultures.
- Social factors that influence health problems include socioeconomic status and poverty.
- Prejudice and discrimination against certain minorities are the historical underpinnings for the fact that those minorities are disproportionately represented in the ranks of the poor.

II. NUTRITION AND EATING

A. Nutrition and Eating Behavior
1. THE FOOD GUIDE PYRAMID

   The Food Guide Pyramid consists of recommended daily servings of different types of food; changes in the pyramid are expected in 2005.

2. CULTURAL VARIATIONS
   - Cross-cultural as well as animal studies provide evidence of the negative effects of poor nutritional choices.
   - Many researchers believe that the high fat intake of Americans and the low fat intake of the Japanese are implicated in differences between the countries in the rates of certain types of cancer.

3. EATING AND LONGEVITY
   - There is considerable evidence that restricting caloric intake can lengthen the lives of animals in the laboratory; research on the effect of calorie restriction on humans is planned.
   - Leaner men do live longer, healthier lives than heavier men.
   - One theory holds that antioxidants (which include vitamin C, vitamin E, and beta-carotene) counteract the cell damage caused by free radicals, which are produced by the body's metabolism and by environmental factors.
   - Researchers are studying whether antioxidants help slow the aging process and improve the health of older adults.

B. **Eating Problems**

1. OBESITY
   - According to 2004 statistics, more than 60 percent of U.S. adults are overweight or obese.
   - Obesity is linked to increased risk for hypertension, diabetes, and cardiovascular disease.
   - Body mass index, a measure of weight in relation to height, is used to determine whether an individual is a healthy weight.
   - Factors that appear to be involved in obesity include heredity, leptin (a protein released by fat cells that signals satiety), set point (the weight maintained when no effort is made to gain or lose weight), basal metabolism rate (BMR, the minimal amount of energy an individual uses in a resting state), environmental factors, and ethnicity and gender.

2. DIETING
   - Restrained eaters are individuals who chronically restrict their food intake to control their weight.
   - Although many Americans regularly embark on a diet, few are successful in keeping weight off long-term.
   - The most effective weight-loss programs include exercise, which burns up calories and raises the metabolic rate.
   - Recurring cycles of dieting and weight gain are risky: researchers have found links between frequent changes in weight and chronic disease.

- When overweight people do lose weight, they become less depressed and lower their risk for a number of health-impairing disorders.

ADJUSTMENT STRATEGIES *for*

Losing Weight*

1. Exercise regularly.
2. Keep a food diary.
3. Shop from a list and don't shop when you are hungry.
4. Minimize your exposure to food cues.
5. Use a smaller plate with smaller servings.
6. Eat at the table with the TV off.
7. At restaurants, eat only half of your meal and take the rest home.
8. Don't starve yourself all day and then eat one big meal in the evening.
9. Seek support from family and friends.
10. Be realistic about weight-loss goals.

* Based on National Institute of Diabetes & Digestive & Kidney Diseases, *Better Health and You* (Washington, D.C.: National Institute of Diabetes & Digestive & Kidney Diseases, 2003).

---

3. ANOREXIA NERVOSA
   - Anorexia nervosa is an eating disorder that involves the relentless pursuit of thinness through starvation; it can be fatal.
   - Anorexia nervosa typically begins in the early to middle teenage years, and it is about ten times more likely to occur among females than among males.
   - Anorexia nervosa has been linked to a person's tendency to set high standards and to see weight as the one thing that he or she can control.

4. BULIMIA NERVOSA
   - Bulimia nervosa is an eating disorder in which the individual keeps binging and then purging.
   - Unlike anorexics, people who binge and purge typically fall within a normal weight range, which makes bulimia more difficult to detect.
   - Bulimia nervosa typically begins in late adolescence or early adulthood; about 90 of the cases are female.
   - About 70 percent of people who display anorexia or bulimia eventually recover.

III. EXERCISE

A. The Benefits of Exercise
- Aerobic exercise is sustained exercise that stimulates the heart and lung activity.
- Exercise helps prevent heart disease and also benefits mental health.
- Both moderate and intense activities bring physical and psychological benefits.

B. Exercise and Longevity
- Regular exercise can lead to a healthier life in middle age and late adulthood and can increase longevity.
- Gerontologists recommend strength training in addition to aerobic activity and stretching for older adults.

- A recent review of research on exercise and aging concluded that exercise can influence physiological changes in brain tissue and optimize body composition; that exercise is related to the prevention of common chronic diseases and to improvement in the treatment of many diseases; that exercise is related to the prevention of disability and can facilitate the treatment of disability; and that exercise is linked to increased longevity.

ADJUSTMENT STRATEGIES *for*

Exercising Regularly

1. Consult with your doctor and get a physical examination.
2. Make exercise a high priority in your life.
3. Reduce TV time.
4. Chart your progress.
5. Get rid of excuses.
6. Learn more about exercise.

IV. DRUGS AND ADDICTION

Psychoactive drugs are substances that act on the nervous system to alter consciousness, modify perceptions, and change moods.

A. Psychoactive Drugs

Psychoactive drugs have been classified as depressants, stimulants, and hallucinogens.

B. Addiction

- Psychological addiction exists when a person is preoccupied with obtaining a drug for emotional reasons.
- Physical addiction exists when discontinuing use of a drug creates unpleasant, significant changes in physical functioning and behavior; these changes are called withdrawal symptoms.
- The disease model of addiction describes addiction as a biologically based, life-long disease that involves a loss of control over behavior and requires medical or spiritual treatment for recovery.
- The life-process model of addiction holds that addiction is a habitual response and source of gratification or security that can be understood best in the context of social relationships and experiences.

C. Alcohol

- Alcohol acts primarily as a depressant, slowing down the brain's activities.
- Activities that require decision making and motor skills become increasingly impaired as more alcohol is consumed.
- With extreme intoxication, a person may lapse into a coma and die.
- Effects of alcohol vary with the way the person's body metabolizes alcohol, body weight, amount consumed, and whether previous drinking created tolerance.
- Alcoholism is the third leading killer in the United States.

  1. DRINKING AMONG COLLEGE STUDENTS AND YOUNG ADULTS
     - Binge drinking often increases in college and is linked to missed classes, physical injuries, and drunk driving.
     - Chronic binge drinking is more common among college men than women.
     - By the time individuals reach their mid-20s, many have reduced their use of alcohol.

2. CULTURAL VARIATIONS

   Alcohol consumption varies with gender, religion, and nationality.

3. ALCOHOLISM

   - Alcoholism is a disorder that involves long-term, repeated, uncontrolled, compulsive, and excessive use of alcoholic beverages and that impairs the drinker's health and social relationships.
   - About one third of alcoholics recover whether they are in a treatment program or not.
   - The likelihood that people will recover from alcoholism increases if they have a strong negative experience related to alcohol, find a substitute dependency, have new social supports, or join an inspirational group.

ADJUSTMENT STRATEGIES *for*

Curbing Alcohol Use

1. Admit that you have a problem.
2. Write your reasons for cutting down or eliminating your drinking.
3. Set a drinking goal and keep a drinking diary.
4. Don't ignore what others are saying to you.
5. Don't go out with people who make you feel uncomfortable if you are not drinking.
6. Don't keep beer, wine, or hard liquor at home.
7. Seek help for your problem.
8. Use the resources in the textbook and at the Online Learning Center.

D. Smoking

- The prevalence of smoking has decreased in the United States in recent decades.
- Nicotine, the active drug in cigarettes, is a stimulant that increases the smoker's energy and alertness and stimulates neurotransmitters that have a calming or pain-reducing effect.

ADJUSTMENT STRATEGIES *for*

Quitting Smoking

1. Develop a strong self-motivation to quit.
2. Use a substitute source of nicotine.
3. Take the antidepressant Zyban.
4. Control the stimuli associated with smoking.
5. Undergo aversive conditioning.
6. Go cold turkey.
7. Stay smoke free.

V. THE PATIENT AND THE HEALTH CARE SETTING

A. Recognizing and Interpreting Symptoms

- When our attention is directed outward, we are less likely to detect symptoms than when attention is directed inward.
- We use schemas to interpret information about ourselves and our world, including symptoms.

B. Seeking Treatment

Whether we seek treatment depends on our perception of the severity of symptoms and of the likelihood that medical treatment will relieve or eliminate them.

C. The Patient's Role

- People who take on the "good patient role" are passive and unquestioning and behave properly.
- People who take on the "bad patient role" complain, demand attention, disobey staff orders, and generally misbehave.
- Realistic expectations about hospitalization, predictable events, and social support reduce the stress of hospitalization.

D. Adherence to Medical Advice and Treatment

An estimated one-third of patients fails to follow recommended treatments.

E. Socioeconomic Status and Ethnicity

- Individuals with low socioeconomic status use medical services less than other individuals.
- There are not as many medical services for the poor as for others.
- There are also cultural barriers to health care, such as language differences and differing belief systems.

F. Gender

- Women and men experience health and the health-care system differently.
- Gender differences exist in the health-care professions, in medical research, in how medical services are provided, and in how the health-care system is used.

Learning Goals

After reading and studying this chapter, you should be able to

1. **Describe some key factors in health and illness.**
   a. Define the biopsychosocial model of health.
   b. Outline psychological influences on health.
   c. Outline social influences on health.

2. **Discuss nutrition, eating behavior, and eating problems.**
   a. Discuss the food guide pyramid, cultural variations in eating behavior, and links between nutrition and longevity.
   b. Discuss obesity, dieting, anorexia nervosa, and bulimia nervosa.

3. **Summarize the role of exercise in health.**
   a. Outline the benefits of exercise.
   b. Discuss the connection between exercise and longevity.

4. **Explain drug use and addiction.**
   a. Discuss psychoactive drugs and how they are classified.
   b. Explain addiction and describe two models of addiction.
   c. Discuss the use of alcohol and alcoholism.
   d. Discuss smoking and efforts to quit smoking.

5. **Characterize some important aspects of health care.**
   a. Discuss how people recognize and interpret symptoms.
   b. Outline factors that influence whether people seek treatment.
   c. Describe the role of the hospitalized patient.
   d. Discuss adherence to medical advice and treatment.
   e. Outline the influence of socioeconomic status and ethnicity on health care.
   f. Outline the relationships between gender and health care.

Guided Review

After you have read this chapter in the textbook, complete these statements. Topics are discussed in the same order as in the chapter. Answers are provided at the end of the study guide chapter.

Learning Goal 1: Describe some key factors in health and illness

Goal 1a: Define the biopsychosocial model of health

1. Today, seven of the ten leading causes of death in the United States are related to personal _____ and life styles.

2. The contemporary view is that _____ and _____ can exert important influences on health.

3. The biopsychosocial health model states that health is best understood in terms of a combination of biological, psychological, and _____ factors.

Goal 1b: Outline psychological influences on health

4. Factors that may cause health problems include lack of self-control, emotional turmoil, and

   _____ _____.

5. Hostility and chronic _____ _____ are linked with cardiovascular problems.

6. Positive emotional states are linked with healthy functioning in both the cardiovascular system and the _____ system.

Goal 1c: Outline social influences on health

7. Most health problems are found in most cultures, but the _____ and _____ of problems vary across cultures.

8. Social factors that influence health problems include socioeconomic status, _____, prejudice, and discrimination.

9. Social factors can influence health through their effects on the frequency of _____ in daily life and through life styles.

Learning Goal 2: Discuss nutrition, eating behavior, and eating problems

Goal 2a: Discuss the food guide pyramid, cultural variations in eating behavior, and links between nutrition and longevity

10. The _____ _____ _____ consists of recommended daily servings of food, but changes in the current version are planned.

11. A good strategy for eating in healthier ways is to substitute plenty of _____,

    _____, and grain products for unhealthy foods.

12. Cancers of the breast, colon, and prostate are _____ in the United States but _____ in Japan.

13. Animals fed diets restricted in _____ but adequate in protein, vitamins, and minerals live as much as 40 percent longer than animals given unlimited access to food.

14. Some scientists believe calorie restriction might lower the level of _____ _____ or potentially toxic particles created by the breakdown of food.

15. Leaner men live _____ lives.

16. Recent research suggests the possibility that _____—which include vitamin C, vitamin E, and beta-carotene—help slow the aging process and improve the health of older adults.

17. It is thought that antioxidants might counteract the cell damage caused by _____ _____.

Goal 2b: Discuss obesity, dieting, anorexia nervosa, and bulimia nervosa

18. Obesity is linked to increased risk of _____, _____, and _____ disease.

19. _____ _____ _____, a measure of weight in relation to height, is used to determine whether an individual is underweight, a healthy weight, overweight, or obese.

20. Individuals can inherit a tendency to be _____.

21. _____ is a protein released by fat cells that results in decreased food intake and increased energy expenditure.

22. _____ _____ is the weight maintained when no effort is made to gain or lose weight.

23. _____ _____ _____ is the minimal amount of energy an individual uses in a resting state.

24. BMR varies with _____ and _____.

25. _____ declines precipitously during adolescence and then more gradually in adulthood.

26. Strong evidence of the influence of the _____ on weight comes from the doubling of the rate of obesity in the United States since 1900.

27. _____ _____ chronically restrict their food intake to control their weight.

28. When restrained eaters stop dieting, they tend to _____.

29. _____ Americans who diet are successful in keeping weight off long-term.

30. Most effective programs for losing weight include _____.

31. Researchers have linked frequent changes in weight and _____ _____.

32. When overweight people do lose weight and maintain their weight loss, they become less _____ and reduce their risk for a number of health-impairing disorders.

33. _____ _____ is an eating disorder that involves the relentless pursuit of thinness through starvation.

34. People with anorexia nervosa weigh less than 85 percent of normal weight, have an intense fear of gaining weight, and have a _____ _____ of their body shape.

35. Anorexia nervosa typically begins in the early to middle teenage years and is about ten times more common among _____ than among _____.

36. Most anorexics are _____-_____.

37. _____ _____ is an eating disorder in which the individual consistently follows a binge-and-purge pattern.

38. Most bulimics are preoccupied with _____, have a strong fear of being overweight, and are depressed or anxious.

39. Unlike anorexics, people who binge-and-purge typically are a _____ _____.

Learning Goal 3: Summarize the role of exercise in health

Goal 3a: Outline the benefits of exercise

40. _____ exercise is sustained exercise that stimulates heart and lung activity.

41. Exercise helps to prevent _____ _____, improves self-concept, and reduces anxiety and depression.

Goal 3b: Discuss the connection between exercise and longevity

42. Regular exercise can increase _____.

43. A recent review concluded that exercise influences physiological changes in the _____ that are associated with aging, can increase _____ and _____ mass, and can reduce the risk of common chronic diseases, among other benefits.

Learning Goal 4: Explain drug use and addiction

Goal 4a: Discuss psychoactive drugs and how they are classified

44. _____ _____ are substances that act on the nervous system to alter states of consciousness, modify perceptions, and change mood.

45. Psychoactive drugs have been classified into three main categories: _____, _____, and hallucinogens.

46. _____ slow down the central nervous system, body functions, and behavior.

47. _____ are drugs that modify an individual's perceptual experiences and can produce hallucinations; LSD, marijuana, and Ecstasy are examples.

Goal 4b: Explain addiction and describe two models of addiction

48. _____ dependence exists when a person is preoccupied with obtaining a drug for emotional reasons.

49. _____ dependence exists when discontinuing use of a drug creates withdrawal symptoms — unpleasant, significant changes in physical functioning and behavior.

50. The _____ _____ of addiction describes addictions as biologically based, life-long diseases that involve a loss of control over behavior and require medical or spiritual treatment for recovery.

51. The _____-_____ model of addiction describes addictions as habitual responses and sources of gratification or security that can be understood best in the context of social relationships and experiences.

Goal 4c: Discuss the use of alcohol and alcoholism

52. Alcohol primarily acts on the body as a _____.

53. As people drink more, their _____ decrease; extreme intoxication may lead to death.

54. Effects of alcohol vary with how the person's body metabolizes alcohol, body weight, amount consumed, and whether previous drinking has led to _____.

55. _____ is a disorder that involves long-term, repeated, uncontrolled, compulsive, and excessive use of alcoholic beverages that impairs the drinker's health and social relationships.

56. Both _____ and environmental factors play a role in alcoholism.

57. About _____-_____ of alcoholics recover whether they are in a treatment program or not.

Goal 4d: Discuss smoking and efforts to quit smoking

58. Smoking is linked to deaths from _____, _____ _____, and chronic pulmonary disease.

59. _____, the active ingredient in cigarettes, is a _____ that increases the smoker's energy and alertness and stimulates neurotransmitters that have a calming or pain-killing effect.

60. Methods for quitting smoking include using a _____ _____ of nicotine, undergoing _____ _____, and simply stopping.

Learning Goal 5: Characterize some important aspects of health care

Goal 5a: Discuss how people recognize and interpret symptoms

61. People are better at recognizing the symptoms of illness that they are _____ with.

62. _____ influence how we perceive and interpret symptoms.

63. When people direct their attention outward, they are _____ likely to notice symptoms than when they direct their attention inward.

Goal 5b: Outline factors that influence whether people seek treatment

64. Whether people seek treatment for symptoms depends on their perception of the _____ of the symptoms and of the likelihood that medical treatment will help.

65. Confidence in medical treatment may encourage _____ _____ of medical intervention.

Goal 5c: Describe the role of the hospitalized patient

66. Hospitalized people may take on the role of _____ _____ or _____ _____.

67. The stress of hospitalization can be reduced by _____ _____, predictable events, and social support.

Goal 5d: Discuss adherence to medical advice and treatment

68. An estimated _____-_____ of patients fail to follow recommended treatments.

69. Failure to follow recommended treatment sometimes reflects lack of trust in the doctor's advice, and that mistrust can be exacerbated when doctors use overly _____ _____.

Goal 5e: Outline the influence of socioeconomic status and ethnicity on health care

70. Individuals from low socioeconomic status use medical services _____ than other individuals.

71. Health services for the poor in the United States are often _____.

72. Cultural barriers to adequate health care include inadequate resources, language differences, and differing _____ _____ about the causes and appropriate treatments for disease.

Goal 5f: Outline the relationships between gender and health care

73. The women's movement of the 1960s and 1970s gave women _____ _____ over their health care.

74. In the past most medical research was conducted with _____ and then generalized without justification.

75. Men are _____ likely than women to go to a doctor when they have an illness.

Key Terms

Briefly define each key term and provide an example or application.

1. biopsychosocial health model

2. leptin

3. basal metabolism rate (BMR)

4. restrained eaters

5. anorexia nervosa

6. bulimia nervosa

7. aerobic exercise

8. psychoactive drugs

9. depressants

10. stimulants

11. hallucinogens

12. psychological dependence

13. physical dependence

14. disease model of addiction

15. life-process model of addiction

16. alcoholism

17. aversive conditioning

18. "good patient" role

19. "bad patient" role

Practice Test A

Answer these multiple-choice questions to assess your understanding of the chapter. Answers are provided at the end of the study guide chapter.

____ 1. The biopsychosocial model of health
a. holds that the mind controls the body.
b. holds that biological, psychological, and social factors are all involved in health.
c. has been replaced as a result of genetic research.
d. has been replaced as a result of stem cell research.

____ 2. According to recent comparisons of the health of various groups of Americans,
a. African-American women are three times more likely than white non-Latino women to have high blood pressure.
b. diabetes occurs at an above-average among Latinos.
c. African-American women have a 35 percent higher death rate for diabetes than white non-Latino women.
d. all of the above are true.

___ 3. Laboratory animals fed diets restricted in calories but adequate in vitamins, minerals, and proteins
a. lived longer than animals that had unlimited access to food.
b. developed kidney disease at an early age.
c. showed a rise in cholesterol at an early age.
d. developed symptoms of malnutrition and died at an early age.

___ 4. Studies of obesity indicate that
a. heredity is not a factor.
b. heredity is the most important factor.
c. heredity, set point, metabolism, and the environment may all play a role.
d. heredity, free radicals, and antioxidants hold the key.

___ 5. Restrained eaters are individuals who
a. occasionally diet.
b. chronically restrict their food intake to control their weight.
c. habitually eat small portions of food.
d. eat out of necessity only, not for pleasure.

___ 6. Anorexia nervosa is an eating disorder that
a. is most often found among those with low socioeconomic status.
b. usually first appears in young adulthood.
c. often begins after an episode of dieting or some type of stress.
d. is most often found among ethnic minorities.

___ 7. Which of the following is true?
a. About 70 percent of individuals who develop anorexia or bulimia nervosa eventually recover.
b. About 30 percent of individuals who develop anorexia or bulimia nervosa eventually recover.
c. Most people who develop bulimia but few people who develop anorexia eventually recover.
d. None of the above is true.

___ 8. Aerobic exercise is
a. the only type of exercise that brings health benefits.
b. sustained exercise that stimulates heart and lung activity.
c. light exercise.
d. exercise aimed at strengthening muscles and improving flexibility.

___ 9. Nicotine acts on the brain
a. as a hallucinogen.
b. much like alcohol.
c. as a stimulant.
d. as a depressant.

___ 10. The chances that a person will seek medical treatment increase when
a. there is a potential cure for the problem.
b. the person has had the problem before.
c. the person recognizes the symptoms as serious.
d. all of the above.

_____ 11. The stress of hospitalization can be relieved by
a. taking on the role of bad patient.
b. demanding the attention of the staff.
c. social support.
d. the distraction offered by unpredictable events.

_____ 12. Recent research on the health care system indicates that
a. female patients demand less of health care providers than male patients do.
b. female patients are more demanding than male patients in their interactions with health care providers.
c. gender differences in how patients interact with health care providers have disappeared.
d. none of the above is true.

Identifying Concepts

Answers are provided at the end of the study guide chapter.

1. BIOLOGY OF HEALTH   Identify the substance or concept described in each statement.

a. Protein released by fat cells that results in decreased food intake and increased energy expenditure

b. Unstable compound formed as a byproduct of a cell's metabolism

c. Weight maintained when no effort is made to gain or lose weight

d. Neutralizes free radicals

2. THREATS TO HEALTH   Identify the condition described in each statement.

a. Eating disorder in which the person pursues thinness to the point of starvation

b. Eating disorder in which the person binges and purges

c. Condition in which a person is preoccupied with obtaining a drug for emotional reasons

d. Condition in which withdrawal symptoms occur if use of a drug is discontinued

Understanding Concepts

Complete these exercises to develop your understanding of important ideas in this chapter.

1. Describe the 2003 study by Sheldon Cohen and his colleagues on the role of positive emotion.

2. Summarize the differences between the recommendations in the Food Guide Pyramid and Americans' actual consumption (shown in Figure 16.1).

3. Summarize the factors that might contribute to obesity.

4. What is the evidence that leptin plays a role in eating behavior?

5. What is the evidence that environmental factors influence weight?

6. Why should exercise be a component of any weight-loss program?

7. What are the key characteristics of anorexia nervosa and bulimia nervosa? What do these eating disorders have in common, and how are they different?

8. Summarize the benefits of exercise.

9. Summarize the effects of drinking alcohol and the costs of alcohol abuse.

10. What factors predict recovery from alcoholism?

Applying Concepts and Strategies

Complete these exercises to develop your ability to apply this chapter's material to your life and the world. Your responses will differ from those of other students in the class, and it is helpful to share your ideas with other students.

1. Describe stressors that you might expect a poor person but not a middle-class person in the United States to experience on a typical day. What other factors do you think might account for the different mortality rates of different ethnic groups discussed in the textbook?

2. How does your typical daily diet compare with the recommendations of the Food Guide Pyramid? Do you think you should make changes in order to have a healthy diet? If you were going to change your diet, what strategies for eating in healthier ways would you use, and why?

3. Suppose you needed to lose weight. What strategies would you use?

4. Describe the disease model and the life-process model of addiction. What difference does it make if addiction follows the life-process model rather than the disease model?

5. Suppose you are a consultant in interpersonal communications. A clinic is troubled by the fact that so many of its patients are not following the directions from their doctors and nurses about taking medications or other treatments. The clinic has come to you for advice. What would you tell them?

Practice Test B

Answer these multiple-choice test questions to help you assess your understanding of the textbook chapter. Answers are provided at the end of the study guide chapter.

____ 1. Over the past century the leading causes of death in the United States
a. have been infectious diseases.
b. have changed from being infectious diseases to being diseases related to personal habits.
c. have remained tuberculosis and smallpox.
d. have changed from being chronic diseases to being diseases caused by overcrowding.

____ 2. The frequent use of humor as a coping strategy
a. has no effect on health.
b. has been linked to decreased levels of the antibody S-IgA.
c. has been linked to increased levels of the antibody S-IgA.
d. causes the blood to clot more rapidly.

____ 3. A 1993 study of more than 19,000 men who were Harvard alumni found that
a. the most overweight men had a 67 percent higher risk of dying than the thinnest men.
b. the heaviest men also had 2.5 times the risk of death from cardiovascular disease.
c. as body mass increased, so did risk of death.
d. all of the above are true.

_____ 4. Basal metabolism rates tend to
a. increase with age.
b. remain stable until middle age.
c. decline steeply in adolescence.
d. rise in early adulthood.

_____ 5. According to the National Center for Health Statistics, from 1970 to 2000
a. U.S. men and women increased the number of calories they took in each day.
b. the number of calories consumed each day in the United States went down despite the rise in obesity.
c. the number of calories consumed each day stayed the same while obesity rose.
d. U.S. women but not U.S. men increased the number of calories eaten each day.

_____ 6. The effects of exercise include
a. burning up calories.
b. raising the metabolic rate.
c. lowering the set point.
d. all of the above.

_____ 7. Effective strategies for losing weight include
a. using a smaller plate with smaller servings.
b. eating while watching television.
c. setting very challenging goals for weight loss.
d. all of the above.

_____ 8. To reap physical benefits from exercise,
a. you may engage in moderate or intense activities.
b. you must burn at least 2,000 calories a week through exercise.
c. you must burn at least 300 calories a day through exercise.
d. you must engage in exercise 45 minutes a day on most if not all days.

_____ 9. Marijuana is
a. a stimulant much like amphetamines.
b. a depressant much like barbiturates.
c. a hallucinogen.
d. not a psychoactive drug.

_____ 10. A longitudinal analysis of binge drinking by Jerald Bachman found that
a. binge drinking increased when people reached their mid-20s.
b. youths who ended their education after high school drank more than college students.
c. drinking was heaviest among singles and divorced individuals.
d. all of the above are true.

_____ 11. A long-term study of 700 individuals over 50 years found that by age 65
a. only one tenth of alcoholics were abstinent or drinking socially.
b. about one third of alcoholics were abstinent or drinking socially.
c. about two thirds of alcoholics were still trying to beat their addiction.
d. alcoholics do not recover unless they enter a professionally run treatment program.

_____ 12. Taking Zyban to help you quit smoking
a. is likely to be far more effective than using a nicotine spray.
b. is likely to be far less effective than using a nicotine spray.
c. is likely to be as effective as using a nicotine spray.
d. is against the law.

Answers to Chapter Questions

Guided Review

1. habits
2. body; mind
3. social
4. negative thinking
5. emotional stress
6. immune
7. frequency; intensity
8. poverty
9. stressors
10. Food Guide Pyramid
11. vegetables; fruits
12. common; rare
13. calories
14. free radicals
15. longer
16. antioxidants
17. free radicals
18. hypertension; diabetes; cardiovascular
19. body mass index
20. overweight
21. leptin
22. set point
23. basal metabolism rate
24. age; sex
25. BMR
26. environment
27. restrained eaters
28. binge
29. few
30. exercise
31. chronic disease
32. depressed
33. anorexia nervosa
34. distorted image
35. females; males
36. high-achieving
37. bulimia nervosa
38. food
39. normal weight
40. aerobic
41. heart disease
42. longevity
43. brain; muscle; bone
44. psychoactive drugs
45. depressants; stimulants
46. depressants
47. hallucinogens
48. psychological
49. physical
50. disease model
51. life-process
52. depressant
53. inhibitions
54. tolerance
55. alcoholism
56. genetics
57. one third
58. cancer; heart disease
59. nicotine; stimulant
60. substitute source; aversive conditioning
61. familiar
62. schemas
63. less
64. severity
65. excessive use
66. good patient; bad patient
67. realistic expectations
68. one-third
69. technical language
70. less
71. inadequate
72. belief systems
73. more control
74. men
75. less

Practice Test A

1. b
2. d
3. a
4. c
5. b
6. c
7. a
8. b
9. c
10. d
11. c
12. b

Identifying Concepts

1. BIOLOGY OF HEALTH
   a. leptin
   b. free radical
   c. set point
   d. antioxidant
2. THREATS TO HEALTH
   a. anorexia nervosa
   b. bulimia nervosa
   c. psychological dependence
   d. physical dependence

Practice Test B

1. b
2. c
3. d
4. c
5. a
6. d
7. a
8. a
9. c
10. c
11. b
12. c